"Wonderfully comprehensive while foc(
when there is an increased understanding
can be overwhelming to introduce r.
However, Lips concisely outlines the key issues with excellen..
of current and classic theories and research from around the world while
using stimulating examples that will keep students engaged as they
develop the foundation needed in order to master the complexity of
gender."

– Dr. Emily Keener, Slippery Rock University

"From first to last, this is a thoroughly scholarly and feminist review of
theory and research in the psychology of women and gender. Dr. Lips
has accomplished the difficult feat of providing a succinct overview that
is nevertheless impressive in scope. Topics will be engaging to students
at the introductory level and will be practical refreshers for more
advanced study. Importantly, chapters provide a structure for comparisons among perspectives that will facilitate civil and tolerant class conversations. Ultimately, students will gain intellectual maturity and a
more nuanced understanding of gender and feminism."

– Dr. Cheryl Travis, University of Tennessee, Knoxville

"*Gender: The Basics* offers an excellent and comprehensive introduction
to gender and its intersections with other systems of power , privilege,
and oppression. Reading the second edition, I was reminded in vivid
detail of how gender is embedded in all aspects of biological, psychological, and social life, from the way in which our personal relationships
unfold to the power dynamics governing institutional practices. New to
the second edition is a chapter on theoretical frameworks regarding
gender that will delight students and scholars from multiple disciplines
for distilling many complex theories to an accessible level. Hilary Lips is
a magnificent writer, relying on a deep knowledge of gender as identity,
relationship, and social structure in lifespan and global contexts."

*– Katherine R. Allen, Ph.D., Professor of Human Development and
Family Science, Virginia Tech*

"In *Gender: The Basics*, Dr. Hilary Lips outlines the major topics needed
to understand all things gender while bringing every page to life. She
uses her expertise to break down complicated theories and explain
empirical studies in an approachable and engaging manner. Plan to finish
The Basics with a thorough understanding of just how pervasive, and
complicated gender is in today's world."

– Dr. Alynn Gordon, Research Consultant, Atlanta, Georgia

Gender: The Basics is an engaging introduction to the influence of cultural, historical, biological, psychological, and economic forces on ways in which we have come to define and experience femininity and masculinity, and on the impact and importance of gender categories. Highlighting that there is far more to gender than biological sex, it examines theories and research about how and why gender categories and identities are developed and about how interpersonal and societal power relationships are gendered. It takes a global and intersectional perspective to examine the interaction between gender and a wide range of topics including:

- Relationships, intimacy, and concepts of sexuality across the lifespan
- The workplace and labor markets
- Gender-related violence and war
- Public health, poverty, and development
- Gender and public leadership

This new edition includes increased coverage of trans visibility and activism, LGBTQ studies and critical masculinity studies, global developments in women's political leadership, links between gender and economic well-being, and cyberbullying.

Supporting theory with examples and case studies from a variety of contexts, suggestions for further reading, and a detailed glossary, this text is an essential read for anyone approaching the study of gender for the first time.

Hilary M. Lips is Emerita Professor of Psychology and Research Professor at Radford University, USA, where she served for many years as Chair of the Psychology Department, and Director of the Center for Gender Studies.

THE BASICS

For a full list of titles in this series, please visit www.routledge.com/
The-Basics/book-series/B

GENDER

THE BASICS
SECOND EDITION

HILARY M. LIPS

Routledge
Taylor & Francis Group

LONDON AND NEW YORK

Second edition published 2019
by Routledge
2 Park Square, Milton Park, Abingdon, Oxon OX14 4RN

and by Routledge
711 Third Avenue, New York, NY 10017

Routledge is an imprint of the Taylor & Francis Group, an informa business

First edition published by Routledge 2014

British Library Cataloguing-in-Publication Data
A catalogue record for this book is available from the British Library

Library of Congress Cataloging-in-Publication Data
Names: Lips, Hilary M., author.
Title: Gender : the basics / Hilary M. Lips.
Description: Second Edition. | New York : Routledge, 2019. | Revised edition
of the author's Gender, c2014. | Includes bibliographical references and
index.
Identifiers: LCCN 2018013012| ISBN 9781138036888 (hardback) |
ISBN 9781138036895 (pbk.) | ISBN 9781315178233 (ebook)
Subjects: LCSH: Sex role. | Sex differences (Psychology) | Sex differences.
Classification: LCC HQ1075 .L578 2019 | DDC 305.3–dc23
LC record available at https://lccn.loc.gov/2018013012

ISBN: 978-1-138-03688-8 (hbk)
ISBN: 978-1-138-03689-5 (pbk)
ISBN: 978-1-315-17823-3 (ebk)

Typeset in Bembo and Bliss
by Wearset Ltd, Boldon, Tyne and Wear

To Marian, Karen, and Tom: Siblings who are also friends.

CONTENTS

FIGURES

ACKNOWLEDGMENTS

I am grateful to Gerhard Boomgaarden at Routledge, who first suggested I should take on this second edition and provided initial guidance. I have also much appreciated the help and encouragement of Mihaela Diana Ciobotea. Thanks are also due to the reviewers of the initial proposal and sample chapters, who provided suggestions and insights to make this a better book.

I owe a special deep debt of gratitude to Wayne Andrew, who designed all the charts and graphs for this book, and whose caring and enthusiastic participation in this and so many other projects over the years has made them better, more meaningful, and more fun.

Finally, thanks go out to my colleagues, who have always been supportive, and to my students, who inevitably asked tough questions, reminded me when things were not clear, and pushed me to find out what I did not know.

Hilary Lips
June 2018

GENDER

EVERYBODY HAS/DOES ONE

Years ago, Ursula LeGuin (1969) described a fictional world in which there were no "women" or "men," but only individuals. *Gender* categories were absent from this society—except for a few days in each individual's monthly cycle when sexual desires became insistent and individuals became "female" or "male" for the time it took to establish a sexual relationship. Even then, no persistent biological or social tendency toward maleness or femaleness was established: one individual could be the father of some children and the mother of others.

My students have been intrigued but discomfited by this fantasy. Most say they cannot imagine a world without gender categories. It would be boring, bland, they protest. Everyone would be the same; relationships would be uninteresting. And how would anyone decide who was supposed to do what? Most react with similar perplexity and stubbornness when I ask them to "imagine yourself as still 'you,' but as a different gender." They argue that they would not, could not, be the same person if they were a different gender—and anyway they would be unskilled and awkward at doing what the other gender is supposed to do.

These responses provide some clues to the pervasive importance of gender categories in our lives. They also suggest that we view gender not as a category that someone simply biologically "is" but as something that individuals do or act out. So what exactly is gender?

GENDER AND SEX: IS THERE A DIFFERENCE?

Most of us are used to dividing people into two categories: female and male. If pressed, we might say the distinction is based on simple biology: male and female individuals look different, have different reproductive organs. Women have breasts. Men can grow beards. A woman can get pregnant and give birth. A man can inseminate a woman—even against her will.

However, we also know that individual women and men vary a great deal in how close they are to society's ideals of femininity and masculinity. Simply being biologically female does not ensure that a person is "womanly," and being biologically male does not mean that an individual is "manly." Some people who are clearly men are described as not very masculine; some women are termed unfeminine. Clearly, there is something more complicated going on than placing people into well-defined biological categories. In fact, with respect to these issues, there seem to be two broad dimensions on which individuals might be categorized: biological and socio-cultural.

In recognition of these two dimensions, people who study the differences and similarities between women and men have sometimes made a distinction between sex and gender. They may use the term *sex* to mean biological femaleness and maleness, and the term *gender* to refer to culturally-mediated expectations and roles associated with masculinity and femininity (e.g., Oakley, 1972; Unger, 1979). Although this is the general approach taken in this book, it must be acknowledged that the biological and social dimensions that define women and men cannot be cleanly separated. For example, the biological fact that women can become pregnant helps shape social expectations for femininity. Men's biologically based propensity to have larger, stronger bodies is enhanced by social norms that encourage men to work at becoming strong and reward them for doing so. Thus sex and gender are intertwined, and it is usually impossible to separate them completely. In fact, one researcher has suggested using *gender/sex* as "an umbrella term for both gender (socialization) and sex (biology, evolution) […] [that] […] reflects social locations or identities where gender and sex cannot be easily or at all disentangled" (van Anders, 2015, p. 1181). Furthermore, gender itself is multi-dimensional. One dimension is *gender identity*: thinking of oneself as male, female, or as someone who does not fit neatly into these categories. Another is *gender role* or *gender expression*: behaving in ways considered appropriate for women or men in the surrounding culture. Still another is *sexual orientation*: attraction to members of one's own and/or other genders.

IS GENDER "BUILT IN," OR DO WE CONSTRUCT IT?

As will be obvious in the discussion of theories about gender in Chapter 2, one key to the arguments surrounding gender is the debate about how strongly it is rooted in biology. Do our bodies predispose us to be, feel, and behave differently as males and females? How much are such differences affected by the way we are raised, by the culture in which we grow up? This *nature-versus nurture* question has haunted researchers who study every aspect of human behavior; however, it is particularly perplexing and complicated in the realm of gender. And the more we explore the role of nature and nurture, the more we confront the conclusion that virtually nothing in gender development is the result of only one or the other of these forces. Nature and nurture cannot be separated: they are intertwined and work together at every stage of human development. Thus, most people who have studied these issues deeply claim an *interactionist* position: they do not argue about *how much* nature or nurture influences particular aspects of development, but try instead to figure out *how* the two sets of influences interact to produce certain results.

THE ROLE OF BIOLOGY

THE STEPS IN HUMAN SEXUAL DIFFERENTIATION

The path to joining the category of male or female begins at conception. Through a series of developmental steps, a fertilized egg moves toward developing a body that will be classified as male or female:

- *Step 1: Chromosomes.* When sperm meets egg to produce fertilization, each normally contributes a set of 23 chromosomes, which pair up to form the genetic basis for the new individual. The twenty-third pair, known as the *sex chromosomes*, is the pair that initially determines sex. Normally, this pair comprises an X chromosome contributed by the mother's egg and either an X or Y chromosome contributed by the father's sperm. If the pair is XX, the pattern of development is predisposed to be female; if it is XY, the pattern is predisposed to be male. If some unusual combination, such as XO or XXX, occurs, development tends to proceed in a female direction—as long as no Y chromosome is present. Only the sperm, not the egg, can contribute a Y chromosome. Thus the genetic basis of sex is determined by the father.
- *Step 2: Gonads.* During the first seven weeks after conception, the embryo develops "neutral" gonads (proto-gonads) and the beginnings of both female and male sets of internal reproductive structures. Up until this point, the embryo has the potential to go either way, to develop either female or male reproductive equipment. In the eighth week, if a Y chromosome is present, the SRY gene on that chromosome promotes the organization of the neutral gonad into an embryonic testis. If there is no Y chromosome, a neutral gonad will start to become an ovary.
- *Step 3: Hormones.* Once formed, the testes or ovaries begin to secrete sex hormones, and these hormones influence the remaining steps in sexual differentiation. Testes secrete both testosterone, which influences the male reproductive tract to develop, and Mullerian Inhibiting Substance (MIS), which causes the female reproductive tract to atrophy and disappear.

Ovaries secrete estrogens and progesterone, which organize the development of the female reproductive system.

- *Step 4: Internal reproductive tract.* Over the next four weeks, the sex hormones gradually organize the internal reproductive structures in a male or female direction. Under the influence of testosterone, these internal ducts become the vas deferens, epididymis, seminal vesicles, urethra, and prostate. If no significant amount of testosterone is present, the internal structures differentiate in a female direction: as fallopian tubes, uterus, and vagina.
- *Step 5: External genitalia.* Also by the end of the twelfth week, the external genitalia, which are indistinguishable by sex at eight weeks, differentiate as either male or female. Under the influence of testosterone, the "neutral" genitalia develop into a penis and scrotum; without the influence of testosterone, the genitalia develop as a clitoris and labia.

A careful reader may have noticed an overall pattern in these steps: at each stage, without the effect of a Y chromosome or male sex hormone, development apparently proceeds in a female direction. This is also true in other mammals. Some biologists like to say that the basic pattern of mammalian development is female—unless testosterone interferes.

Although we tend to think of female and male as two distinct, non-overlapping categories, the fact that sex develops through a series of sequential steps shows that there are some possibilities for these categories to be fuzzy. If, for example, a genetic male (XY) reaches step 3, in which testosterone is being secreted, but happens to have an inherited condition (androgen insensitivity syndrome) that makes cells unable to respond to testosterone, step 4 will not proceed in a male developmental direction. At birth, the baby will probably appear female and be classified as such; the male genetic configuration and testes may well not be discovered until young adulthood. There are varieties of ways in which the steps of sexual differentiation may be inconsistent, producing an individual whose indicators of biological sex are mixed. Such *intersex* individuals make up between 1 and 4 percent of the population.

There are two other aspects of the journey toward maleness or femaleness which appear even more complex than the development of a body that may be classified as male or female. One concerns the sexual differentiation of the brain. The other concerns the different ways in which individuals are treated and taught once they have been classified as female or male.

FEMALE BRAINS AND MALE BRAINS?

If different levels of prenatal hormones can affect the development of internal and external genitalia, might they not also affect the developing brain—producing different kinds of brains in females and males? For decades, popular books and articles have argued that women and men think and behave differently because their brains are different. In general terms, this notion is not new. Late in the nineteenth century, women were said to be intellectually inferior to men because they had smaller brains. When it was demonstrated that women's brains were proportionately larger than men's by weight, the argument shifted to the size of particular areas of the brain—first, the frontal lobes, then, when that proved untenable, the parietal lobes—that were said to be smaller in women. More recently, researchers have examined the size, shape, and density of various brain structures in women and men and have found some evidence for sex differences, for instance, in the corpus callosum (the structure that connects the right and left hemispheres of the brain). Since there is a tremendous amount of individual variation in brain size and shape, it is difficult to draw definitive conclusions about sex differences in brain morphology. Furthermore, it is not clear what functional significance these differences may have. Finally, it is uncertain whether the differences are "built in" or are the results of different life experiences—since brains are very plastic and responsive to experience.

The complexity of the issues is illustrated in the story of one set of researchers (Wood, Heitmiller, Andreasen, and Nopoulos, 2008) who set out to find a brain difference that would mesh with the often-reported finding that women show more interpersonal awareness than men. After using magnetic resonance imaging (MRI) to examine the brains of 30 women and 30 men matched on age and IQ, they concluded that one particular brain structure, the straight gyrus (SG)—part of a brain region that had already been linked to the ability to interpret nonverbal cues—was proportionately larger in women than in men. Furthermore, size of the SG was correlated with scores on a test of interpersonal perception. Thus far, this may sound like a clear case of sex differences in brain structure causing sex differences in a particular ability. It turns out not to be so simple, however. In this study, both the size of the SG and the interpersonal perception scores were also correlated with a third variable: respondents' scores on a measure of psychological femininity and masculinity. Respondents (both female and male) who described themselves as having more "feminine" qualities tended to have larger SGs *and* higher interpersonal perception scores. Furthermore, a subsequent study that examined the brains of children aged 7 to 17 found a surprising result: the SG was larger in boys than in girls, and interpersonal awareness scores were associated with smaller, not larger, SGs (Wood, Murko, and Nopoulos, 2009). In this younger sample, both higher interpersonal awareness and smaller SGs were associated with higher scores on psychological femininity. This complicated set of findings illustrates how perilous it can be to try to draw sweeping conclusions about sex differences in the brain and their relationship to female–male differences in behavior. It suggests, for example, the possibility that children's experiences as boys or girls may affect brain development. It leaves us wondering whether women's larger SGs come from many years of being socially sensitive, or whether their social sensitivity stems from their larger SGs—or whether both things may be true.

Another research emphasis has been on exploring possible sex differences in the organization of various cognitive abilities within the brain. Researchers cannot discern this organization by examining brains directly; rather, they ask respondents to perform specific tasks, such as reading, listening, and recognizing objects, and they use various methods to determine which part of the brain is activated and used to accomplish these tasks. Using this approach, some investigators have found results consistent with the idea that women and men may differ in how basic abilities, such as language, are distributed across the two hemispheres of the brain or among the different areas within hemispheres. The findings often involve small differences, are complex, and often contested, so it is not possible to sum them up in brief generalizations. This complexity has not prevented media commentators from trumpeting misleading headlines such as "Women are significantly more right-brained than men."

If there were differences in the organization of female and male brains, how might this occur? For decades, there have been efforts to understand the extent to which prenatal hormones may be involved and may organize the developing brain in ways that produce average differences between girls and boys in certain interests and social behaviors. This too is a complicated area, but a reasonable amount of evidence suggests that levels of prenatal androgens are associated with later levels of certain kinds of interests (e.g., interest in babies) and behaviors (e.g., rough-and-tumble play) which are more strongly associated with one gender than with the other. For example, one study measured testosterone levels in amniotic fluid (the fluid that surrounds the fetus in the womb), and tested the association between those levels and the levels of masculine-typical play, measured when the children were aged 6 to 10 years (Auyeung *et al.*, 2009). For both boys and girls, parents reported more masculine-typical activities and interests for children whose samples of amniotic fluid *in utero* had shown higher levels of testosterone. The association between prenatal hormone levels and later behavior does not prove definitively that one causes the other. However, this and other studies have been used to suggest that prenatal concentrations of sex hormones may contribute to female–male behavioral differences, and that, to the extent that hormones are responsible for these differences, they may also contribute to the large individual differences in such qualities *among* both girls and boys.

When we learn about scientific findings of differences in the brains of men and women in any particular sample—findings that involve sophisticated techniques such as neuroimaging—it is tempting to conclude that something really definitive has been proven about brain sex differences. However, experts caution that it would be wise to remain skeptical. Neuroimaging results can be affected by extraneous variables such as breathing rates or caffeine intake—a problem if samples are small. Furthermore, it is difficult to interpret the functional significance of differences in the size of brain structures or of more or less activation of a certain area of the brain. And if scientists are trying to link brain differences to behavior that is "feminine" or "masculine," they have to define what behaviors fall into these categories—a daunting and controversial task.

The role of biology in producing gender-related behavior is complex and fascinating; we have only scratched the surface of it here, and much more research remains to be done. However, biology always works in interaction with the environment, and that interaction is always a "work in progress" as each individual develops (Berenbaum and Beltz, 2016). As one eminent group of reviewers noted (Berenbaum, Blakemore and Beltz, 2011: 814),

> biology is not destiny. Genes are activated or suppressed by environmental factors. Hormones and brain functioning are almost certainly influenced by the different environments in which girls and boys are raised, by their different behaviors, and by joint effects of genes and the social environment.

THE ROLE OF CULTURE

SOCIALIZATION: LEARNING TO BE GENDERED

By the age of 6 months, infants can distinguish women's from men's voices; by 9 months, most can discriminate between photographs of men and women—and sometime between the ages of 11 months and 14 months, they show the ability to accurately pair women's voices with pictures of women and men's voices with pictures of men (Martin and Ruble, 2004). Clearly, children learn very early on of the existence of gender categories and quickly become competent at figuring out who fits into which category.

Not only do children discern these categories very early, they also quickly become adept at associating activities and items with the appropriate gender. By the middle of their second year, infants reliably look at a female face when presented with images of items such as ribbons and dresses, and at a male face when presented with pictures of things such as fire hats and hammers (Eichstedt, Serbin, Poulin-Dubois, and Sen, 2002). By this age, too, children have learned to link more metaphorical, abstract qualities with gender. Infants in this same study associated bears, fir trees, and navy blue with men, and hearts, cats, and bright pink with women. Children are unlikely to have seen all these items with women and men (for example, most infants will not have seen men with bears); however, they may have learned to connect the attributes of these things with gender. For example, a bear may be seen as strong and fierce; a cat may be seen as soft and quiet. Even very young children have absorbed the message that these characteristics connect to gender. Young children also seem to absorb cultural stereotypes that link very high intellectual ability more with men than with women. One US study found that, among 6-year-olds, girls were less likely than boys to believe that members of their own gender were "really, really smart." In contrast to boys, girls at this age also began to avoid activities that were described as being for "really, really smart" children (Bian, Leslie, and Cimpian, 2017).

How do children arrive at these conclusions? According to psychologists, they respond to instructions, rewards, and punishments from people such as parents, teachers, and peers, who let them know how to act as girls or boys and try to shape their behavior to fit gender expectations. A boy may be praised for acting "like a little man"; a girl may reap approval for behaving "just like Mommy." Peers may tease a boy for "throwing like a girl"; teachers may criticize a girl for being "unladylike." To cultivate approval and avoid criticism, children bring their behavior into line with the gendered expectations communicated to them. However, children do not simply react to rewards and punishments; they are not mere putty in the hands of socializing agents. On the contrary, it is clear that children are active searchers for cues about how to behave in gender-appropriate ways.

Once children figure out that there are two gender groups and that they belong to one of them, there appear to be some important consequences. They begin to evaluate their own group as better than the other group (although this effect may be limited to qualities thought to be gender-appropriate): children as young as 3 years old like their own gender group more, attribute more positive qualities to members of that group, and show a strong preference for same-gender playmates. They also display more interest in information about their own group, and tend to use gender stereotypes to form impressions of others. They do not seem to need much of a push to conform to gendered expectations; rather, they seem to be motivated to learn as much as they can about this significant social category—gender—which is so important to their social identity. Thus the instructions, the presence of adult or peer models who can be imitated, rewards, and punishments are all used by children as sources of guidance to doing the best possible job of fitting into the "girl" or "boy" category. In fact, children become quite rigid for a while as they try to work this out. During early childhood, children try to consolidate their knowledge about gender into hard-and-fast categories; these categories can be very inflexible, particularly between the ages of 5 and 7 years. During this period, children are prone to make quick and strong judgments about people based solely on gender, and they are likely to be "sure" that women and men cannot do certain things (Martin and Ruble, 2004). After the age of 7, children tend to relax the categories a little and become more flexible.

Socialization does not end with childhood. It is a continuing process that affects how individuals understand and enact gender at each life stage. As children approach adolescence, they fall more and more under the influence of peers and less under the influence of parents. Older children and adolescents who are not "typical" for their gender often feel peer pressure to conform to gender norms; when this happens, they are vulnerable to low self-esteem and depression. Adolescents who view themselves as gender-atypical but feel accepted by their peers are less likely to face such difficulties. Through the media, children, adolescents, and adults are presented with a continuous stream of gendered expectations and models to imitate. One study, for example, examined the portrayals of male and female characters in 500 top-grossing US films released across the 5-year period from 2007 to 2012. They found that, in 2012, male characters outnumbered females 2.51 to 1—the lowest percentage of females on screen over the 5 years (S.L. Smith, Choueiti, Scofield, and Pieper, 2013). In 2015, male characters had twice as much screen time and spoke twice as often as female characters in the 100 top-grossing US films (Geena Davis Institute, 2016). Researchers studying US films have also found that female characters were more likely than males to be depicted as young, as parents, and as being in a married or committed relationship (S.L.

Smith, Pieper, Granados, and Choueiti, 2010). Males were more likely than females to be portrayed as strong and funny; females were more likely to be presented as physically attractive. Both male and female characters were likely to be in gender-traditional occupations. Another study (Paek, Nelson, and Vilela 2011), which examined gender portrayals in television advertising across seven countries, found that males were reliably shown in more prominent visual and auditory roles than females, and that both women and men were used to advertise gender-typed products. A study of women's portrayal in 15 Arab and 3 Turkish television dramas found women underrepresented, less likely to have recognizable jobs, and more likely than men to be shown in gender-typed occupations, activities, and settings (Kharroub and Weaver, 2014). In general, research shows that in television programs and commercials, video games, and popular films, whether created for children, adolescents, or adults, male characters are portrayed more often than females and gender stereotypes are very common (Collins, 2011). We swim in a cultural sea of gendered images and, at every stage, a desire to "fit in" pushes individuals to conform to those images.

THE INFLUENCE OF THE GENDER HIERARCHY

It may appear that gender socialization involves fitting people into a relatively arbitrary division of activities and qualities labeled masculine and feminine. Indeed, a look at varying gender prescriptions across cultures or historical eras does suggest a strong streak of arbitrariness. In some cultures, men wear long, flowing garments as a matter of course, but in some the idea of a man in a "dress" is viewed with alarm. In some cultures, men who are good friends walk down the street holding hands, but in others, that behavior is considered a violation of masculinity norms. There was a time in North America when the now-familiar mantra that "pink is for girls, blue is for boys" was reversed and pink was considered a strong, "masculine" color.

However, not all gender prescriptions are arbitrary. Many, in fact, help maintain a hierarchy in which men hold more power than women do. If we consider the behaviors, personal qualities, and appearances that are considered desirable for men, many involve strength, dominance, and leadership; those considered desirable for women encompass delicacy, flexibility, and agreeableness—and a willingness to bend to a situation rather than take charge. A man often demonstrates his masculinity by wielding power; a woman can often indicate her femininity by behaving submissively. Thus, when people violate gender norms, they are sometimes also challenging the gender hierarchy.

For example, traditional gender roles tend to be entwined with the kinds of work women and men do. The expectation that women will be warm and nurturing means that they are considered a good fit for jobs or tasks that emphasize caretaking and supporting others. The expectation that men will be achievement-oriented and assertive implies that they will be viewed as good candidates for positions that involve taking charge and making decisions. Alice Eagly's (1987) *social roles theory* proposed that we expect women to be warm and compassionate and men to be tough and decisive *because* we so often observe them performing roles that require these very qualities. The gendered division of labor is both based on, and gives credibility to, gender stereotypes. Furthermore, Eagly argued, the requirements of the roles reinforce these qualities: women in "feminine" roles have more opportunity to practice compassion and so develop in that direction; men in "masculine" roles have more scope for decisiveness and so become more used to such behavior and better at it. Thus gender stereotypes reproduce themselves: people are selected for roles congruent with gender stereotypes, and they learn to perform the requirements of these roles, thereby enacting the gender stereotypes and helping maintain both the stereotypes and the gendered division of labor. In maintaining the gendered division of labor, this circular process also maintains the gender hierarchy, since roles requiring masculine-stereotyped qualities such as leadership abilities are almost guaranteed to involve more status and higher pay than those requiring feminine-stereotyped qualities such as warmth and flexibility.

Another approach, *social dominance theory* (Pratto and Walker 2004), suggests that in societies that emphasize hierarchical social arrangements, the values toward which men are socialized are hierarchy-enhancing—values that emphasize the promotion of the interests of powerful groups. Women, on the other hand, are encouraged to adopt hierarchy-attenuating values—values that stress equality and minimize intergroup status and power differences. The expectation that women and men will hold different values promotes their perceived suitability for different kinds of occupations: men for roles that involve wielding power and influence, women for roles that involve supporting and empowering others. Indeed, even a cursory examination of labor statistics in Western countries indicates that men are far more likely than women to be in powerful, high-status positions such as corporate, professional, and political leadership, whereas positions such as social worker, counselor, secretary, and nurse, which involve helping and supporting others, are dominated by women.

Gender stereotypes and roles, then, represent more than the expression of biologically based sex differences and more than an accidental or random division by societies of qualities and behaviors into "feminine" and "masculine." They are expressions of cultural values, social constructions that help organize behavior and maintain a society's power structures. Since gender is socially constructed, there is room for variation in the ways it is defined.

DOES GENDER HAVE TO BE A BINARY?

Historically, cultures have differed in their accommodation of individuals who are uncomfortable with the gender assigned to them or who do not fit neatly into either the feminine or the masculine gender. Among many Native American groups, for example, there is a tradition of categorizing such individuals as "two-spirit" people. Two-spirit people may be individuals with male bodies who identify and live as women, people with female bodies who identify and live as men, individuals of either sex who are sexually attracted to same-sex others, or anyone who lives outside the traditional definitions of gender and combines elements of both female and male genders. Having two spirits has traditionally been considered a special gift in these cultures. Two-spirit persons have been respected and, in some groups, given special roles in religious ceremonies.

Formal exceptions to a simple two-gender system and fluid gender categories have a long and varied history. Scholars note that ancient gods were often considered gender-fluid and that the hidden name of God, the four-Hebrew-letter YHWH, used by the early Israelites, was Hebrew for "He/She"; God was understood to be dual-gendered (Sameth, 2016). In parts of Polynesia, a category called *mahu* incorporates male-bodied individuals who adopt a feminine appearance and perform women's work. In India, the *hjiras* are male-to-female transgender people who belong to a religious sect devoted to a particular goddess. They are often called upon to provide blessings at ceremonies such as weddings and births. Some researchers define two-spirit people, mahu, hjiras, and other similar groups as separate gender categories, referring to them as a *third gender*. They argue that such a label is appropriate, since these individuals are not completely incorporated into either the female or male gender, but live by a separate set of rules and expectations. It is probably too simplistic to categorize all these groups in the same way, given the many differences among them. However, the notion that gender categories need not be limited to male and female underlines the idea that gender is a social construction, maintained by agreement among members of a culture.

If gender as a binary concept is a social construction, can people resist, change, or modify that construction? In recent years, a significant number of young people have answered yes to that question. One survey of millennials aged 18 to 34 in the United States revealed that fully half of the respondents (57 percent of women and 44 percent of men) said gender exists on a spectrum and that not everyone fits neatly into female or male categories (Rivas, 2015). A poll of 1000 teenagers in the United Kingdom showed that only 78 percent of the men identified as 100 percent male, and 80 percent of the women identified as 100 percent female (Barr, 2016). Among a sample of more than 2000 adults, Israeli researchers found that more than 35 percent reported that they felt to some extent as the other gender, as both men and women, or as neither (Joel, Tarrasch, Berman, Mukamel, and Ziv, 2014). The findings led these researchers to call for "a new conceptualization of gender, which relates to the multiplicity and fluidity of the experience of gender" (p. 291). Discomfort with traditional binary gender categories is evident in the rise of terms such as genderfluid, gender nonconforming, genderqueer, agender, bi-gender, and pangender—all of which are labels that express resistance to the idea that everyone identifies clearly, easily, and permanently as either female or male. But what shapes an individual's gender identity?

WHAT SHAPES GENDER IDENTITY?

Earlier in this chapter, we considered the difficulty of imagining oneself as a member of a different gender. For most people, this is quite difficult—perhaps not least because of strong cultural messages that every individual fits into one of two binary, non-overlapping gender categories. Gender identity, the powerful conviction that one is female or male, or that one does not fit into either of these gender categories, develops very early in life for most individuals. What is responsible for this conviction? Do most children simply accept the category to which they are told they belong? Do they try to figure out which category is the "best"? Are there biological underpinnings to gender identity? One thing we know with certainty is that there are limits to the extent children will passively accept their assignment to a gender category. In one very famous case, a circumcision accident destroyed a young boy's penis when he was only 7 months old (Diamond and Sigmundson, 1997). Following what they believed was the best expert advice, this child's parents decided to raise him as a girl. Starting at the age of 17 months, "John" became "Joan." This child had an identical twin brother, and, for the first few years, the doctor supervising his case wrote optimistic descriptions of how the two children were developing: one as a traditional masculine boy and the other (reassigned) as a well-adjusted, feminine girl. The case was offered as proof of the malleability of gender identity in individuals younger than 24 months: at such an early age, it was said, a child would adopt the gender identity she or he was given, regardless of biological factors.

However, this case did not turn out well. As a young teenager, "Joan," who, according to her family, had never been happy as a girl despite their best efforts to support that identity and to socialize her in a feminine direction, discovered the truth about her history and demanded to reclaim a masculine gender identity. He went through genital surgery, adopted a masculine name, and began living life as a young man. Eventually, he married and became the father of an adopted family. He spoke about his experience in an attempt to protect other children from what he viewed as tragic manipulation by the medical community. Yet he remained troubled for the rest of his life, and later committed suicide.

Supporting the notion that gender identity is fixed very early and not easy to change are the first-person accounts of many people who identify as *transgender* or *trans*: individuals whose gender identity does not match their body's configuration. Most of the people who have written about this experience report that they became aware in early childhood that their bodies did not match their inner conviction about their gender—and that they found it impossible to change that inner conviction despite considerable external pressure. One therapist who collected such narratives reported that 85 percent of her clients recognized before they entered grade school that their gender identities and bodies were discrepant (Brown and Rounsley, 1996).

Transgender issues have increasingly become a topic of popular discussion, in part because of a very public gender transition by celebrity Caitlyn Jenner in 2015 and the high media profiles of other trans individuals such as Laverne Cox and Jazz Jennings. With growing awareness of transgender issues has come controversy. In the United States, there has been bitter and angry debate about whether high school students should be forced to use school bathrooms consistent with the sex listed on their birth certificate, even if they identify and are living as the other gender. A recent decision by the Boy Scouts of America to admit trans boys generated both fierce negative reactions and enthusiastic approval. The hostile reactions appear to stem from discomfort about whether trans individuals should be categorized according to their gender identity or whether they are simply disguising themselves. Some parents argue, for instance, that they do not want their daughter to have to use a bathroom in which she may encounter a (perhaps predatory) male presenting as a female. However, all the available evidence points to the conclusion that trans individuals are not disguising themselves but expressing their deeply experienced conviction that they belong in a gender that does not match their assigned sex. What the evidence has not told us so far is the *source* of this deep and powerful conviction.

If an awareness of a mismatch between inner identity and bodily form occurs so early and is so intractable, may there be some neurobiological dimension to gender identity? There is some limited research suggesting differences between one small aspect of the brains of transgender and *cisgender* (persons whose experience of gender aligns with their assigned gender) individuals (e.g., Kruijver *et al.*, 2000), but samples are small, and conclusions are based only on correlations. There is no definitive proof that such differences are routinely present or that they *cause* variations in gender identity (Smith, Junger, Derntl, and Habel, 2015). It is reasonable to assume, however, that biology and environment interact in complicated processes to produce gender identity—and that the details are simply not yet fully understood.

Adding to the complexity are reports suggesting that, under some circumstances, gender identity has proven to be flexible. In one case, a male child who was the victim of a surgical accident to his penis at the age of 2 months was reassigned as female at the age of 7 months. That individual, who was later followed up as an adult, apparently successfully adopted a feminine gender identity (Bradley, Oliver, Chernick, and Zucker, 1998). The researchers speculated that her successful transition to a feminine gender identity was due to the early age (7 months) at which she was reassigned, in contrast to the later age (17 months) in the unsuccessful case described above.

In cases of variations in prenatal sexual differentiation, the outcome for gender identity tends to be mixed. One study of 14 genetic males who were assigned as females at birth because they were born without a normal penis found that 8 of them later declared themselves male (Reiner and Gearhart, 2004). In another set of cases, children in the Dominican Republic born with male (XY) genetic configurations and ambiguous genitalia were raised as girls, but were then found to change to a masculine gender identity at puberty when male secondary sex characteristics developed (see Imperato-McGinley, Peterson, Gautier, and Sturla, 1979). In these cases, some researchers argue, the children's early gender identity was not "set" as female because their ambiguous genitalia caused them to be recognized in their community as members of a special category: "first woman, then man." This ambiguity paved the way for them to slip easily from a feminine to a masculine gender identity. Clearly, the causes, processes, and timing of the formation of core gender identity are still in need of clarification.

The tension between, on the one hand, thinking of gender as less binary, more of a spectrum, and more fluid, and, on the other hand, trans individuals' often intractable desire to "join" the gender category with which they identify shows the complexity of gender identity. Clearly, in terms of gender identity, having a male body does not make one a man, and having a female body does not make one a woman. However, the desire to change one's body to match one's identity suggests that the body is experienced as critically important. Yet, even if bodily change is achieved, others may reject one's self-categorization as fraudulent. For example, when Caitlyn Jenner was chosen as *Glamour Magazine*'s 2015 "Woman of the Year," some commentators protested that she was not a real woman. Even within feminist movements with the stated aim of dismantling sex/gender as a limiting category, there have been uncomfortable debates about whether trans women should be included as women. Does identifying as female, taking female hormones, and having a surgically constructed vagina qualify an individual as a woman? Or does a person have to be born with XX chromosomes and have ovaries to qualify? If the determination is based on biology, does that not reinforce the very notion that feminist movements have been fighting against for years: that women and men are biologically destined for different roles? And how can a women's movement flourish if there is disagreement about who counts as a woman? Perhaps, as Lee (2010: 43–44) suggests,

> movement building must become less about identity and more about imagining a livable world regardless of the stake we hold in being women, or men, or gay, or black, or white, or indigenous, or abled, or trans. [...] [however] [...] that seems to dismiss the pressing issues represented by these stakes, namely, the subjugation of human beings, and among them, those who occupy bodies that fail to conform to ... binary logic.

GENDER INTERSECTS WITH OTHER CATEGORIES

There is more to gender than the basic, private experience of belonging to a gender category. The ways in which that category is defined and expressed may vary a great deal across social and cultural environments.

Some years ago, two researchers (Sugihara and Katsurada, 1999) asked a group of Japanese college students to complete the Bem Sex Role Inventory (BSRI), a test often used in North America to assess psychological masculinity and femininity. In North American samples, men usually score as more "masculine" and women as more "feminine" on this measure, meaning that men tend to describe themselves as more like the US men, and women as more like the US women on whom the test was developed. For Japanese students, however, these differences did not appear. There were no differences between Japanese women and Japanese men on either the Masculinity or Femininity scales of the BSRI, and both genders scored higher on the Femininity scale than on the Masculinity scale. The authors noted that traits desirable for women and men in Japan may be different from those thought desirable in American culture, and they commented that "Japanese have described the 'ideal' woman as 'Yamato-nadeshiko' which represents a gentle and quiet female with internal strength," and that the ideal man is someone with "internal strength rather than physical strength" (p. 645). In a later study using a scale developed specifically for Japanese respondents, these authors again found minimal differences between women and men in their self-descriptions; they commented that, in contrast to Western cultures, gendered personality expectations in Japan may be meaningful only when considered within social contexts (Sugihara and Katsurada, 2002).

Clearly, the ideals and norms for femininity and masculinity are not identical across all cultures. Research also shows that even within cultures, racial and ethnic identities intersect with gender norms. For example, one researcher (Tabar, 2007) describes a cultural category of ethnicized masculinity, labeled *habiib*, among second-generation Lebanese-Australian youths. The term *habiib* emphasizes not only a sense of kinship and shared experience among young Australian men of Lebanese ancestry, but also, according to Tabar's informants, "a hypersexualised masculinity with a particular style of dressing, posturing and even speaking."

Gender norms, stereotypes, and expressions also intersect with factors such as age, social class, sexual orientation, and ability/ disability. For example, there is evidence from several sources that women develop more confidence and power as they move into middle age. Research also shows that gender stereotypes are different for women of low and middle social class. We will explore these intersections further in later chapters.

THE EMPHASIS ON DIFFERENCES

Sometimes the entire focus of inquiries into gender and sex seems to be on defining the differences between categories. Perhaps this is not surprising; academic researchers know that one sure way to get findings published is to show a "significant" difference between two groups. Indeed, "no-difference" findings often languish, unpublished and unrecognized, in academic file cabinets.

The issue of difference is a loaded one, however: in many times and places, women have been excluded from occupations and from participation in aspects of public life *because* of presumed differences from men that made them unsuitable for such activities. Thus, researchers oriented toward gender equality have often focused on showing that women and men do *not* differ on important abilities and temperamental qualities.

But might an emphasis only on debunking differences cause us to miss some important issues? A focus only on illustrating differences may solidify gender stereotypes and uphold the status quo. However, a focus only on showing similarities may result in the glossing over of important issues: differences among women and men of different cultures, ethnicities, racial identities, sexualities, ages, and social classes; the different resources and sources of power available to women and men; or the different needs of women and men with respect to biologically connected issues such as health, reproduction, and longevity.

Clearly, a single-minded emphasis on either differences or similarities is likely to miss something important. Canadian researcher Meredith Kimball (1995) argued that it is important not to choose one emphasis over the other, but instead to practice "double visions," engaging the tension between the two approaches. Maintaining this perspective is difficult, but it is more consistent with the complexities of women's and men's lives and the ways they entwine and connect. In the following chapters, as we excavate the assumptions and ideas underlying gender stereotypes and prejudice, we will repeatedly run up against this tension between seeing similarities and seeing differences.

FOR FURTHER EXPLORATION

Blakemore, Judith E.O., Berenbaum, Sheri A., and Liben, Lynn S. (2009). *Gender development* (New York: Psychology Press, Taylor and Francis Group). This detailed yet reader-friendly book provides a fascinating and balanced look at different aspects of the development of gender. Chapters on the history of the field and on biological, social, and cognitive approaches to understanding how gender takes shape will leave the reader well informed.

Boylan, Jennifer (2003). *She's not there: A life in two genders* (New York: Broadway Books). This lively and personal book is one of several interesting autobiographies of individuals who have transitioned as adults to a different gender expression.

Colapinto, John (2001). *As nature made him: The boy who was raised as a girl* (New York: HarperCollins). A journalist tells the fascinating story of the famous "John/Joan" case.

Fausto-Sterling, Anne (2000). *Sexing the body: Gender politics and the construction of sexuality* (New York: Basic Books). A biologist uses her expertise to warn against over-simplified interpretations of research on biological sex differences. Among the controversies she takes up are the idea that there should be only two genders, and the notion that scientific language is neutral.

Fine, Cordelia (2010). *Delusions of gender: How our minds, society, and neurosexism create difference* (New York: W.W. Norton). An accessible critique of research on sex differences in the brain.

Jordan-Young, Rebecca M. (2010). *Brain storm: The flaws in the science of sex differences* (Cambridge, MA: Harvard University Press). The author presents a sophisticated analysis of the methodological problems with research linking prenatal hormones to sex differences in the brain. She challenges researchers to come up with a new, dynamic model that focuses on the processes of development instead of trying to measure "essential" male–female differences presumed to be the outcome of prenatal hormone differences.

Maccoby, Eleanor E. (1998). *The two sexes: Growing up apart, coming together* (Cambridge, MA: Harvard University Press). A well-respected pioneer in the psychology of gender development summarizes research showing how the sex-segregated "two cultures of childhood" merge gradually into a more gender-integrated adult culture—and some of the problems that result.

REFERENCES

Auyeung, B., Baron-Cohen, S., Ashwin, E., Knickmeyer, R., Taylor, K., Hackett, G., and Hines, M. (2009). Fetal testosterone predicts sexually differentiated childhood behavior in girls and boys. *Psychological Science, 20*, 144–148. doi: 10.1111/j.1467-9280.2009.02279.x.

Barr, C. (2016). Who are Generation Z? The latest data on today's teens. *Guardian*, December 10. www.theguardian.com/lifeandstyle/2016/dec/10/generation-z-latest-data-teens.

Berenbaum, S.A. and Beltz, A.M. (2016). How early hormones shape gender development. *Current Opinion in Behavioral Sciences, 7*, 53–60. doi: 10.1016/j.cobeha.2015.11.011.

Berenbaum, S.A., Blakemore, J.E.O., and Beltz, A.M. (2011). A role for biology in gender-related behavior. *Sex Roles, 64*, 804–825. doi: 10.1007/s11199-011-9990-8.

Bian, L., Leslie, S., and Cimpian, A. (2017). Gender stereotypes about intellectual ability emerge early and influence children's interests. *Science, 355* (6323), 389–391.

Bradley, S.J., Oliver, G.D., Chernick, A.B., and Zucker, K.J. (1998). Experiment of nurture: Ablatio penis at 2 months, sex reassignment at 7 months, and a psychosexual follow-up in young adulthood. *Pediatrics, 102*(1), e9.

Brown, M. and Rounsley, D. (1996). *True selves: Understanding transsexualism for families, friends, coworkers, and helping professionals.* San Francisco, CA: Jossey-Bass.

Collins, R.L. (2011). Content analysis of gender roles in media: Where are we now and where should we go? *Sex Roles, 64*, 290–298. doi: 10.1007/s11199-010-9929-5.

Diamond, M. and Sigmundson, H.K. (1997). Sex reassignment at birth: Long-term review and clinical implications. *Archives of Pediatric Medicine, 151*, 298–304.

Eagly, A.H. (1987). *Sex differences in social behavior: A social role interpretation.* Hillsdale, NJ: Erlbaum.

Eichstedt, J.A., Serbin, L.A., Poulin-Dubois, D., and Sen, M.G. (2002). Of bears and men: Infants' knowledge of conventional and metaphorical gender stereotypes. *Infant Behavior and Development, 25*, 296–310. doi: 10.1016/S0163-6383(02)00081-4.

Geena Davis Institute (2016). *The reel truth: Women aren't seen or heard. An automated analysis of gender representation in popular films.* https://seejane.org/research-informs-empowers/data/.

Imperato-McGinley, J., Peterson, R.E., Gautier, T., and Sturla, E. (1979). Androgens and the evolution of male gender identity among male pseudohermaphrodites with a 5-alph-reductase deficiency. *New England Journal of Medicine, 310*, 839–840.

Joel, D., Tarrasch, R., Berman, Z., Mukamel, M., and Ziv, E. (2014). Queering gender: Studying gender identity in "normative" individuals. *Psychology & Sexuality, 5*, 291–321. doi: 10.1080/19419899.2013.830640.

Kharroub, T. and Weaver, A.J. (2014). Portrayals of women in transnational Arab television drama series. *Journal of Broadcasting & Electronic Media, 58*, 179–195. doi:10.1080/08838151.2014.906434.

Kimball, M. (1995). *Feminist Visions of Gender Similarities and Differences.* Binghamton, NY: Haworth.

Kruijver, F., Zhou, J-N., Pool, C., Hofman, M., Gooren, L., and Swaab, D. (2000). Male-to-female transsexuals have female neuron numbers in a limbic nucleus. *Journal of Clinical Endocrinology and Metabolism, 85*, 2034–2041.

Lee, W.L. (2010). *Contemporary feminist theory and activism: Six global issues.* Peterborough, Ontario: Broadview Press.

LeGuin, U.K. (1969). *The left hand of darkness.* New York: Ace Books.

Martin, C.L. and Ruble, D. (2004). Children's search for gender clues. *Current Directions in Psychological Science, 13*, 67–70. doi: 10.1111/j.0963-7214. 2004. 00276.x.

Oakley, A. (1972). *Sex, gender and society.* London: Maurice Temple Smith.

Paek, H., Nelson, M.R., and Vilela, A.M. (2011). Examination of gender-role portrayals in television advertising across seven countries. *Sex Roles, 64*, 192–207. doi:10.1007/s11199-010-9850-y.

Pratto, F. and Walker, A. (2004). The bases of gendered power. In A.H. Eagly, A.E. Beall, and R.J. Sternberg (eds), *The Psychology of Gender* (2nd edn), pp. 242–268. New York: Guilford Press.

Reiner, W.G. and Gearhart, J.P. (2004). Discordant sexual identity in some genetic males with cloacal exstrophy assigned to female sex at birth. *New England Journal of Medicine, 350*, 333–341.

Rivas, J. (2015). Half of young people believe gender isn't limited to male and female. Fusion.net, February 3. http://fusion.net/story/42216/half-of-young-people-believe-gender-isnt-limited-to-male-and-female/.

Sameth, M. (2016). Is god transgender? *The New York Times*, August 12. https://mobile.nytimes.com/2016/08/13/opinion/is-god-transgender.html?_r=0&referer=.

Smith, E.S., Junger, J., Derntl, B., and Habel, U. (2015). The transsexual brain—A review of findings on the neural basis of transsexualism. *Neuroscience and Biobehavioral Reviews, 59*, 251–266. doi: 10.1016/j.neubiorev.2015.09.008.

Smith, S.L., Choueiti, M., Scofield, E., and Pieper, K. (2013). *Gender inequality in 500 popular films: Examining on-screen portrayals and behind-the-scenes employment patterns in motion pictures released between 2007–2012.* Annenberg School of Communication. http://annenberg.usc.edu/sites/default/files/2015/04/28/Gender%20Inequality%20in%20500%20Popular%20Films.pdf.

Smith, S.L., Pieper, K.M., Granados, A., and Choueiti, M. (2010). Assessing gender-related portrayals in top-grossing G-rated films. *Sex Roles, 62*, 774–786. doi:10.1007/s11199-009-9736-z.

Sugihara, Y. and Katsurada, E. (1999). Masculinity and femininity in Japanese culture: A pilot study. *Sex Roles,* 40, 635–646. doi: 10.1023/A:1018896215625.

Sugihara, Y. and Katsurada, E. (2002). Gender role development in Japanese culture: Diminishing gender role differences in a contemporary society. *Sex Roles,* 47, 443–452. doi:/10.1023/A:1021648426787.

Tabar, P. (2007). "Habiibs" in Australia: Language, identity and masculinity. *Journal of Intercultural Studies, 28*, 157–172.

Unger, R. (1979). Toward a redefinition of sex and gender. *American Psychologist, 34*, 1085–1094.

van Anders, S.M. (2015). Beyond sexual orientation: Integrating gender/sex and diverse sexualities via Sexual Configurations Theory (SCT). *Archives of Sexual Behavior, 44*, 1177–1213. doi: 10.1007/s10508-015-0490-8.

Wood, J.L., Murko, V., and Nopoulos, P. (2009). Ventral frontal cortex in children: Morphology, social cognition and femininity/masculinity. *Social Cognitive and Affective Neuroscience, 3*, 168–176.

Wood, J.L., Heitmiller, D., Andreasen, N.C., and Nopoulos, P. (2008). Morphology of the ventral frontal cortex: Relationship to femininity and social cognition. *Cerebral Cortex, 18*, 534–540.

2

THEORETICAL FRAMEWORKS FOR THINKING ABOUT GENDER

More than four decades ago, many feminists in the United States adopted a small but powerful shorthand for the experience of suddenly beginning to see one's world differently. Click! A "click!" moment, as first described by Jane O'Reilly (1971) in the inaugural issue of *Ms. Magazine*, was a sudden shift in one's view of the world—a eureka moment when a woman noticed, in a visceral way, how much everything was organized around the assumption that men were more important, more competent, than women, and were shaken by that realization. It was the moment when, for instance, a woman noticed that any woman in an office was assumed to be a secretary, that a husband doing housework was assumed to be "helping" rather than sharing, that a family vacation was never a vacation if one was a housewife. A "click!" moment was the instant, as reported by many women, when they became radicalized—when they shifted away from an androcentric (male-centered) perspective, and began to define themselves as feminist.

We see our world through frameworks provided by our culture, our families, our peers. Changing those frameworks, whether stimulated by a single critical event or a long period of reflection and analysis, forces us to interpret our observations in new ways, to notice different things. And we may not always be aware of our frameworks unless and until they change. Thus, it can be useful to examine different possible frameworks for interpreting and making sense of what is going on around us. Such frameworks, often called theories, are systematic ways of making sense of what we observe.

A change in the framework or theory we use can change the questions we ask when we try to understand an issue—which is why arguments about theoretical perspectives can be so intense, even if theoretical issues may appear dry and abstract. In terms of women and gender, a critical task of theory has been to make "gender visible and problematic across intimate social contexts," to challenge assumptions about social arrangements that have been accepted as normal (Allen, 2016). For example, Naomi Weisstein (1971) ignited the beginnings of a revolution in the way psychologists studied women and gender with a single publication, *Psychology constructs the female*. In that study, she castigated psychologists for uncritically assuming that female–male behavioral differences were "natural," and stemmed merely from biological differences. In the wake of her call for psychologists to consider the impact of the social environment upon gender differences, many more researchers began to study ways in which female–male differences in behavior might result from differing expectations, opportunities, and rewards for women and men. In a similar way, a shift in the way historians studied women and gender was accelerated by Sheila Rowbotham's (1975) ground-breaking study, *Hidden from history*. In that work, she interrogated the notion of what was considered worthy of historical study and documentation, and noted the pervasive tendency to omit women and their activities from the historical record. Her work helped stimulate historical investigations into many aspects of women's lives and an increased recognition of how social/historical context shaped women's roles. In turn, this focus on women's experiences led eventually to the recognition that important differences among women based on race, class, ethnicity, sexual orientation, age, and other dimensions also needed to be part of the analysis (Hannam, n.d.).

In every academic discipline concerned with gender, preferred theories have shifted and changed over time under the influence of political and social forces and movements such as *feminism* and anti-racism. In this chapter, we will examine some of the theoretical perspectives that have shaped the study of women and gender.

THEORIES ABOUT GENDER

There are so many different theories concerned with gender that it is impossible to cover all of them in one short chapter. Not only does every discipline have its own set of dominant theories, but disciplines do not even necessarily align in the scope of their theories, or in what criteria they use to designate a theory as useful. In the sciences, such as biology or psychology, a useful theory is one that can be tested to determine whether it fits with observations. In some humanities disciplines, such as philosophy, however, a useful theory is one that provides a systematic and logical way of analyzing and explaining a given situation, but that may not actually be testable. Political theory, reflecting yet another approach, may sometimes refer to a set of beliefs about how the political and governing process should work and what gives legitimacy to a government. In the following sections, we will examine two major categories of theories of gender: theories about why and how gender categories develop, are experienced and enacted, and theories about why and how gender inequalities persist.

THEORIES ABOUT THE WHY AND HOW OF GENDER DEVELOPMENT

There exists a long tradition of theories about differences between women and men, some centered on the notion of women as deficient or incompletely developed human beings, and some based on the idea of men and women as complementary—but relatively equal—opposites. Proponents of the "deficiency" view have included Western philosophers, theologians, and scientists, including Aristotle, Thomas Aquinas, and Sigmund Freud. Advocates of the complementary opposites view have included early medical researchers who viewed female and male reproductive organs as being the same except "inside out;" Chinese philosophers who conceived of two complementary energies as "yin" (darkness, coldness, femininity) and "yang" (heat, brightness, masculinity) and taught that they should be properly balanced in each person; and a variety of theorists—from Carl Jung to present-day psychologists—who have explicated the concept of *androgyny*: the joining of masculine and feminine qualities in a single individual. The hierarchical and complementary approaches may overlap, as in cases where people argue that women have special qualities (such as unselfishness) that complement those of men but are not sufficiently competent or tough to be placed in leadership positions.

PSYCHOANALYTIC THEORIES

Psychoanalytic theory, developed by Sigmund Freud (1960), is often linked to his controversial idea that "anatomy is destiny." He postulated that children learn to identify with their gender through complicated childhood processes centering on their response to having or not having a penis. This process, in which 3- to 5-year-old children of both sexes attach a high value to the possession of a penis, so that boys learn to fear castration and girls develop "penis envy," was said by Freud to result in feminine or masculine identification. Boys, according to his theory, suppress their early attraction to their mothers and identify with their fathers because they fear their fathers will see them as rivals and castrate them. Girls identify with their mothers as a kind of resigned, fall-back strategy: they realize they cannot have a penis of their own, so they hope they can instead attract a man and have a male child.

Freud's theory, unpopular with anyone who takes issue with the notion that girls automatically feel inferior because of their anatomy, has been modified by many subsequent theorists. For example, his one-time student, Karen Horney (1926), posited that it was boys, not girls, who experienced anatomical envy. Males, she argued, unconsciously envied the female womb and tried to compensate for that lack by engaging in other forms of creativity. Later, psychologist Ellyn Kaschak (1992) proposed that, within patriarchal families, both boys and girls developed unconscious feelings that men were central and women peripheral—and that both had to resolve and move beyond such feelings to achieve mature relationships. Sociologist Nancy Chodorow (1978) also used a psychoanalytic approach to analyze family relationships and their impact upon gender development. She argued that a traditional Western family arrangement, with the mother as primary caretaker and nurturer and the father as a more remote parent, helped create a situation in which girls find it easier than boys to form intimate bonds, whereas boys, driven by the need to separate from the mother in order to form a masculine identity, learn to devalue women and femininity. All variations of psycho-analytic theory stress early child–parent relationships and uncon-scious processes as reasons for gender development.

EVOLUTIONARY THEORIES

Also controversial are theories about gender that are grounded in *evolutionary psychology*. Such theories, originated by Charles Darwin (1871), posit that every species, including human beings, changes over time as a result of genetic changes that are passed along across generations. Qualities that enhance the likelihood of survival are more likely to be passed on because individuals who have them are more likely to grow to maturity, find a mate, and reproduce. This approach argues that some qualities relevant to reproductive success are different for males and for females; the theory locates female–male differences in the different mating strategies that favor women's and men's reproductive success. For instance, this approach suggests that because men have millions of sperm, their best bet for reproducing their genes is to scatter them as widely as possible by mating with many different women. Women, on the other hand, have to devote a lot of time and energy to each pregnancy and birth, so they maximize their chances of passing on their genes by being careful and selective in choosing a mate. Thus men have evolved to be promiscuous and women to be selective, according to this theory.

Traditional evolutionary theories have been challenged and expanded to accommodate observations that simply do not fit with the traditional notion that males have evolved to compete for females and to mate promiscuously, whereas females have evolved to be more selective. For example, primatologist Sarah Hrdy (1981) wrote about the many instances in which female primates mate with multiple partners to enhance the survival chances of their off-spring. Biologist Bruce Begemihl (1999) noted that traditional evolutionary theory did not explain, or even encompass, same-sex attraction and relationships or other forms of sexual diversity. He gathered a great deal of evidence for what he called biological exuberance—a vast and complex variety of sexual and gender expression in the animal world that does not fit neatly into the idea that all evolution is driven by competition and oriented toward the narrow objective of reproducing individuals' genes. Seeking to develop a more inclusive theory, evolutionary biologist Joan Roughgarden (2004) posited the idea of social selection, arguing that evolution favors not just traits that attract a mate, but also social-inclusionary traits (traits that confer an advantage in terms of acceptance by one's group). For example, female–female pair bonding does not achieve the successful passing along of an individual's genes; however, in some species and in some situations, such bonding may contribute to an individual's access to resources. Thus, traits that facilitate female–female pair bonding may be evolutionarily adaptive. All variations of evolutionary theory rest on the notion that, over many generations, traits that confer survival advantages are more likely to be passed along—to be "selected for." Whereas the traditional approaches were colored by cultural assumptions about the natural differences between women and men, later approaches have made it clear that the impact of evolutionary pressures cannot be summed up by the simple idea that men are promiscuous and women selective.

SOCIALIZATION THEORIES

A third category of theories of gender development involves *socialization*. These approaches emphasize that children learn from their culture to identify as male or female and how to behave in masculine or feminine ways. As noted in Chapter 1, such lessons may be directly taught by parents, teachers, or peers, or simply absorbed through observation. The theories assume that conformity to expectations about being feminine or masculine is motivated by individuals' desire to "fit in" and to be socially competent. One such approach, *social cognitive theory*, posits that children first learn gender roles through external rewards and punishments, but later learn to regulate their own behavior through internal rewards and punishments (Bandura, 1986). Another approach, the *cognitive approach to gender development*, suggests that children adopt gender roles as a result of identifying with a gender category and developing ideas about what is appropriate behavior for that category (Martin, Ruble, and Szkrybalo (2002). *Gender schema theory* (Bem, 1981) asserts that, beginning in childhood, individuals develop mental representations or schemas relevant to gender, and use those schemas to organize their thinking and behavior. According to this theory, the more emphasis there is on gender dichotomy in a child's upbringing, the more that child will elaborate and use the gender schema. All of these theoretical approaches stress that the child's rearing and social environment shape the development of gender.

SOCIAL-CULTURAL THEORIES

Finally, there are *social-cultural theories* that focus on how women's and men's behavior is shaped by the way power is distributed in the broader culture. These theories posit that, because so many cultures assign higher status and power to men, behavior associated with masculinity tends to be powerful behavior and feminine behavior tends to be powerless behavior. Such approaches focus not on anatomy, biology, or childhood learning to explain gender development, but on the direct impact of the social-cultural environment upon women's and men's behavior. They suggest that, in the process of accommodating a society's assignment of more powerful, high-status roles to men and less powerful roles to women, men tend to develop more dominant, directive, controlling behaviors, whereas women tend to develop more submissive, conciliatory, cooperative behaviors. *Social roles theory* and *social dominance theory*, described in Chapter 1, are examples of social-cultural theories. These theories suggest that gender differences in behavior stem from contextual cultural differences—and that gender differences in behavior are likely to be greatest in societies that emphasize male dominance and hierarchical organization (e.g., Pratto, 1996; Sanday, 1981).

FEMINIST THEORIES: FRAMEWORKS FOR UNDERSTANDING GENDER INEQUALITY

Feminism, as a social movement, has the goal of removing inequalities between women and men. Thus, feminist theories focus on analyzing and understanding the reasons for gender inequalities and figuring out the best strategies for reaching that goal. Most such theories start with the idea that gender inequality is produced and reproduced within a power structure called *patriarchy* (literally the rule of the father), a system of male dominance that involves male authority figures in the family and elsewhere, men's competitive relationships with other men, and the exclusion or restriction of women (Lerner, 1986; Ortner, 2014). However, with a proliferation of viewpoints and voices, "the issue of male dominance or patriarchy has become on the one hand more muted, and on the other hand more complicated, more intertwined with other forms of inequality like race, class, and sexuality" (Ortner, 2014, p. 533).

The number and variety of feminist theories may seem overwhelming, and there is not complete agreement on how to characterize them. One authoritative overview of feminist theories (Lorber, 2012) describes 13 different broad theoretical approaches to understanding and undermining gender inequality. Lorber sorts the various approaches into three general categories of feminism: gender reform, gender resistance, and gender rebellion—an organization that we will follow in this chapter.

GENDER REFORM THEORIES

Some of the earliest attempts to classify feminisms (e.g., Jaggar and Struhl, 1978) identified what Lorber (2012) labels reform theories: *liberal feminism*, *Marxist feminism*, and *socialist feminism*. These types of feminism characterized some of the earliest ("first-wave") movements for women's rights. Lorber argues that reform-oriented theories rest on the notion that there are two gender groups that have not been treated equally, and they explore ways to understand the reasons for that, to make the system fair, to erase the disadvantages (such as pay inequity, employment discrimination, unfair distribution of household labor) that have accrued to women. The theories in this category differ in their analysis of the root causes of gender inequalities, but they all begin with the acceptance of the idea that there are two gender groups and that men are advantaged over women.

Liberal feminism focuses on economic and political equality. This approach posits that the socialization of girls and boys into different life patterns, the division of household and occupational labor between women and men, the devaluing of women and their work, and the generally more restricted choices for women than men all contribute to gender inequality and must be challenged. The thrust of this theoretical approach is toward more gender neutrality in the way opportunities, challenges, and rewards are divided. One way of characterizing this approach is captured in a quote by U.S. Supreme Court Justice Ruth Bader Ginsburg, who said that she had spent years of her life "devoted to—I don't say women's rights—I say the constitutional principle of the equal citizenship status of women and men" (quoted in Carmon and Knizhnik, 2015: 43). This eminently practical and necessary approach of striving for equal status and opportunities for women and men does, however, have some limitations. Some have argued, for instance, that it can be androcentric—that it risks making men and masculinity the standard or goal toward which women should be able to move. It tends to privilege the importance of paid work and give less attention to the importance of the unpaid family and household work that women have traditionally done, to issues such as sexual violence, and to race, class, and ethnic differences among women (Lorber, 2012).

Marxist feminism views gender inequality not as an isolated issue but as a symptom of a larger problem: pervasive class inequality in societies. This approach argues that one important driving force in the subordination of women is the exploitation of women as unpaid workers in the home. Women's free labor makes it possible for corporations to pay male employees less because they do not have to consider the cost of childcare, cooking, housecleaning, and other domestic necessities of family life. Another source of gender inequality, according to this theory, is the use of women as an auxiliary or reserve pool of workers—who are hired and fired in response to fluctuating economic forces and paid less than their male counterparts. This analysis is important because it highlights the economic importance of women's traditional unpaid domestic work. Indeed, it has proven difficult to eradicate gender inequality, even when governments or corporations take on more financial responsibility for childcare solutions (e.g., by providing on-site childcare and/or parental leave). Responsibility for childcare and domestic work continues to rest more heavily on women than on men, even when such options are provided.

Traditionally, Marxist feminist theory ignored differences among women based on factors other than class. However, more recent approaches have theorized that economic class may be understood as both racialized and gendered—that the subordination of gender and racial or ethnic groups is partially created and maintained by, for example, hiring practices that privilege young white women for certain jobs, or the use of images and stereotypes that associate certain kinds of people, in terms of gender and race, with certain occupations (Acker, 2006).

Socialist feminist theory built on Marxist theory by developing a new focus on the complex inequalities among people and groups who differ on several important dimensions: gender, race, class, and ethnicity. Theorists within this framework emphasize that the statuses attached to each of these dimensions have interlocking effects, so that, for example, a wealthy white woman who becomes a research scientist has a different status (and different experiences, different barriers) than a wealthy woman of color or a wealthy white man in the same occupation. The combined effects of these different statuses, the way they operate jointly to produce various levels of status and advantage/disadvantage, has in recent years become known as *intersectionality*. Factoring into the complex inequalities of gender, race/ethnicity and class are the burdens of family and household responsibilities on women. These burdens pervasively fall on women, but they differ, and may be handled differently, for women in different economic classes and different racial or ethnic groups. The socialist feminist analysis of this injustice emphasizes that government intervention can provide potential solutions: through policies based on acknowledging that childcare is a responsibility of societies as a whole, rather than simply of individual parents.

Feminist theories have become increasingly complex and nuanced as they have expanded to cover a broader range of issues. Thus, a newer inclusion in reform-oriented feminisms is *transnational feminism*. Within this framework, theorists have been exploring the interplay of economic globalization forces and gender inequality. The relationships are complicated, and cannot be easily summarized. However, the focus is on understanding the ways in which global movements of persons and goods, the production of goods, and ideas are gendered. For example, women and men emigrate or flee their countries at different rates, under different kinds of pressure, for different reasons. Factories move from developed countries to countries where they can pay workers less— and different kinds of factories hire younger, single, or older married women. Women are more likely than men to be trafficked as sex workers. Violence against women takes different forms in different cultures, and certain forms of violence may follow women when they move to new countries. Ideas about women's rights and gender equality also flow across borders—and women in Third World countries may resent Western feminists' assumptions about what the most important issues are and how they should be tackled. The challenge of theorizing about gender from a transnational perspective is immense, but in a world where national borders are increasingly permeable, and where the pressures toward maximizing profits through globalization may well be exacerbating gender inequalities, many feminist theories believe it is crucial.

GENDER RESISTANCE THEORIES

According to Lorber (2012), gender resistance theories have in common the notion that simply balancing opportunities for women and men is not enough to achieve gender equality. That approach ignores the positive aspects of cultural femininity, and would result in women becoming more and more like men in order to achieve equality. For example, psychological theorists such as Jean Baker Miller (1977) and Carol Gilligan (1982) have emphasized the strengths and importance of qualities traditionally assigned to women, such as caring, responsible nurturing, cooperation, and accommodation. They and many others have argued that simply trying to get more and more women into high-status, traditionally male positions implicitly devalues women's qualities and reinforces the idea that men and men's lives form the standard against which women should be judged. By contrast, gender resistance theories celebrate women's qualities and experiences, and stress the importance of taking women's perspective. Among the theoretical approaches Lorber includes within this category are *radical feminism*, *lesbian feminism*, *cultural feminism*, and *standpoint feminism*.

Radical feminism identifies the oppression of women by men as the most basic form of oppression. Its analysis focuses on uncovering the dismissiveness, *misogyny*, and violence against women built into institutional systems of law, medicine, religion, science, the media, education, and other social structures. Within this approach, there has been an emphasis on highlighting and understanding the control, exploitation, and objectification of women's bodies manifested in restrictions on women's reproductive choices, pornography, prostitution, rape, sexual assault, and harassment. Proponents of this approach argue that even if women achieve equality with men in terms of occupational opportunities or pay, they will still be vulnerable to this kind of threat—and so the equality will be a mirage. However, theorists using this framework do not analyze women's sexuality simply in terms of victimhood. They argue, rather, that an important aspect of gender equality is an understanding of and respect for women's sexual pleasure and sexual agency. If women were not viewed as subordinate to men, they note, women would not be regarded as "conquests" or as promiscuous when they had sex with men, but rather as partners choosing to share in a pleasurable act. Radical feminist theory also focuses on the important positive qualities associated with women's traditional nurturing roles and argues that these qualities must not be overlooked in attempts to craft a culture that is supportive of women. The celebration of feminine nurturance is extended to caring for the environment (eco-feminism).

Radical feminism has generated plenty of controversy. Some radical feminist theorists may argue that, because society has encouraged male dominance and female sexual display, most men are capable of violence against women, and heterosexual relationships are almost always potentially dangerous to women. These arguments, which gloss over the differences among men and the possibility that men, like women, can recognize and transcend cultural pressures, have often been painful for men and for women in heterosexual relationships. Radical feminism may also suggest that some cultural institutions are so imbued with misogyny that they cannot be reformed and must instead be rejected and re-created as completely different. For instance, theologian Mary Daly, who critiqued the Christian tradition for its pervasive *sexism* and sought reform (Daly, 1968), eventually decided she had to turn her back on the Church and develop a feminist philosophy and spirituality outside that institution.

Some have argued that the focus on women's positive qualities of nurturance and caring presents an unrealistic idealization of women—and that it is perhaps not so far from such idealization to the old condescending idea that women should be protected and kept on a pedestal. Women who do not see themselves fitting into the nurturing, caring feminine stereotype may be uncomfortable with this approach. Finally, some have argued that a theory which is centered on women's positive qualities, although providing a needed correction to androcentrism, may inadvertently reinforce the notion that women and men are essentially different and contribute to gender polarization (Bem, 1993).

Lesbian feminist theories rest on the idea that gender is maintained because of society's organization of its institutions around heterosexuality. If there were not an assumption of heterosexuality, if heterosexual couple relationships were not considered the norm, if everyone were not expected to find a partner of the "opposite" sex, why would there be so much invested in feminine and masculine roles, in masculine or feminine identity? Like radical feminist theory, this approach is pessimistic about heterosexual relationships; it goes a step further by suggesting that gender equality is most likely to be served when women focus their energy on close relationships with other women. Lesbian sexuality is celebrated in this approach, as are the emotional bonds of strong female friendships and women's communities. *Cultural feminist theories* overlap with lesbian feminist theories in foregrounding the importance of female–female relationships and women's social spaces. This approach also emphasizes the importance of woman-created art, literature, and music as ways to celebrate women's experiences and push back against a male-dominant view of the world. Some have argued that both of these approaches may tend to idealize women's relationships—making it seem that women are more understanding, caring, and compassionate toward other women than perhaps they really are. Some evidence on this point is discussed in Chapters 4 and 7. Other critiques focus on the separatism implied in these theories. If women withdraw to their own social spaces, they may be more comfortable, but male dominance may not be challenged.

Standpoint feminist theories emphasize that gender equality depends in large part on developing a society in which women's perspectives are included and valued as much as men's. For example, women must be included in science, medicine, business, and law, so that their experiences can inform decisions about what problems are important and need to be addressed. Such inclusion would make it clear that many male-centered assumptions have been treated as facts rather than as conclusions based on limited perspectives. This theoretical approach makes an important contribution by suggesting that any given situation may well not be viewed in the same way by women and men, and that it is critical to avoid automatically privileging masculine perspectives. However, by highlighting the importance of different perspectives, it also lays bare a much bigger problem: there are vast differences among women and among men. The standpoint of a middle-class Black North American woman is likely to be quite different from that of a working-class Southern European man.

GENDER REBELLION THEORIES

Theories in this group share the principle that a social order based on a binary system of two discrete gender categories is not a given, but may be challenged. They focus on how gender categories are created and maintained by our actions—and how the gendered social system can be undercut if people stop doing or performing gender. They argue that gender is not necessarily a useful general category, since it intersects with so many other dimensions (race, ethnicity, class, age, sexuality). Instead of simply focusing on gaining equal treatment for women and men, they ask: What is a woman, what is a man, and why do we have to have these categories at all? Among the theoretical approaches belonging to this group are *social construction feminism, multiracial/multiethnic feminism, feminist studies of men, postmodern feminism,* and *queer theory* (Lorber, 2012).

According to *social construction feminism,* gender categories are created and maintained by behaviors and social organizational structures that emphasize the differences between two non-overlapping categories: male and female. As noted in Chapter 1, biological sex is not neatly divided into two discrete categories. However, our society is organized around the male/female gender dichotomy (e.g., different clothes, toys, books, and hairstyles for girls and boys, girls' and boys' teams, different occupations, recreations, and behaviors thought to be appropriate for women and men) and people are expected to tailor their behavior and identity to fit one of the two categories—thus constructing gender. "By doing gender, we impose categorical divisions on physiological and behavioral continuums" (Lorber, 2012: 204). The categories "male" and "female" are legal ones (hence, for instance, the usual requirement to list one's sex on identity documents and the often fierce insistence that marriage be legally defined as a union between one man and one woman). They also form the basis for the division of labor in the home and the workplace. Social construction feminism theorizes that if binary gender categories were disrupted, if there were multiple categories and/or a refusal to fit neatly into the expectations for femininity and masculinity by doing gender, the social order that supports higher status to one group could not be maintained. This kind of rebellion against binary gender categories is not easily accomplished, however. An interesting case in point is the story of two psychologists who tried as hard as they could, with only partial success, to raise children for whom gender was not important (Bem, 1998).

Other theoretical approaches have also emphasized the importance of disrupting a social order based on categories. *Multiracial/multiethnic feminist theories* focus on the intersecting effects of multiple categories of identity, status, and dominance: not just gender, but race, ethnicity, social class, sexuality, and others. This approach simultaneously recognizes the particular experiences of specific groups (e.g., African American women), and analyzes the web of oppressive forces that produce the injustices affecting many groups. As Patricia Hill Collins (2000), a pioneer in the chronicling of this approach, notes, "Since Black women cannot be fully empowered unless intersecting oppressions themselves are eliminated, Black feminist thought supports broad principles of social justice that transcend U.S. Black women's particular needs" (p. 22).

The *feminist study of men* also provides an approach that examines interlocking structures of power and subordination based on gender, race, class, ethnicity, sexuality, and other categories. This approach focuses, in part, on the dominance relations between men, the factors that give some men power over other men. However, a major emphasis is on the ways in which, *within* categories such as race and class, male perspectives and male dominance tend to prevail. As noted by Jensen (2017), "Patriarchy is a system that delivers material benefits to men—unequally depending on men's other attributes (such as race, class, sexual orientation, nationality, immigration status) and on men's willingness to adapt to patriarchal values—but patriarchy constrains all women" (p. 59). A key concept in the feminist study of men is *hegemonic masculinity*, which refers to a cultural ideal of manhood or the most favored form of masculinity within the gender hierarchy (e.g., a masculinity that includes strength, toughness, potential for violence, competence as a breadwinner, heterosexuality) that underlies male dominance over women and some men's dominance over other men (e.g., Connell and Messerschmidt, 2005). The dominant ideal of masculinity may be enacted and reinforced through cultural rituals such as sport, male bonding in fraternities, and the visibility and importance accorded to all-male groups of political or business leaders. When that ideal is threatened, the reflexive tendency to defend it is aptly captured in this book title by an insightful female athlete: *The stronger women get, the more men love football* (Nelson, 1994). Some men have argued cogently that analyses of masculinity are critical to the advancement of social justice (e.g., Jensen, 2017; Kilmartin and Smiler, 2014; Marche, 2017).

Perhaps the theoretical approaches that are most unsettling and challenging to anyone used to thinking of gender categories as binary, essential, and stable are *postmodern feminist theories* and *queer theories.* A ground-breaking theorist for this approach is Judith Butler (1990), who developed and articulated the idea of gender *performativity*: the notion that gender is not something that individuals have, but rather something they do. Butler argued that gender categories are not essential but fictional—that they are constructed by the behavior of people endeavoring to conform to cultural structures of power and knowledge that organize humans into female–male binary categories. In other words, individuals do not act as males or females because of their inner gender identities; rather, the identities themselves are constructed by the cultural categories and the attempts to enact them. According to Butler, we do not have male and female categories of people because individuals identify as either male or female; rather individuals identify as male or female (and perform masculinity or femininity), because the categories exist and are enforced by cultural norms. The identities do not produce the categories; the categories produce the identities and the performance of those identities.

Queer theories take the idea of the arbitrariness of gender boundaries even further, and challenge the dualities of sex (female–male), gender (feminine–masculine), and sexuality (heterosexuality–homosexuality). They argue that these categorical boundaries are blurry, shift with time and circumstance, and thus provide no logical basis on which to divide people and favor one group over another. Such an approach, which advocates ignoring sex/gender/sexuality categories, is a fundamental challenge to the entire gender system. As noted in the previous chapter, emerging evidence suggests that, indeed, for many people, the experience of gender does not map neatly onto a binary system and that dichotomous gender categories do not capture the complexity of gender experience.

Postmodern and queer theories have been useful in bringing attention to the broad spectrum of gender performances and sexualities—making it clear that there are many varieties of "normal." This approach has, however, been critiqued on the basis that it does not provide useful frameworks for the political activism of, say, challenging sex discrimination. It is hard to fight discrimination against women, for instance, if everyone is arguing about what the category "woman" means and whether the woman–man distinction is valid. Another challenge comes from the experiences and activism of trans persons. As noted in Chapter 1, trans individuals may report an extremely strong feeling of identifying with a gender that does not match the sex to which they were assigned or their bodily configuration as female or male. They may, for instance, have been performing masculinity for most of their lives without ever claiming a masculine identity. Such examples make it more difficult to argue that identities are simply products of performing gender. On the other hand, trans politics may provide the most uncomfortable interrogation of the idea that gender is essential, fixed, and binary. When an individual can make a transition from living as a female to living as a male, it indicates that the boundaries between male and female are fluid, that a multitude of unknown factors affect individual gender identities, and that the clear, dichotomous categories which society takes for granted are fundamentally suspect.

HOW IMPORTANT ARE THEORIES?

The leader of the Roman Catholic Church, Pope Francis, has been quoted as commenting, cryptically yet dramatically, that gender theory was an attack on the family (Associated Press, 2016). He did not specify precisely which gender theory he was describing as so dangerous, but it was probably not the conservative theory of gender that portrays female–male behavioral and identity differences as biologically based and their family roles (mother as nurturer, father as breadwinner and authority) as divinely inspired. His comment makes it clear that how we think about, understand, and analyze problems may have important consequences in terms of how we view the world. It is also a reminder that, although we may tend to define theories as rather dry, rational sets of ideas about how the world works, our allegiance to them may be quite emotional. Scientists and scholars regularly have pointed, even nasty, disagreements over which theories are correct. When the theoretical domain in question is gender—already a fairly emotional topic for many people—debates can become very heated. Certainly, scientists who study gender development may have fierce disputes about, for instance, the degree and manner in which biology plays a role in behavioral gender differences; feminist scholars may disagree passionately about, for example, whether liberal, transnational, or social construction feminist theory is more useful for understanding and ameliorating gender inequality. A theory can become, for some, more like an ideology or doctrine, not susceptible to counterfactual evidence or logical arguments. Disagreements over theories can become the basis for insulting or rejecting others who are trying to solve the same problems ("she's not a real feminist"), but dialogue is probably more useful.

In fact, regardless of how long and how hard we ponder the theories described in this chapter, it will be impossible to determine one that is "correct." Most people engaged in deep study of gender and gender inequality find bits of what appears to be truth in many different theoretical approaches. Moreover, they find themselves modifying their ideas in response to new arguments, new evidence, new perspectives. The most useful way to analyze gender relations may fluctuate according to the particular issue under study, the historical and cultural context, and the unique and collaborative insights of those doing the analyzing. Understanding a complicated problem requires openness to a multitude of perspectives.

FOR FURTHER EXPLORATION

Bem, Sandra L. (1993). *The lenses of gender: Transforming the debate on sexual inequality* (New Haven, CT: Yale University Press). Bem, a psychologist, argues here that gender inequality is maintained through our adherence to three basic notions: that female–male differences are rooted in biology, that males are superior to females, and that society should be organized around these differences. She challenged these ideas, arguing that the focus on sexual difference was misguided and that biological sex need not be central to an individual's identity and sexuality.

Butler, Judith (1990). *Gender trouble: Feminism and the subversion of identity* (New York: Routledge). In this pioneering book, Butler questions the binary view of gender, and suggests that gender, rather than being "who we are," exists only when we perform it. From her perspective, gender and sexuality are fluid, and we should always be questioning what is supposedly normal about them.

Collins, Patricia Hill (2000). *Black feminist thought: Knowledge, consciousness, and the politics of empowerment,* (2nd edn) (New York: Routledge). The author explores the impact of intersecting oppressions upon Black women's experiences, and links African American women's activism with Black feminist thought.

Feminist Theory Website. Hosted by the Center for Digital Discourse and Culture, Virginia Tech University, this site contains historical information in English, French, and Spanish about feminists and their work in many countries. www.cddc.vt.edu/feminism/index.html.

Hrdy, Sarah B. (1981). *The woman that never evolved.* Cambridge, MA: Harvard University Press. Hdry, a primatologist and evolutionary theorist, reorients the focus of evolutionary theory to female strategies for reproduction and survival, thus challenging many traditional assumptions of evolutionary theory. She has also written further on the social aspects of evolution in later books, particularly in *Mother and others: The evolutionary origins of mutual understanding* (Cambridge, MA: Harvard University Press, 2009). In that book, she focuses on the importance of cooperative parenting, as opposed to rearing by one caretaker, in the evolution of the human tendency for cooperation and engagement with others.

Jensen, Robert (2017). *The end of patriarchy: Radical feminism for men* (North Melbourne, Australia: Spinifex Press). The author applies radical feminist theory to an analysis of human communities. He calls for an end to male dominance and a re-examination and overhaul of patriarchal structures.

Lorber, Judith (2012). *Gender inequality: Feminist theories and politics* (5th edn) (New York: Oxford University Press). The author, a scholar with deep expertise in sociology and women's studies, presents an overview of 13 different feminist theories, categorized by her as theories of reform, resistance, or rebellion.

Roughgarden, Joan (2004). *Evolution's rainbow: Diversity, gender and sexuality in nature and people* (Los Angeles, CA: University of California Press). The author, an evolutionary biologist, critiques the sexual selection emphasis of evolutionary theory and postulates instead a theory of social selection, which focuses on sexual partners' cooperation in pursuit of mutual benefit. She continues her development of the latter approach in a later book, *The Genial Gene: Deconstructing Darwinian Selfishness* (2009) (Los Angeles, CA: University of California Press). Her approach, which challenges traditional evolutionary approaches to sex, gender, and sexuality, is controversial among biologists, and very provocative.

REFERENCES

Acker, J. (2006). *Class questions: Feminist answers.* Lanham, MD: Rowman & Littlefield/AltaMira.

Allen, K.R. (2016). Feminist theory in family studies: History, reflection, and critique. *Journal of Family Theory & Review, 8,* 207–224. doi: 10.1111/ jftr.12133.

Associated Press (2016). Pope says gender theory part of "global war" on marriage. *Newsmax* October 2. www.newsmax.com/Newsfront/pope-gender-theory-war/2016/10/02/id/751239/.

Bandura, A. (1986). *Social foundations of thought and action: A social cognitive theory.* Englewood Cliffs, NJ: Prentice-Hall.

Begemihl, B. (1999). *Biological exuberance: Animal sexuality and natural diversity.* Durham, NC: St. Martin's Press.

Bem, S.L. (1981). Gender schema theory: A cognitive account of sex typing. *Psychological Review, 88,* 354–364.

Bem, S.L. (1993). *The lenses of gender: Transforming the debate on sexual inequality.* New Haven, CT: Yale University Press.

Bem, S.L. (1998). *An unconventional family.* New Haven, CT: Yale University Press.

Butler, Judith (1990). *Gender trouble: Feminism and the subversion of identity.* New York: Routledge.

Carmon, I. and Knizhnik, S. (2015). *Notorious RBG: The life and times of Ruth Bader Ginsburg.* New York: HarperCollins.

Chodorow, N. (1978). *The reproduction of mothering: Psychoanalysis and the sociology of gender.* Berkeley, CA: University of California Press.

Collins, P.H. (2000). *Black feminist thought: Knowledge, consciousness, and the politics of empowerment* (2nd edn). New York: Routledge.

Connell, R.W. and Messerschmidt, J.W. (2005). Hegemonic masculinity: Rethinking the concept. *Gender & Society, 19,* 829–859. doi: 10.1177/ 0891243205278639.

Daly, M. (1968). *The church and the second sex*. Boston, MA: Beacon Press.

Darwin, C. (1871). *The descent of man, and selection in relation to sex*. London: John Murray.

Freud, S. (1960). *A general introduction to psychoanalysis* (trans. J. Riviere). New York: Washington Square Press. (Original work published 1924.)

Gilligan, C. (1982). *In a different voice: Psychological theory and women's development*. Cambridge, MA: Harvard University Press.

Hannam, J. (n.d.). Women's history, feminist history. In *Making history: The changing face of the profession in Britain*. www.history.ac.uk/makinghistory/resources/articles/womens_history.html.

Horney, K. (1926). The flight from womanhood. *International Journal of Psychoanalysis, 7*, 324–329.

Hrdy, S.B. (1981). *The woman that never evolved*. Cambridge, MA: Harvard University Press.

Jaggar, A.M. and Struhl, P.R. (1978). *Feminist frameworks: Alternative theoretical accounts of the relations between women and men*. New York: McGraw-Hill.

Jensen, R. (2017). *The end of patriarchy: Radical feminism for men*. North Melbourne, Australia: Spinifex Press.

Kaschak, E. (1992). *Engendered lives: A new psychology of women's experience*. New York: Basic books.

Kilmartin, C. and Smiler, A. (2014). *The masculine self*. Cornwall-on-Hudson, NY: Sloan Publishing.

Lerner, G. (1986). *The creation of patriarchy*. New York: Oxford University Press.

Lorber, J. (2012). *Gender inequality: Feminist theories and politics* (5th edn). New York: Oxford University Press.

Marche, S. (2017). What are men to do in the age of Trump? *Guardian*, February 3. www.theguardian.com/world/2017/feb/03/men-womens-march-feminism-donald-trump.

Martin, C.L., Ruble, D.N., and Szkrybalo, J. (2002). Cognitive theories of early gender development. *Psychological Bulletin, 128*, 903–933. doi: 10.1037/0033-2909.128.6.903.

Miller, J.B. (1977). *Toward a new psychology of women*. Boston, MA: Beacon Press.

Nelson, M.B. (1994). *The stronger women get, the more men love football: Sexism and the American culture of sports*. New York: Houghton Mifflin.

O'Reilly, J. (1971). The housewife's moment of truth. *Ms., 1*. Reproduced in *New York Magazine*, December 20. http://nymag.com/news/features/46167/.

Ortner, S.B. (2014). Too soon for post-feminism: The ongoing life of patriarchy in neoliberal America. *History and Anthropology, 25*, 530–549. doi: 10.1080/02757206.2014.930458.

Pratto, F. (1996). Sexual politics: The gender gap in the bedroom, the cupboard, and the cabinet. In D.M. Buss and N.M. Malamuth (eds), *Sex, power, conflict: Evolutionary and feminist perspectives* (pp. 179–230). New York: Oxford University Press.

Roughgarden, J. (2004). *Evolution's rainbow: Diversity, gender and sexuality in nature and people*. Los Angeles, CA: University of California Press.

Rowbotham, S. (1975). *Hidden from history: Rediscovering women in history from the 17th century to the present*. New York: Pantheon Books.

Sanday, P.R. (1981). *Female power and male dominance: On the origins of sexual inequality*. Cambridge: Cambridge University Press.

Weisstein, N. (1971). *Psychology constructs the female or, the fantasy life of the male psychologist*. Boston, MA: New England Free Press.

3

POWER, INEQUALITIES, AND PREJUDICE

Beliefs about the differences between women and men have consequences. In a demonstration of this principle, two Canadian researchers (Funk and Werhun, 2011) brought men into their lab and asked them to squeeze a handgrip as hard as they could. Afterward, some of the men were told they squeezed "like a girl." Would such a judgment make men feel badly? Interfere with later performance? Indeed. On later tests, men who received this feedback showed a threatened sense of masculinity, reduced performance on a cognitive task, and less attentional self-control than men who were not told their grip strength was girl-like. And, when given another chance to use the handgrip, these men squeezed more strongly than other men—perhaps trying to prove their masculinity. Believing that they had violated gender-related expectations apparently shook these men's self-confidence, interfered with their ability to think straight, and motivated them to work hard to prove their masculinity.

The finding that gender stereotypes can exert such effects is a clue to how integral they are to societal norms. These stereotypes are so pervasive that often we don't even see them as stereotypes, but rather as "the way things are."

GENDER STEREOTYPES: INSTRUMENTALITY VERSUS EXPRESSIVENESS

Decades ago, two sociologists (Parsons and Bales, 1955) characterized the main themes in gender stereotypic expectations for femininity and masculinity. Women were viewed as more expressive, with qualities that emphasized an orientation toward emotion and relationships; men were viewed as more instrumental, with qualities that focused on action, leadership, and accomplishment. The core aspects of these stereotypes appear repeatedly, even across cultures. For example, 75 percent of adults surveyed in 25 countries associated 6 adjectives (adventurous, dominant, forceful, independent, masculine, strong) with men and three (sentimental, submissive, superstitious) with women (Williams and Best, 1990).

Gender stereotypes change over time, but relatively slowly—and the feminine stereotype seems to have been more fluid in recent decades. Between 1973 and 1993, US college women's attribution of masculine-stereotyped qualities to themselves increased significantly, while men's attribution of feminine-stereotyped qualities to themselves did not change (Twenge 1997). When asked what women and men would be like in the future, respondents predicted that women would take on more masculine-stereotyped qualities and roles (Diekman and Eagly, 2000). Research in Spain (Lopez-Zafra and Garcia-Retamero, 2012) and Germany (Wilde and Diekman, 2005) has also shown that ideas about women's roles and characteristics are changing faster than ideas about men's roles and characteristics.

Individuals adjust their expectations and self-views to accommodate social changes in gender roles (Diekman, Johnston, and Loescher, 2013). In the United States, women have increasingly moved into the paid workforce and taken on occupational roles previously held by men, whereas men's roles have not changed so much. It is not surprising, then, that only women's self-views and the perceptions of women have changed. In countries such as Chile and Brazil, social change has pushed both men and women into more urban, industrial environments and greater technological competence, leading to an increased emphasis on the masculine-stereotyped qualities of independence and problem-solving skills.

Not surprisingly, increases in stereotypically masculine characteristics were perceived in both women and men in these countries (Diekman, Eagly, Mladinic, and Ferreira, 2005).

DESCRIPTIONS AND PRESCRIPTIONS

Gender stereotypes are, in part, descriptive—implying beliefs about what typical men and women are like. *Descriptive gender stereotypes* influence our expectations and even what we notice or ignore about individual men and women. However, gender sterotypes also incorporate a very important prescriptive element. Prescriptive stereotypes specify what women and men *should* be like; they are unwritten but powerful rules about what women and men should do to conform to society's expectations about femininity and masculinity. The men in the opening example who were told they squeezed "like a girl" were implicitly being told not just that they differed from the typical man, but that they had violated one of the prescriptions for masculinity by being weak. No wonder they had trouble thinking straight!

The prescriptive aspects of gender stereotypes may be broken down into several categories (Prentice and Carranza, 2002). *Intensified prescriptions* are positive qualities considered especially desirable for either women or men. For example, in North America, women should be warm, kind, and interested in children. Such qualities are also judged positively in men, but for women they are more important. *Relaxed prescriptions* are positive qualities viewed as desirable for anyone, but for which either women or men are more easily forgiven if they fall short. For example, intelligence is valued in both men and women, but women are judged less harshly than men if they are seen as lacking in this quality. *Intensified proscriptions* are undesirable qualities that are viewed as especially undesirable in one gender or the other. For example, promiscuity is viewed as a bad thing—but promiscuous women are the targets of more disapproval than promiscuous men. Finally, *relaxed proscriptions* are socially undesirable traits that nonetheless receive less disapproval when displayed by one gender than the other. For example, it would be hard to argue that it is a good thing to be shy, but a shy woman is more likely than a shy man to be excused for this quality.

There are important implications of the notion that one gender may be more likely than the other to be stigmatized or punished for a particular undesirable quality. For example, it is considered more important for women than for men to be physically attractive—and one key aspect of attractiveness in Western cultures is thinness. Being overweight is considered undesirable—but more so for women than for men. Employers attribute laziness, emotional instability, incompetence, lack of self-discipline, and low supervisory potential to heavy women (Puhl and Brownell, 2001), and women's (but not men's) body mass is associated with lower wages and lower career success (Glass, Haas, and Reither, 2010). Overweight women are less likely than other women to earn college degrees (Glass et al., 2010). For men, on the other hand, weight seems to have no relationship with educational attainment. Why would heavy women be less likely to complete college? Perhaps their high school teachers and peers judge them more harshly and are less likely to provide encouragement. Stereotypes may appear ephemeral and unimportant, but they have very tangible consequences.

The prescriptive masculine stereotype appears more rigid than the feminine one; indeed, a significant and very upsetting form of harassment for men is the claim that an individual is "not man enough" (Waldo, Berdahl, and Fitzgerald, 1998). Men and boys react strongly to feedback that they are gender-deviant: in one study, men who were told they scored high on a feminine knowledge test declined to publicize their scores and later expressed stronger masculine interests (Rudman and Fairchild, 2004). In another study, men who were told falsely that their personality score was similar to that of a typical woman were more likely than other men to harass a female partner by sending her pornographic material (Maass, Cadinu, Guarnieri, and Grasselli, 2003). The association of communal qualities with femininity creates both cultural and psychological barriers to men's adoption of stereotypically feminine careers such as early childhood education and participation in tasks such as childcare (Croft, Schmader, and Block, 2015).

Both women and men experience *double binds* in which the prescriptive stereotype for their gender directly conflicts with the prescriptions for an occupational or social role they are performing. A woman in a leadership position must display decisiveness and toughness that are antithetical to the feminine role. If she appears too tough and decisive, she is criticized as unfeminine. A man who works as a nurse may find that the compassion and accommodation necessary for the performance of this role signal to others that he is not sufficiently masculine.

"TRUTH" AND STEREOTYPES

Some argue that stereotypes contain a "grain of truth." This claim is difficult to evaluate with respect to gender stereotypes, particularly since gender stereotypes are somewhat dynamic. Women's and men's self-descriptions differ less than their estimates of male–female differences in general. Thus, apparently, people do not see themselves in ways that match the stereotypes—even if they think those stereotypes are accurate for others. Janet Swim (1994) found that respondents' estimates of gender differences fairly mirrored research findings, but that they underestimated the impact of situations on such differences. An international study compared perceived gender differences in personality traits (i.e., gender stereotypes) to self- and observer-assessed gender differences on the same traits. Perceived and assessed gender differences were relatively similar—and quite consistent across age groups and countries (Löckenhoff *et al.*, 2014). This finding suggests that there is some accuracy and universality to gender stereotypes. However, both assessed and perceived gender differences were small, and reflected the aggregated responses of many people. Individuals' gender stereotypes are likely to be less accurate than consensual stereotypes shared across many people. In addition, gender stereotypes tended to be greater in countries in which measured gender differences were also greater, suggesting that culture affects both gender expression and attitudes about gender. Indeed, this is the main problem with evaluating the accuracy of stereotypes. As noted in Chapter 2, many attributes we associate with women and men are not essential, built-in aspects of personality, but responses to social conditions and expectations that differ for the two genders. If gender is to some extent a social construction, as argued in Chapter 1, then gender stereotypes are also social constructions.

THE IMPACT OF THE MEDIA UPON GENDER STEREOTYPES

In one episode of the old television sitcom *Friends*, Ross, a recent father divorced from his wife, spends time caring for his infant son. Dismayed to find the boy clinging to a Barbie doll, Ross tries to get him interested in a GI Joe "action figure" instead. The message that boys don't play with dolls (and that, if they do, those dolls are actually not "dolls" but "action figures") comes through loud and clear. Whereas the episode pokes fun at gender stereotypes, it also reinforces both the descriptive and prescriptive aspects of stereotypes. It reminds viewers that boys don't play with dolls and, perhaps more importantly, it reminds them that the adults in a boy's social environment get very upset if he *does* seem to be interested in dolls.

A steady stream of media images in film and television reinforces the stereotypic instrumental–expressive distinction between women and men. Content analyses of prime-time television programming, commercials, and films have shown for years that male characters are portrayed more often in work-related roles, whereas female characters tend to occupy interpersonal roles in families, friendships, and romance. Both female and male characters are most likely to be portrayed in gender-traditional roles and occupations (Smith, Choueiti, Prescott, and Pieper, 2013). The work roles for female characters usually involve clerical or service occupations and are unlikely to include the exercise of authority and instrumental behavior. These portrayals do affect viewers: a stream of studies in different countries has shown that the more television young viewers watch, the more they accept stereotypical beliefs about gender. It is difficult to see how gender stereotypes can change if media portrayals do not.

STEREOTYPES AND BEHAVIOR: GENDER-TYPED PLAY AND WORK

Exposure to stereotypes affects not only attitudes but also behavior. For instance, differences in girls' and boys' play are linked in part to exposure to gender stereotypes. Researchers measured the amount of time preschool children watched superhero programs on television; they then examined the relationship between viewing such programs and children's behavior (male-stereotyped play and weapons play) one year later (Coyne *et al.*, 2014). Boys' viewing of superhero programs significantly predicted their male-stereotyped play and weapons play one year later. The more such programs boys watched, the more gender-stereotyped their play became—and, because the researchers controlled for initial exposure levels, the result could not be explained simply by saying that boys who were already inclined toward male-stereotypical play simply chose to watch more superhero programs. Watching superhero programs also affected girls: they became more likely to engage in weapons play, but not to engage in other forms of male-stereotyped play.

Research findings also link gender stereotypes to occupational choice. For example, "unfeminine" stereotypes of computer scientists apparently prevent many women from exploring computer science as a career. US college students view computer science majors as lacking interpersonal skills and being rigidly focused on computers rather than people—traits that are incompatible with stereotypical femininity (Cheryan, Plaut, Handron, and Hudson, 2013). After reading articles that debunk the "unfeminine" image of computer scientists, female students report more interest in participating in computer science.

Gender stereotypes also influence behavior by affecting others' expectations of us. One study revealed that when primary school students' math exams were graded anonymously by outside examiners, girls scored higher than boys, but on exams that were marked by teaches who knew the students' names, boys did better (Lavy and Sand, 2015). The teachers' higher expectations of boys in primary school appeared to result not only in boys' immediate higher academic achievement, but also, in the longer term, in a greater likelihood of their enrollment in advanced math and science courses in high school (Lavy and Sand, 2015). At the same time, these teacher expectations produced lower achievement and less likelihood of enrollment in high school advanced math and science classes for girls. This matters greatly, the researchers note, because of the implications for later occupational choices.

PUSHING BACK: CHILDREARING WITHOUT GENDER STEREOTYPES?

Could we rear children without the constraints of gender stereotypes: letting each individual find and develop her or his own strengths, interests, aspirations? Some parents have found to their chagrin that this is not as easy as it sounds. Psychologists Sandra and Daryl Bem (Bem, 1998) tried diligently to rear their son and daughter so that they would not look at themselves or others "through a gender-polarizing lens," and that they would not think of males as normative or as "the main characters in the drama of social life and females as the supporting cast" (p. 179). They also raised them not to be *heteronormative*—so that they would view both cross-sex and same-sex love and sexuality as equally normal, and to be sex-positive: to appreciate and take responsibility for their own bodies and bodily desires. Their children grew up to be more flexible than most with respect to gender expression, but they never felt they had completely transcended gender. No matter how conscientiously parents try to remove gender categories as legitimate reasons for constructing one's self or judging others, children grow up in a gendered culture.

Efforts toward rearing children free from gender stereotypes do have their success stories. One mother, for example, recounted that her 7-year-old son had been assigned by his teacher to draw a picture showing "Mummy in the kitchen." The child's completed drawing did show his mother in the kitchen, but it also, without prompting, included his father washing the dishes (Bates, 2015).

WOMEN ARE WONDERFUL—BUT INCOMPETENT? EVALUATING WOMEN AND MEN

Are gender stereotypes really harmful to women? The qualities stereotypically attributed to women tend to be rather desirable: warm and caring, empathic, supportive. By contrast, masculine qualities (assertiveness, dominance, leadership orientation) may not seem quite so likable. Such reflections are a reminder that stereotypes imply more than beliefs about the qualities associated with particular groups—they also involve feelings about favorability, approval, liking, and admiration. In other words, they involve evaluation. As we move from the notion that women and men have certain qualities to the notion that we like, admire, or disdain women or men because of those qualities, we are moving from stereotyping to prejudice. Evaluative judgments based on individuals' gender represent a type of prejudice labeled *sexism*.

There is plenty of evidence that women are frequently the targets of sexist discrimination. Historically, they have often been excluded from roles, places, and behaviors. Currently, they are underrepresented in most powerful positions, underpaid in comparison to men, and, in many parts of the world, have less access than men to education, medical care, and political power. Strangely, this does not seem to mean that people *like* women less than men. Indeed, both women and men evaluate women as a group more favorably than men—a finding dubbed the "women are wonderful" effect (Eagly, Mladinic, and Otto, 1991). However, liking does not necessarily translate into respect, and favorable attitudes toward women do not translate into confidence that they will perform well in situations that require competence, decisiveness, or leadership. Similarly, unfavorable stereotypes that men are less empathic and sensitive than women may support the notion that men are less likable than women—but make better leaders. Masculine qualities may be less "warm and fuzzy," but they are associated with power. One group of researchers argues that a succinct summary of gender stereotypes and prejudice would be "Men are bad, but bold, and women are wonderful but weaker" (Glick *et al.*, 2004: 714).

STEREOTYPES AND STATUS

Social psychologists Laurie Rudman and Peter Glick (2008) argue that the prescriptive aspect of gender stereotypes is largely rooted in twin factors: a social structure that assigns men more power and status than women, and the intimate interdependence of gender roles. Prescriptive masculine stereotypes support gender hierarchy by ensuring that boys and men are trained in, and reinforced for, behaviors that keep their status and power high: leadership, decision-making, dominance, achievement-oriented behavior.

Prescriptive feminine stereotypes safeguard the hierarchy by pressuring girls and women to assume traditional supportive, nurturing roles. Because these two sets of status-differentiated roles are interdependent, promoting a great deal of everyday role-guided social contact between women and men (e.g., female secretaries interacting with male executives, female dental assistants interacting with male dentists, female aides interacting with male political leaders), there are many opportunities to reinforce the prescriptive stereotypes.

Prescriptive gender stereotypes surrounding power and emotionality affect heterosexual attraction. In one study, respondents saw photographs of female or male adults displaying happiness, pride, shame, or no emotion. Across ethnicities and a wide age range, respondents saw men as most sexually attractive when displaying pride and least attractive when displaying happiness. By contrast, women appeared more attractive when displaying happiness and least attractive when displaying pride (Tracy and Beall, 2011).

The different reactions to female and male political leaders reflect the impact of associating power and status with masculinity. Participants in one study reacted negatively to female politicians portrayed as interested in seeking power, but men's power-seeking intentions did not affect participants' reactions to them (Okimoto and Brescoll, 2010). Not only did respondents express less desire to vote for a "power-seeking" woman politician than for a woman not perceived as seeking power but they were also more likely to express feelings of moral outrage toward her: contempt, anger, and disgust, as illustrated in Figure 3.1. The researchers concluded that this moral outrage was based on the woman's violation of the prescription that she should be communal in her focus. Outraged reactions to women's ambitious or power-oriented behavior block women from powerful positions and maintain a status difference between women and men. On the flip side, men who are perceived as too modest—violating prescriptive norms of masculinity—also experience prejudice and dislike (Moss-Racusin, Phelan, and Rudman, 2010).

In support of the idea that prescriptive gender stereotypes reinforce status differences between women and men, Rudman and Glick note that the most intensified proscriptions for women, the traits or

Power-seeking intentions

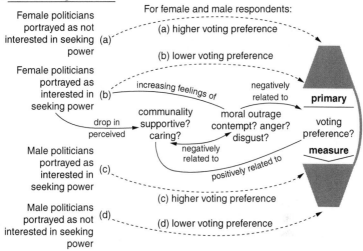

Figure 3.1 Power seeking and the backlash against female politicians. When respondents in this study read a description of a hypothetical female politician, they responded differently, depending on whether or not she appeared interested in seeking power. If she was interested in seeking power, they viewed her as less communal and caring, expressed more reluctance to vote for her, and reacted with more negative emotions than they did if she appeared uninterested in power. Male politicians, on the other hand, were not penalized for being interested in power.

Source: Based on Okimoto and Brescoll (2010, Study 2).

behaviors that generate the most negative reactions, are those that involve women in claiming or asserting power: rebelliousness, stubbornness, dominance. For men, on the other hand, the most intensified proscriptions involve traits or behaviors that undermine masculine power: emotionality, approval-seeking, readiness to yield to others. These proscriptions are evident in the derogatory labels flung at individuals who fail to conform: women who act "uppity" are called bitches; men who are too easy-going and do not enact masculine prerogatives for power are labeled wimps.

Since men are likely to gain the most from a gender hierarchy that puts them on top, it makes sense that they would hold stronger prescriptive gender stereotypes than women. Research supports this prediction. Men score higher than women on endorsement of traditional gender roles, and react more negatively than women to people who violate gender prescriptions (Glick, Diebold, Bailey-Werner, and Zhu, 1997; Glick et al., 2004).

We have been discussing the explicit endorsement of gender stereotypes, but researchers have demonstrated that stereotypes can also operate implicitly—below levels of awareness. *Implicit stereotypes* guide our reactions and judgments of others even when they are contrary to our explicit beliefs. For example, women may explicitly reject the idea that women should be subservient, yet be just as likely as men to show automatic negative reactions to women who act authoritatively, ambitiously, or competitively (Rudman and Glick, 1999). Thus, both women and men, knowingly or unknowingly, enforce gender prescriptions by their negative reactions to individuals who violate them.

SEXISM IS COMPLICATED

Types of prejudice abound. We can think, for example, of racism, *ageism*, classism: each one an evaluative reaction to individuals based on their group membership. Every type of prejudice is complicated, but sexism is perhaps more complicated than most. This is because, unlike forms of prejudice in which the prejudiced individual is motivated to, and often can, avoid contact with the target group, people who harbor sexist beliefs are usually in close, even intimate contact with members of the target group. Men and women who hold very sexist attitudes form intimate partnerships with members of the other gender. Women and men work together, parent children together, make decisions together, and often enjoy each other's company a great deal, sometimes while holding firmly to sexist beliefs. Thus theorists and researchers have struggled to analyze sexism and its different manifestations.

OLD-FASHIONED VERSUS MODERN SEXISM

How frequently do we hear openly sexist statements such as "women have no head for politics," or "men are just overgrown babies"? Such overtly derogatory comments reflect blatant sexism and, over the decades, have become less acceptable, less "politically correct." Does that mean sexism is on the wane? Perhaps, but equally likely is the possibility that it has gone underground. Openly sexist comments that endorse stereotypic judgments about women and men and differential treatment of them epitomize *old-fashioned sexism*, and are often greeted with disapproval. However, researchers have identified a more subtle form of prejudice, labeled *modern sexism* (Swim, Aikin, Hall, and Hunter, 1995) or *neosexism* (Tougas, Brown, Beaton, and Joly, 1995). Modern sexism entails a lack of support for policies designed to promote gender equality, antagonism toward women's demands for access and inclusion, and denial that gender discrimination still exists. An expression of modern sexism may be, for example, "I'm all for women's rights, but these women complaining about discrimination in employment are going too far: they're too pushy and unreasonable."

HOSTILE AND BENEVOLENT SEXISM

A breakthrough in understanding the maintenance of sexist attitudes even in the context of intimate relationships came when researchers zeroed in on the ambivalence that often characterizes gender-related attitudes. Remember the evidence that people like women more than men, but still don't necessarily respect their abilities or leadership potential? Those mixed feelings are a sign of *ambivalent sexism*: a constellation of attitudes made up of both hostile and benevolent feelings toward the other gender.

Whereas most theories of prejudice have focused only on the hostility directed at the targets, Peter Glick and Susan Fiske (1996) developed an analysis of sexism that explored how individuals maintain the balance between male dominance and intimate inter-dependence in female–male relationships. They identified two intertwined sets of attitudes that support gender ideologies: *hostile sexism* and *benevolent sexism*. Whereas hostile sexism comprises derogatory beliefs about the other gender, benevolent sexism entails warmer but condescending attitudes. Hostile sexism toward women includes attitudes that men should be in charge of women, that women are incompetent and untrustworthy, and that heterosexual relationships with women are dangerous and confining for men. Benevolent sexism directed at women includes the attitudes that men should be protective and chivalrous toward women, put women on a pedestal, and that a man needs an intimate relationship with a woman to be complete.

Hostile sexism directed at men includes resentment of their presumed control and dominance, the belief that men are incompetent in certain domains, and the idea that male–female relationships tend to be adversarial. Benevolent sexism toward men includes the attitude that men need to be taken care of, the belief that men are naturally better at some things (especially dangerous or difficult things), and the notion that women need romantic partnerships with men to feel fulfilled.

Why would hostile and benevolent attitudes coexist? Despite the resentments that can accompany the hierarchical relationship between men and women, each gender gets something out of that relationship and so has some stake in maintaining and feeling good about it (Rudman and Glick, 2008). The traditional masculine and feminine gender roles are interdependent: despite resenting men for their dominating behavior, women may depend on men and feel grateful to them for protection; despite viewing women as incompetent and so feeling superior to them, men may depend on, and feel grateful for, women's warmth, care, and nurturing.

Women are consistently less likely than men to endorse hostile sexist attitudes toward women. However, women do not always see benevolent sexist attitudes as a problem, often endorsing these attitudes as strongly, or even more strongly, than men do. It is tempting to think that benevolent sexism cannot be so bad if it entails positive feelings toward the target. However, as Rudman and Glick (2008) argue, benevolent sexism produces patronizing, even if affectionate, behavior, such as "treating her like a pet or mascot, just as one might love a particularly clumsy and not-too-bright pet dog or cat whose incompetence is endearing." Patronizing behavior undermines the target's self-confidence and promotes an image of superiority for the patronizer and inadequacy for the target—effectively reinforcing the dominance of one over the other. In addition, benevolent attitudes are directed mainly toward women who conform to traditional femininity; women who "break the rules" are not necessarily viewed as meriting chivalry or protection. Furthermore, benevolent sexism, by seeming positive and "nice," can undermine women's resistance to gender inequality.

Hostile and benevolent sexism toward men also tends to support traditional male dominance. High hostility toward men is associated with the idea that male dominance is inevitable, even if unpleasant—a necessary evil that women have to cope with. Interestingly, the women who score highest on hostility toward men tend to be not feminists, but rather those with the most traditional gender-role attitudes and the lowest support for feminism. For women, an adversarial view of men may imply a manipulative approach to heterosexual relationships, such as the idea that men have to be "tricked" into marriage. Such an approach is congruent with benevolent sexism toward men, which implies that a woman needs a man to provide for her and protect her—even though she has to take care of him.

Hostile and benevolent sexist attitudes toward both women and men are strongest in societies where gender equality is lowest (Glick *et al.*, 2004). In such cultures, women are encouraged to accept male dominance in return for male protection; men are encouraged to provide materially for women in exchange for emotional support, nurturance, and submissiveness.

SEXISM IN THE EVALUATION OF WORK

What kind of person comes to mind when we think of a nurse? An airline pilot? The CEO of a multinational corporation? Most people automatically generate images that conform to gender expectations: a female nurse, a male pilot, a male corporate leader. This tendency would not be problematic if it did not also entail a tendency to be a little suspicious of gender-non-traditional occupants of such roles and to expect them to perform poorly. In fact, judgments about work performance are often affected by the gender of the person doing the work and the perceived fit between gender roles and certain kinds of work.

If gender stereotypes say generally that men are more competent than women, we might expect men's work to be evaluated more highly than women's. Such a pattern was shown clearly in an early study by Philip Goldberg (1968). He asked female respondents to judge the quality of a written article attributed to either a female or male author. Respondents judged the same article better on several dimensions when they thought it was written by a man than when they thought the author was a woman. These results were all the more unsettling because the people making these biased judgments were women. Many years later, Goldberg's study was extended to include both male and female respondents and articles designed to reflect traditionally masculine (politics), traditionally feminine (psychology of women), or neutral (education) areas of expertise (Paludi and Strayer, 1985). In that study, both women and men evaluated the articles—even those in the feminine and gender-neutral fields—more favorably when they were attributed to male authors. Researchers have since demonstrated that such a pro-male bias is not always found (Top, 1991). It is most likely to occur in certain kinds of situations: when the domain in question is stereotypically masculine, when raters do not have much specific information about the expertise of the person whose work is being judged, and when people are evaluating a résumé rather than other kinds of written work (Swim, Borgida, Maruyama, and Myers, 1989).

Many of us would protest that we do not allow gender stereotypes to bias our judgments of others' work, competence, or potential. Yet, as noted earlier in this chapter, stereotypic judgments need not necessarily be explicit; they may occur without our awareness. Researchers uncover implicit gender stereotypes by presenting respondents with a series of trait adjectives and asking them to pair those traits with either women or men as quickly as possible. The speed with which someone responds is a measure of how easily the association fits into her or his network or associations for that gender. Respondents with strong implicit gender stereotypes may, for example, respond more quickly to the pairing of *kind—woman* than to the pairing of *kind—man*. Using this approach, researchers have found, for example, that respondents associate women more readily with egalitarian words and men with hierarchical words (Schmid Mast, 2004), and that they associate women with subordinate roles and men with authority roles (Rudman and Kilianski, 2000).

Implicit gender stereotypes affect perceptions of workers and work. For example, people implicitly associate women with traits considered characteristic of elementary schoolteachers and men with traits stereotypic of accountants and engineers (White and White, 2006). An interesting example of implicit stereotyping in the realm of work appears in a study of attitudes toward female and male managers (Latu *et al.*, 2011). College students responded to questionnaires measuring hostile and benevolent sexism and to a questionnaire measuring how motivated they were to respond without sexism. In addition, researchers measured students' implicit associations between gender and traits of successful or unsuccessful managers. All participants showed explicitly positive views of women in the workplace. Furthermore, those who had the strongest internal motivation to avoid responding in a sexist way did not show implicit prejudice against women as managers. However, the men implicitly associated men with the traits of successful managers and women with the traits of unsuccessful managers. Female respondents linked successful manager traits more strongly with women than with men. The more participants implicitly associated men with the traits of successful managers, the higher was their recommended salary for a male employee.

Outside the laboratory too, individuals apply prejudiced evaluations without realizing they are doing so. Faculty members at large, research-intensive US universities evaluated an application from a graduate student for a lab manager position (Moss-Racusin *et al.*, 2012). Some faculty members received an application ostensibly from a woman; others received the identical application ostensibly from a man. As shown in Figure 3.2, the gender of the applicant made a significant difference: respondents rated the applicant as more competent and worthy of hiring, proposed to provide more mentoring, and suggested a higher salary when the name on the application was male than when it was female. Given high national concern about attracting more women into science fields, these faculty members had no doubt been encouraged to support and foster female graduate students, yet they favored male applicants.

Benevolent sexism can have a particularly complicated impact upon gender equality in the workplace. Individuals who endorse

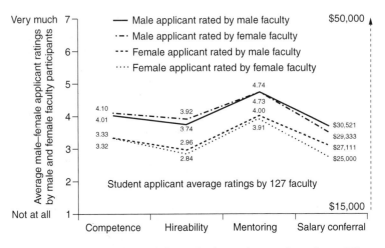

Figure 3.2 Science faculty's subtle gender biases favor male students. When faculty members in science departments of research-intensive US universities evaluated identical male and female applicants for a lab manager position, male applicants received higher ratings and higher salary offers.

Source: Based on data from Moss-Racusin *et al.* (2012).

benevolent sexist attitudes seem to be "compassionate sexists" (Hideg and Ferris, 2016). Because they feel sympathetic toward women, they tend to support gender-based employment equity policies—but only when those policies promote the hiring of women into stereotypically feminine positions, not into masculine positions. Thus, while believing they are supporting women, benevolent sexists may inadvertently undermine gender equality by helping to maintain occupational gender segregation.

SEXISM AND THE MEDIA

We have seen that the media reinforce and strengthen gender stereotypes—a process that can lead indirectly to sexism. However, there is ample evidence that the media also promote sexism directly. Blatant misogyny—hatred of or disdain for women—is all too common in the words of performers and media commentators and in the depictions of women in television, film, music, and videogames. Some rap music, for example, includes derogatory and hostile statements about women, lyrics approving rape and physical violence against women, claims that women are "beneath" men, and references to women as objects to be used and discarded (Adams and Fuller, 2006). Rap or hip-hop music by certain male artists fairly drips with hostile sexism and is more likely than other genres to use words such as "bitch" and "hoe" to define women (Frisby, 2010). Female rappers sometimes present a counter-force to these themes, incorporating messages of sexual empowerment, resistance, independence, and economic success for women (Herd, 2015). Themes of benevolent sexism are rampant in pop and country music, where the lyrics often emphasize that women are valued and appreciated mainly for their bodies and appearance or for their "sweetness." Female characters are under-represented, stereotyped, and sexualized in videogames (Stermer and Burkley, 2015), and some games glorify the rape or other abuse of women.

An often-overlooked venue for sexism in the media is the computer search engine. Information scientist Safiya Noble (2012) notes that commercial search engines are powerful influences on the kinds of information that is easily discoverable through online searches. Search results that appear at the top of the results page all too often reflect sexism and racism. For example, Google searches for "black girls" or "Latinas" may bring up a list of results for which pornographic sites are at the top. A search for "women's magazines" produces hits for pages-long lists of traditional magazines, such as *Women's Day* or *Cosmopolitan*, before listings for any feminist periodicals; and a search for "women athletes" is likely to produce something like "25 sexiest women athletes" high up in the results. The influence of search engines on what we know about the world is profound, and scholars are just beginning to come to grips with it.

Even in the staid world of media political punditry, prejudice against women is often evident. In one documentary examining the media portrayal of gender, a collection of nasty remarks by radio or television commentators about female political leaders includes reference to "that ugly hag, Madeleine Albright," and a description of U.S. Supreme Court Justice Sonia Sotomayor as having "not the sort of face you'd like to see on a five-dollar bill" (All Things

Considered, 2011). In Argentina, the press attacked President Cristina de Kirchner on the basis of her appearance rather than her accomplishments; media in Chile promulgated a nickname for president Michelle Bachelet as "the fat woman" (Frazier, 2016). During the 2016 US presidential race, commentators mocked Hillary Clinton both for not smiling and for smiling too much (Zarya, 2016). Ordinary women who state their political opinions often find themselves critiqued in the press or social media for their appearance (thus, presumably, delegitimizing their opinions). For example, women who participated in the Women's March in January 2017 were mocked for their appearance. One US male state senator posted on Facebook that "Trump managed to achieve something that no one else has been able to do: he got a million fat women out walking" (Simons, 2017). It is clear that negative portrayals of female political leaders impact people's perceptions—particularly among men who already hold sexist attitudes (Schlehofer, Casad, Bligh, and Grotto, 2011). When media portrayals are positive, both women and men view female politicians as both competent and warm, but men high in hostile sexism exposed to negative media portrayals of women politicians are likely to see those women as both incompetent and cold.

IMPACT OF SEXISM UPON ITS TARGETS

Being a target of sexism has consequences: emotional, cognitive, behavioral, and even physiological. We saw in this chapter's opening example that men who were told they "squeezed like a girl" had trouble thinking well of themselves afterwards. Other studies have shown that men in traditionally feminine occupations may be at special risk of bullying or being "hassled," and have higher rates of absences and turnover in their jobs (Evans and Steptoe, 2002).

It is not just being in gender-non-traditional occupations that causes such problems, but the attitudes of an individual's co-workers. One study of German men in non-traditional occupations (e.g., nursing, eldercare, elementary school teaching, hairdressing) found that the attitudes of their female colleagues were directly related to the men's depressive moods and job dissatisfaction

(Sobiraj, Korek, Weseler, and Mohr, 2011). Men whose female colleagues endorsed statements such as "It bothers me when a man does something I consider 'feminine,'" were significantly more depressed than their counterparts whose female colleagues did not endorse such attitudes.

Being a target of sexism produces physiological reactions too: cardiovascular reactivity (rate of change in the cardiovascular system in response to stress) increases after exposure to sexist comments. Hostile and benevolent sexism seem to causes different kinds of physiological responses. In one study, researchers characterized these reactions, respectively, as "flash fire" and "slow burn" (Salomon, Burgess, and Bosson, 2015). In comparison to women who received neutral comments, women recipients of hostile sexist comments reported anger and showed heightened cardiovascular reactivity (increased heart rate, systolic blood pressure, and cardiac contractile force) during a subsequent demanding task. Women who received benevolent sexist comments also showed increased cardiovascular reactivity and anger, but they experienced a significantly slower return to their normal cardiovascular functioning than did women in the other conditions. The researchers suggest that it may be more difficult to recover from benevolent than from hostile sexism because benevolent sexism is more ambiguous and requires more processing—thus slowing down coping.

STEREOTYPE THREAT

It can be uncomfortable to be in a situation where others are skeptical of our qualifications or expect us to perform poorly. That uneasy awareness of being judged according to negative stereotypes about our group has been dubbed *stereotype threat* (Steele, 1997). Knowing that others are applying negative stereotypes to us in our current activities often translates into poor performance. For example, women high in mathematical ability perform more poorly than their male counterparts when told they are taking a math test on which men generally score higher—but not when they are given the same test with the message that women and men generally have similar scores (Spencer, Steele, and Quinn 1999). Researchers theorize that victims of stereotype threat may lose confidence and disengage from tasks associated with the threatened ability, perhaps investing less effort. In the current example, reminding these high-ability women of the stereotype that women are "not good at math" may have made them withdraw effort from the task, resulting in poorer performance.

Stereotype threat may also harm performance by diverting cognitive energy to counter the stereotype. When women who are given math problems to solve are exposed to negative stereotypes about their math performance, they apparently use some of their working memory to counter the stereotype instead of having all that memory available to solve the problems. When women are "retrained" to associate being female with being *good* at math, they show increased working memory capacity and their math performance improves (Forbes and Schmader, 2010). Some researchers suggest that stereotype threat is partially responsible for women's historically lower performance in mathematics and the physical sciences (e.g., Shaffer, Marx, and Prislin, 2013).

Stereotype threat may promote a shift in behavior to avoid conforming to the stereotype. Researchers exposed women to the stereotype that effective leadership is associated with masculine rather than with feminine characteristics. They then gave the women the opportunity to respond to hypothetical situations requiring assertive leadership (von Hippel, Wiryakusuma, Bowden, and Shochet, 2011). Women exposed to the stereotype tended to alter their communication style in a traditionally masculine direction by speaking more directly, using fewer hedges, hesitations and tag questions. Ironically, these changes backfired. Evaluators rated women who used a more masculine communication style as less warm and likeable and they indicated less willingness to comply with these women's requests. Thus in trying to disconfirm the stereotype that "women can't lead effectively," the women may have undermined their own leadership effectiveness. These women faced a stark example of the double bind produced by prescriptive gender stereotypes: no matter what they did they were violating a norm.

Men too can feel the sting of stereotype threat when reminded that another group is expected to perform better than their own. In one study, men performed worse on a test when told that it measured the stereotypically feminine quality of social sensitivity and that women typically performed better (Koenig and Eagly, 2005). In another, White men who had been selected for their high math proficiency performed worse on a math test after being exposed to information suggesting that Asian men excelled in math ability (Aronson, *et al.*, 1999).

The impact of stereotype threat extends far beyond the social psychology laboratory and beyond simple decrements in perform-ance. In life outside the laboratory, individuals are less likely than in previous decades to encounter bald stereotypic statements such as "men do better than women at math" or "men are not good at relationships." However, stereotypes can be communicated and absorbed in many subtle ways. One series of studies of women in various work settings showed that the mere process of comparing themselves with male colleagues seemed to trigger stereotype threat in women (von Hippel, Issa, Ma, and Stokes, 2011). Why would this happen? Probably because, in many workplaces, men are paid more, advance more quickly, and are assigned more "important" work than women. A woman in such a workplace, comparing her career progress with that of male colleagues, may well begin to wonder if she were being evaluated on the basis of her gender. These researchers showed that women who compared themselves with male colleagues were more likely than other women to experience stereotype threat. Further, that stereotype threat con-tributed to a set of problematic work-related attitudes. First, stereo-type threat was related to identity separation: women's differentiation of their identity into a "work self" (perhaps persua-sive, analytical, ambitious) and a "female self" (perhaps warm, sens-itive, accommodating). Such identity separation signals a sense of "not belonging" and may have mental health consequences for women who feel they must not express their "female self" when at work. Second, the threat was associated with women's belief that their career prospects were limited, a lack of confidence that they would achieve their career goals. Finally, both directly and through these two attitudes, stereotype threat led to lowered job satisfaction and increased intention to quit their jobs. The only way out of this kind of situation is for workplaces to become more gender-balanced and for occupational roles to be more evenly distributed by gender.

RESPONDING TO EXPRESSIONS OF SEXISM

Being the target of sexist comments or actions can be upsetting and stressful: experiencing gender prejudice has been linked to depression, anxiety, lowered self-esteem, and anger. Women are far from complacent about such incidents. In one study, women who were targets of scripted sexist remarks by male confederates almost always found the remarks objectionable, viewed the speaker as prejudiced, and felt angry (Swim and Hyers, 1999). Yet these women were restrained and cautious about responding publicly to the remarks. Whereas 81 percent of the women in a simulated version of this study predicted they would confront the person making a sexist comment, only 45 percent of the women in the actual study did this.

In another study, participants kept daily diaries for two weeks about their experiences of gender prejudice (Brinkman, Garcia, and Rickard, 2011). In about one-third of the reported instances of gender prejudice, the women said that they had not responded in the way they would have preferred. Usually, this discrepancy between desired and actual responses took the form of wanting to confront the perpetrator, but not doing so. The women attributed their reluctance to confront to a variety of reasons, such as not being cost-effective (e.g., "it would have escalated the situation"), concern about social norms (e.g., "it would have made someone feel worse"), and being constrained by the situation (e.g., "class was starting"). The most frequent inhibitor of confrontation was concern about social norms—a finding that underlines the power of prescriptive gender stereotypes. Apparently, these women were well aware that if they confronted the perpetrator they would be labeled as prickly, oversensitive, and complaining, and that, as women, they were expected to smooth over the situation rather than make it worse. Thus, even though they were the targets of boorish behavior, these women often felt constrained to avoid rocking the boat and violating the expectation that they would be sociable, agreeable, and "nice." The pressure exerted by social norms makes it difficult for individual women to push back against sexism, even when they feel justified in doing so.

There is little research on men's responses to anti-male sexist comments directed at them. However, men who push back against sexist remarks about women or antigay comments may face negative reactions. For example, a man who confronts another man about antigay prejudice risks being disliked, being viewed as a complainer, and perceived as more likely to be gay (Cadieux and Chasteen, 2015).

FEMINISM AS A COLLECTIVE RESPONSE TO SEXISM

Outside a New York City rock radio station one day in 2002, a group of angry young women, organized by Riot Grrrl NYC, gathered to protest "cock rock," and the station's male-dominated playlist. They carried signs such as "Do women have to be naked to get on the radio?" and "We love girl music," and chanted slogans such as "You're teaching girls that women suck […] we won't give in and we won't give up." These women scoffed at the notion that they should be "reasonable" or that the station was blameless and merely responding to audience demand. As one participant later wrote, she was not interested in "a bigger slice of male-dominated pie—I want a different pie, I want a bigger piece of it, and I don't want to cook it" (Ragonese, 2002: 27).

In New Delhi, on July 31, 2011, hundreds of women marched in India's first "SlutWalk" to protest sexual violence against women. The title of the march underlines the idea that women should not have to fear sexual assault, no matter what they wear (RFI 2011). The event, one of many similar ones around the world, challenged the idea that sexual assault is the fault of the victim, caused by her choice of clothing or behavior. The women felt compelled to march because the problem is so pervasive: one survey showed that 85 percent of New Delhi's women fear sexual harassment when they leave home.

On January 21, 2017, an estimated five million people around the world participated in a Women's March to advocate for legislation and policies supportive of gender and racial equality, LGBTQ rights, immigration justice, protection of the natural environment, and other human rights issues. First planned as a march on Washington, to send a message to an incoming US administration that appeared hostile to such issues, the project spread to many other countries; hundreds of marches occurred worldwide. By some estimates, the events in the United States comprised the largest single-day demonstration in US history (Broomfield, 2017).

These protests represent collective responses to sexism—something that may be easier and more effective than the individual responses discussed in the previous section. It is harder to challenge social norms as an individual than with others (Cialdini and Griskevicius, 2010), and the history of social movements indicates that such movements can succeed over time in changing rules and expectations. Movements challenging traditional inequities between women and men are driven by various versions of feminism. As noted in Chapter 2, the many shades of feminism have in common a desire to challenge gender inequalities and a belief that women's lives and experiences are important. Yet despite the apparent reasonableness of such ideals, the term "feminist" has acquired a dubious reputation in certain circles, and some young women reject the label even while endorsing the goal of gender equality.

Feminist movements around the world have had life-changing impacts: from the early suffrage movements that won women the right to vote, to reproductive rights movements that have strengthened women's right to make decisions about childbearing, to anti-violence movements that have agitated for protection against sexual assault and domestic violence, to a variety of organizations that have pushed for an end to workplace discrimination. Such organizations are driven by the energy and convictions of individual participants—but how and why does an individual identify with, align, and coalesce with a feminist movement?

Psychologists have long favored theories of identity development that involve progression through stages of understanding and commitment. Following in this tradition, Downing and Roush (1985) postulated a model of feminist identity development with five sequential stages: passive acceptance (the woman is unaware of discrimination against her based on her sex); revelation (with the realization that discrimination exists, the woman becomes angry and hostile toward men); embeddedness emanation (she attempts to withdraw from patriarchal culture into a women-only culture); synthesis (she begins to reintegrate with the dominant culture, make more independent decisions, and relate to men as individuals rather than as members of a category of oppressors); and active commitment (she espouses a commitment to social change through feminist collective action). This model proposes that the development of feminist identity is initially triggered by an experience of discrimination, which jolts the woman out of the initial passive acceptance stage.

This model of women's feminist identity development has been popular, but it may not provide an adequate or accurate description of the experience of today's young women. There is little evidence that women move linearly through the five stages. Furthermore, whereas this model may have captured the experiences of women arriving at a feminist identity in the 1980s, women growing up in the 1990s and later may have a very different "take" on discrimination, gender equality, and feminism. Rather than starting with "passive acceptance," women developing a feminist identity in the 1990s said there was never a time when they had accepted male superiority and traditional gender expectations. Rather, they had always assumed they would be able to "have it all," and only later realized that they were still saddled with traditional expectations associated with marriage and motherhood (Horne, Matthews, and Detrie, 2001). A study comparing older and younger self-identified feminists and non-feminists found suggestive evidence that as women age they progress from experiencing anger to activism, as the model predicts. However, the study also revealed differences between the experiences of older and younger women (Erchull *et al.*, 2009). For the younger women, the starting point seemed more likely to be synthesis—and they moved toward stronger feminist identification and activism as they became aware of subtle discrimination. Erchull and her colleagues suggest the necessity for a new model of feminist identity development:

> Such a model would acknowledge that many young women feel empowered and able to accomplish anything but may not understand the complexities of gender discrimination given that they live in a world where sexism is more subtle than it was in the past.

What about feminist identity development for men? Researchers have ignored this question; however, there is a long history of men supporting feminism (Kimmel and Mosmiller, 1992), and pro-feminist men's movements—although not always prominent—have supported the idea that gender equality has benefits for both women and men (Copeland, 2015).

Regardless of the sequence through which feminist identity develops, the collective response to sexism that such an identity supports has proven an effective way to challenge gender inequalities and stereotypes. As we will see in the Chapter 4, both the stereotypes and the challenges to those stereotypes have important implications for relationships between men and women.

FOR FURTHER EXPLORATION

Basu, Amrita (ed.) (2010). *Women's movements in the global era* (Boulder, CO: Westview Press). This reader contains a collection of articles on the origins, development, and challenges confronted by women's movements around the world, including South Africa, Pakistan, China, Russia, Poland, and Latin American countries. The international focus makes it a good place to start to understand the impact of feminist collective responses to sexism.

Kimmel, Michael S. (2010). *Misframing men: The politics of contemporary masculinities* (Piscataway, NJ: Rutgers University Press). The author, a sociologist who has spent his career analyzing masculinities, writes about the social and political changes that have impacted men's lives, takes on those who argue that feminism has harmed men, and examines what the future may hold for masculinity.

Ridgeway, Cecilia L. (2011). *Framed by gender: How gender inequality persists in the modern world* (New York: Oxford University Press). A sociologist describes how we tend to use our traditional beliefs about gender as a framework for organizing new information and dealing with uncertainty—thus unintentionally reproducing old gender stereotypes in new situations.

Rudman, Laurie A., and Glick, Peter (2008). *The social psychology of gender. How power and intimacy shape gender relations* (New York:

Guilford Press). Two social psychologists examine the complex ways in which male dominance coexists with intimate interdependence to produce our current gender stereotypes and roles.

Implicit Association Test Exercise (2011). www.understanding prejudice.org/iat/.

This site allows the user to try out a measure of implicit stereotyping: the *Implicit Association Test*. Versions of the test for both gender and race are available. Trying the test is a good way to gain an understanding of what researchers are measuring when they try to assess implicit stereotypes.

REFERENCES

Adams, T.M. and Fuller, D.B. (2006). The words have changed but the ideology remains the same: Misogynistic lyrics in rap music. *Journal of Black Studies*, 36, 938–957. doi: 10.1177/0021934704274072.

All Things Considered (2011). A look at media, gender in "Miss Representation." National Public Radio, November 13. www.npr.org/2011/11/13/142288599/a-look-at-media-gender-in-miss-representation.

Aronson, J., Lustina, M.J., Good, C., Keough, K., Steele, C.M., and Brown, J. (1999). When White men can't do math: Necessary and sufficient factors in stereotype threat. *Journal of Experimental Social Psychology*, *35*, 29–46. doi:/10.1006/jesp. 1998.1371.

Bates, L. (2015). Young children must be protected from ingrained gender stereotypes. *Guardian*, February 23. www.theguardian.com/lifeandstyle/womens-blog/2015/feb/23/sexist-assumptions-young-children-gender-stereotypes.

Bem, S.L. (1998). *An unconventional family*. New Haven, CT: Yale University Press.

Brinkman, B.G., Garcia, K., and Rickard, K.M. (2011). "What I wanted to do was […]". Discrepancies between college women's desired and reported responses to gender prejudice. *Sex Roles*, 65, 344–355. doi: 10.1007/s11199-011-0020-7.

Broomfield, M. (2017). Women's March against Donald Trump is the largest day of protests in U.S. history, say political scientists. *Independent*, January 23. www.independent.co.uk/news/world/americas/womens-march-anti-donald-trump-womens-rights-largest-protest-demonstration-us-history-political-a7541081.html.

Cadieux, J. and Chasteen, A.L. (2015). You gay, bro? Social costs faced by male confronters of antigay prejudice. *Psychology of Sexual Orientation and Gender Diversity*, 2, 436–446. doi: 10.1037/sgd0000134.

Cheryan, S., Plaut, V.C., Handron, C., and Hudson, L. (2013). The stereotypical computer scientist: Gendered media representations as a barrier to inclusion for women. *Sex Roles*, 69, 58–71. doi: 10.1007/s11199-013-0296-x.

Cialdini, R.B. and Griskevicius, V. (2010). Social influence. In R.F. Baumeister and E.J. Finkel (eds), *Advanced social psychology: The state of the science*, pp. 385–417. New York: Oxford University Press.

Copeland, L. (2015). Michael Kimmel is out to show why feminism is good for men. *The Washington Post*, March 8. www.washingtonpost.com/lifestyle/style/michael-kimmel-is-out-to-show-why-feminism-is-good-for-men/2015/03/08/bedd603e-c50f-11e4-9271-610273846239_story.html?utm_term=.f7428dabe416.

Coyne, S.M., Linder, J.R., Rasmussen, E.E., Nelson, D.A., and Collier, K.M. (2014). It's a bird! It's a plane! It's a gender stereotype! Longitudinal associations between superhero viewing and gender stereotyped play. *Sex Roles*, 70, 416–430. doi:/10.1007/s11199-014-0374-8.

Croft, A., Schmader, T., and Block, K. (2015). An underexamined inequality: Cultural and psychological barriers to men's engagement with communal roles. *Personality and Social Psychology Review*, 19, 343–370. doi: 10.1177/1088868314564789.

Diekman, A.B. and Eagly, A.H. (2000). Stereotypes as dynamic constructs: Women and men of the past, present, and future. *Personality and Social Psychology Bulletin*, 26, 1171–1188. doi: 10.1177/0146167200262001.

Diekman, A.B., Johnston, A.M., and Loescher, A.L. (2013). Something old, something new: Evidence of self-accommodation to gendered social change. *Sex Roles*, 68, 550–561. doi: 10.1007/s11199-013-0263-6.

Diekman, A.B., Eagly, A.H., Mladinic, A., and Ferreira, M.C. (2005). Dynamic stereotypes about women and men in Latin America and the United States. *Journal of Cross-Cultural Psychology*, 36, 209–226. doi: 10.1177/00220 22104272902.

Downing, N.E. and Roush, K.L. (1985). From passive acceptance to active commitment: A model of feminist identity development for women. *The Counseling Psychologist*, 13, 695–709. doi: 10.1177/0011000085134013.

Eagly, A.H., Mladinic, A., and Otto, S. (1991). Are women evaluated more favorably than men? An analysis of attitudes, beliefs, and emotions. *Psychology of Women Quarterly*, 15, 203–216. doi: 10.1111/j.1471-6402.1991.tb00792.x.

Erchull, M.J., Liss, M., Wilson, K.A., Bateman, L., Peterson, A., and Sanchez, C.E. (2009). The feminist identity development model: Relevant for young women today? *Sex Roles, 60*, 832–842. doi: 10.1007/s11199-009-9588-6.

Evans, O. and Steptoe, A. (2002). The contribution of gender-role orientation, work factors and home stressors to psychological well-being and sickness absence in male- and female-dominated occupational groups. *Social Science and Medicine, 54*, 481–492. doi: 10.1016/S0277-9536(01)00044-2.

Forbes, C.E. and Schmader, T. (2010). Retraining attitudes and stereotypes to affect motivation and cognitive capacity under stereotype threat. *Journal of Personality and Social Psychology, 99*, 740–754. doi: 10.1037/a0020971.

Frazier, R. (2016). Sexism in politics 2016: What can we learn so far from media portrayals of Hillary Clinton and Latin American female leaders? Council on Hemispheric Affairs, June 16. www.coha.org/sexism-in-politics-2016-what-can-we-learn-so-far-from-media-portrayals-of-hillary-clinton-and-latin-American-female-leaders/.

Frisby, C.M. (2010). Sticks 'n stones may break my bones, but words they hurt like hell: derogatory words in popular songs. *Media Report to Women*, summer–fall, pp. 12–18.

Funk, L.C. and Werhun, C.D. (2011). "You're such a girl!" The psychological drain of the gender-role harassment of men. *Sex Roles, 65*, 13–22. doi 10.1007/s11199-011-9948-x.

Glass, C.M., Haas, S.A., and Reither, E.N. (2010). The skinny on success: Body mass, gender and occupational standing across the life course. *Social Forces, 88*, 1777–1806. doi: 10.1353/sof.2010.0012.

Glick, P. and Fiske, S.T. (1996). The Ambivalent Sexism Inventory: Differentiating hostile and benevolent sexism. *Journal of Personality and Social Psychology, 70*, 491–512. doi: 10.1037/0022-3514.70.3.491.

Glick, P., Diebold, J., Bailey-Werner, B., and Zhu, L. (1997). The two faces of Adam: Ambivalent sexism and polarized attitudes toward women. *Personality and Social Psychology Bulletin, 23*, 1323–1334.doi: 10.1177/01461672972312009.

Glick, P., Lameiras, M., Fiske, S.T., Eckes, T., Masser, B., Volpato, C., Manganelli, A.M., Pek, J.C.X., Huang, L., Sakalli-Uğurlu, N., Castro, Y.R., D'Avila Pereira, M.L., Willemsen, T.M., Brunner, A., Six-Materna, I., and Wells, R. (2004). Bad but bold: Ambivalent attitudes toward men predict gender inequality in 16 nations. *Journal of Personality and Social Psychology, 86*, 713–728. doi: 10.1037/0022-3514.86.5.713.

Goldberg, P.A. (1968). Are women prejudiced against women? *Trans-action*, 5, 28–30.

Herd, D. (2015). Conflicting paradigms on gender and sexuality in rap music: A systematic review. *Sexuality & Culture, 19*, 577–589. doi:10.1007/s12119-014-9259-9.

Hideg, I. and Ferris, D.L. (2016). The compassionate sexist? How benevolent sexism promotes and undermines gender equality in the workplace. *Journal of Personality and Social Psychology*, *111*, 706–727. doi: 10.1037/pspi0000072.

Horne, S., Matthews, S., and Detrie, P. (2001). Look it up under "F": Dialogues of emerging and experienced feminists. *Women and Therapy*, *23*, 5–18.

Kimmel, M.S. and Mosmiller, T. (1992). *Against the tide: Pro-feminist men in the United States, 1776–1990, a documentary history*. Boston, MA: Beacon Press.

Koenig, A.M. and Eagly, A.H. (2005). Stereotype threat in men on a test of social sensitivity. *Sex Roles*, *52*, 489–496. doi: 10.1007/s11199-005-3714-x.

Latu, I.M., Stewart, T.L., Myers, A.C., Lisco, C.G., Estes, S.B., and Donahue, D.K. (2011). What we "say" and what we "think" about female managers: Explicit versus implicit associations of women with success. *Psychology of Women Quarterly*, *35*, 252–266. doi: 10.1177/0361684310383811.

Lavy, V. and Sand, E. (2015). *On the origins of gender human capital gaps: Short and long term consequences of teachers' stereotypical biases*. Working paper No. 20909, January, National Bureau of Economic Research. www.nber.org/papers/w20909.

Löckenhoff, C.E., Chan, W., McCrae, R.R., De Fruy, F., Jussim, L. De Bolle, M. *et al.* (2014). Gender stereotypes of personality: Universal and accurate? *Journal of Cross-Cultural Psychology*, *45*, 675–694. doi: 10.1177/0022022113520075.

Lopez-Zafra, E. and Garcia-Retamero, R. (2012). Do gender stereotypes change? The dynamic of gender stereotypes in Spain. *Journal of Gender Studies*, *21*, 169–183. doi: 10.1080/09589236.2012.661580.

Maass, A., Cadinu, M., Guarnieri, G., and Grasselli, A. (2003). Sexual harassment under social identity threat: The computer harassment paradigm. *Journal of Personality and Social Psychology*, *85*, 853–870.

Moss-Racusin, C.A., Phelan, J.E., and Rudman, L.A. (2010). When men break the gender rules: Status incongruity and backlash against modest men. *Psychology of Men & Masculinity*, *11*, 140–151. doi: http://dx.doi.org/10.1037/a0018093.

Moss-Racusin, C.A., Dovidio, J.F., Brescoll, V.L., Graham, M.J., and Handelsman, J. (2012). Science faculty's subtle gender biases favor male students. *PNAS*, *109*, 16474–16479. doi: 10.1073/pnas.1211286109.

Noble, S.U. (2012). Missed connections: What search engines say about women. *Bitch*, *spring* (54), 36–41.

Okimoto, T.G. and Brescoll, V.L. (2010). The price of power: Power seeking and backlash against female politicians. *Personality and Social Psychology Bulletin*, *36*, 923–936. doi: 10.1177/0146167210371949.

Paludi, M.A. and Strayer, L.A. (1985). What's in an author's name? Differential evaluations of performance as a function of author's name. *Sex Roles, 12*, 353–361. doi: 10.1007/BF00287601.

Parsons, T. and Bales, R.F. (1955). *Family socialization and interaction process.* Glencoe, IL: Free Press.

Prentice, D.A. and Carranza, E. (2002). What women should be, shouldn't be, are allowed to be, and don't have to be: The contents of prescriptive gender stereotypes. *Psychology of Women Quarterly, 26*, 269–281. doi: 10.1111/1471-6402.t01-1-00066.

Puhl, R. and Brownell, K.D. (2001). Bias, discrimination and obesity. *Obesity Research, 9*, 788–805.

Ragonese, M. (2002). Riot Grrrls castrate "cock rock" in New York. *Off Our Backs, 32*(5/6), 27–31.

RFI (2011). Indian women protest sexual violence in Delhi's first SlutWalk, July 31. www.english.rfi.fr/node/102830.

Rudman, L.A. and Fairchild, K. (2004). Reactions to counterstereotypic behavior: The role of backlash in cultural stereotype maintenance. *Journal of Personality and Social Psychology, 87*, 157–176.

Rudman, L.A. and Glick, P. (2008). *The social psychology of gender. How power and intimacy shape gender relations.* New York: Guilford Press.

Rudman, L.A. and Kilianski, S.E. (2000). Implicit and explicit attitudes toward female authority. *Personality and Social Psychology Bulletin, 26*, 1315–1328. doi: 10.1177/0146167200263001.

Salomon, K., Burgess, K.D., and Bosson, J.K. (2015). Flash fire and slow burn: Women's cardiovascular reactivity and recovery following hostile and benevolent sexism. *Journal of Experimental Psychology: General, 144*, 469–479. doi: 10.1037/xge0000061.

Schlehofer, M.M., Casad, B.J., Bligh, M.C., and Grotto, A.R. (2011). Navigating public prejudices: The impact of media and attitudes on high-profile female political leaders. *Sex Roles, 65*, 69–82. doi: 10.1007/s11199-011-9965-9.

Schmid Mast, M. (2004). Men are hierarchical, women are egalitarian: An implicit gender stereotype. *Swiss Journal of Psychology, 63*, 107–111. doi: 10.1024/1421 0185.63.2.107.

Shaffer, E.S., Marx, D.M., and Prislin, R. (2013). Mind the gap: Framing of women's success and representation in STEM affects women's math performance under threat. *Sex Roles, 68*, 454–463. doi: 10.1007/s11199-012-0252-1.

Simons, M. (2017). Commentary: The politics of calling women ugly. *Chicago Tribune,* January 27. www.chicagotribune.com/news/opinion/commentary/ct-women-politics-appearance-feminists-ugly-20170126-story.html.

Smith, S.L., Choueiti, M., Prescott, A., and Pieper, K. (2013). *Gender roles & occupations: A look at character attributes and job-related aspirations in film and television*. Geena Davis Institute on Gender in Media. https://seejane.org/wp-content/uploads/key-findings-gender-roles-2013.pdf.

Sobiraj, S., Korek, S., Weseler, D., and Mohr, G. (2011). When male norms don't fit: Do traditional attitudes of female colleagues challenge men in nontraditional occupations? *Sex Roles, 65,* 798–812. doi: 10.1007/s11199-011-0057-7.

Spencer, S.J., Steele, C.M., and Quinn, D.M. (1999). Stereotype threat and women's math performance. *Journal of Experimental Social Psychology, 35,* 4–28.

Steele, C.M. (1997). A threat in the air. *American Psychologist, 52,* 613–629.

Stermer, S.P. and Burkley, M. (2015). SeX-Box: Exposure to sexist video games predicts benevolent sexism. *Psychology of Popular Media Culture, 4,* 47–55. doi: 10.1037/a0028397.

Swim, J.K. (1994). Perceived versus meta-analytic effect sizes: An assessment of the accuracy of gender stereotypes. *Journal of Personality and Social Psychology, 66,* 21–36. doi: 10.1037/0022-3514.66.1.21.

Swim, J.K. and Hyers, L.L. (1999). Excuse me—what did you just say?! Women's public and private responses to sexist remarks. *Journal of Experimental Social Psychology, 35,* 68–88. doi: 10.1006/jesp. 1998.1370.

Swim, J.K., Aikin, K.J., Hall, W.S., and Hunter, B.A. (1995). Sexism and racism: Old-fashioned and modern prejudices. *Journal of Personality and Social Psychology, 68,* 199–214. doi: 10.1037/0022-3514.68.2.199.

Swim, J., Borgida, E., Maruyama, G., and Myers, D.G. (1989). Joan McKay versus John McKay: Do gender stereotypes bias evaluations? *Psychological Bulletin, 105,* 409–429. doi: 10.1037/0033-2909.105.3.409.

Top, T.J. (1991). Sex bias in the evaluation of performance in the scientific, artistic, and literary professions: A review. *Sex Roles, 24,* 73–106. doi: 10.1007/BF00288704.

Tougas, F., Brown, R., Beaton, A.M., and Joly, S. (1995). Neosexism: Plus ça change, plus c'est pareil. *Personality and Social Psychology Bulletin, 21,* 842–849. doi: 10.1177/0146167295218007.

Tracy, J.L. and Beall, A.T. (2011). Happy guys finish last: The impact of emotion expressions on sexual attraction. *Emotion, 11,* 1379–1387. doi: 10.1037/a0022902.

Twenge, J.M. (1997). Changes in masculine and feminine traits over time: A meta-analysis. *Sex Roles, 36,* 305–325. doi: 10.1007/BF02766650.

von Hippel, C., Issa, M., Ma, R., and Stokes, A. (2011). Stereotype threat: Antecedents and consequences for working women. *European Journal of Social Psychology, 41,* 151–161. doi: 10.1002/ejsp. 749.

von Hippel, C., Wiryakusuma, C., Bowden, J., and Shochet, M. (2011). Stereotype threat and female communication styles. *Personality and Social Psychology Bulletin, 37*, 1312–1324. doi: 10.1177/0146167211410439.

Waldo, C.R., Berdahl, J.L., and Fitzgerald, L.F. (1998). Are men sexually harassed? If so, by whom? *Law and Human Behavior, 22*, 59–79.

White, M.J. and White, G.B. (2006). Implicit and explicit occupational gender stereotypes. *Sex Roles, 55*, 259–266. doi: 10.1007/s11199-006-9078-z.

Wilde, A. and Diekman, A.B. (2005). Cross-cultural similarities and differences in dynamic stereotypes: A comparison between Germany and the United States. *Psychology of Women Quarterly, 29*, 188–196. doi: 10.1111/j.1471-6402.2005.00181.x.

Williams, J.E. and Best, D.E. (1990). *Sex and psyche: Gender and self viewed cross-culturally*. Newbury Park, CA: Sage.

Zarya, V. (2016). There is literally no facial expression Hillary Clinton can make to please male pundits. *Fortune.com*, September 27. http://fortune.com/2016/09/27/hillary-clinton-smiling-debate/.

4

RELATIONSHIPS, INTIMACY, AND SEXUALITIES

In the rarefied early twentieth-century world of British aristocracy, portrayed in the popular television series *Downton Abbey*, individuals' choices with respect to intimate relationships are shaped and constrained as much by gender as by class. The eldest daughter of the noble house finds herself unable to marry the man she loves because of an impulsive sexual indiscretion she dares not admit lest it bring scandal upon her entire family. A housemaid's liaison with a soldier leads not only to an unplanned pregnancy but also to her rejection by the man in question, disgrace, and the destruction of her chances for a normal life. The valet finds he can divorce his wife for adultery, whereas she would need stronger grounds to divorce him.

Such examples of gender-based uneven distribution of penalties and power in intimate relationships appear quaint and old fashioned—but are they? Persistent acceptance of a *double standard* in which women are judged more harshly than men for sexual activity that "breaks the rules," and men's, but not women's, sexual desires are acknowledged as urgent and insistent, is well documented by researchers in many countries. It appears that the gender stereotypes considered in the previous chapters shape and constrain intimate relationships.

GENDER AND EXPECTATIONS OF POWER AND INTIMACY IN INTERPERSONAL RELATIONSHIPS

Gender stereotypes prescribe authority, leadership, and decisiveness for masculinity, and accommodation, interpersonal sensitivity, subservience, and warmth for femininity. These prescriptions are as strong in the sphere of interpersonal relationships as they are in the public sphere of business, politics, and education—with similar implications for maintaining a system in which men are in charge. Years ago, Australian scholar Dale Spender (1989) used audio recording to document shared speaking time in her male and female academic colleagues' conversations. She found that women did more listening than speaking: women's share of the speaking time in conversation with male colleagues ranged from 8 to 38 percent. When Spender herself tried, as an experiment, to hold three-minute, two-person conversations in which she held the floor for at least half of that time, most of her male colleagues walked away before the time was up. The harder she pushed to try to claim her half of the speaking time, the more uncomfortable she became and the more irritation her male colleagues expressed. Apparently, both her colleagues and she had been trained to think of male conversational dominance as normal, and female attempts at claiming an equivalent share of speaking time as pushy and rude.

The way we talk with each other has implications for both power and intimacy. Controlling the conversation is a type of power in relationships; keeping the conversation flowing supports and encourages the development and maintenance of closeness, or at least comfort, in a relationship. Whereas we expect men to dominate relationships, we expect women to do more of the work of sustaining relationships by encouraging and maintaining conversational exchanges. For example, women self-disclose more than men do—especially in cross-sex conversations, and especially with respect to feelings. Women also do more of the work of sustaining interactions—by using nonverbal signals such as eye contact and nodding to show that they are paying attention, by making "listening noises" such as "Mm-hmm" and "I know," and by following up on topics raised by a speaker. In one of the first demonstrations of how hard women work to sustain close relationships, Pamela Fishman (1978) analyzed 52 hours of recorded spontaneous conversation between members of 3 heterosexual couples in intimate relationships. During these conversations, women did much more support work than did men. Conversational topics raised by the women were far less likely than those raised by the men to "succeed" (result in a discussion of those topics); men were far more likely than women to use delayed minimal responses (e.g., a long pause, followed by a uninterested "umm") after women's statements than vice versa. Women worked much harder than men to keep the lines of communication open, but men were the ones who decided what the communication was to be about. Again, men were adhering to a masculine stereotype that prescribes authority and dominance; women were enacting a feminine stereotype of accommodation, warmth, and supportiveness.

Whereas much of the research on conversational dominance has been conducted with English-speaking dyads, one study of Japanese speakers provided some insights by focusing, not just on quantitative aspects (number of interruptions, total speaking time, number of topics that succeed), but also on the qualitative aspects of conversations (i.e., what people are talking about and how they are speaking). In this study, men displayed a self-oriented conversational style that emphasized storytelling and claiming expertise. Their female partners engaged in an other-oriented speaking style (showing interest, asking for more details), which supported the men. Conversation in these dyads became a dance in which male dominance was mutually constructed and maintained by both parties (Itakura and Tsui, 2004).

Researchers differ as to the reasons for gender differences in communication, but evidence is consistent with social rather than with strong biological explanations. This is because the patterns of differences vary according to the interactive context, such as the relationship between the participants, the type of activity, or the familiarity of the situation. Gender differences in dominance-oriented conversational tactics such as talkativeness and interruptions are more often observed in mixed-gender than same-gender interactions, suggesting that they form part of a tendency for men to try to dominate women rather than simply a gender difference in dominance. And gender differences in both affiliative and assertive speech are more likely in interactions between strangers and in research labs than in natural settings, suggesting that people fall back on gender-related norms and scripts to guide their behavior when in unfamiliar contexts.

Societies institutionalize stereotypes connecting gender, power, and intimacy in certain ways. A venerable tradition in many societies is the practice of asking a father for permission to marry his daughter. In some cultures, single women come under the authority of their brothers should the father die before the women are married. When a woman marries, she often takes her husband's last name. Do such "old-fashioned" ideas of male power and female accommodation have currency in the ways young people think about relationships today? Consider the media representations of love and romance enjoyed by adolescents. In the popular *Twilight* series of books and movies, a young woman, Bella, is courted by a vampire, Edward (and also, for a while, by a werewolf, Jacob). The relationships are marked by numerous instances in which the males rescue Bella from harm—but they often harm her in the process. Bella is stalked, bruised, overpowered, frightened, and ordered around repeatedly by Edward and Jacob. Clearly, the males are portrayed as holding and exercising more power; Bella is portrayed as willing to make huge sacrifices in the service of love and intimacy—and, later in the series, for motherhood. These portrayals are redolent of benevolent sexism, a term introduced in Chapter 3 to describe the attitude that women are vulnerable and need protection and guidance from men. Perhaps because they are so often surrounded by approving depictions of benevolent sexism, adolescent girls may internalize this type of patronizing ideology and fail to recognize it as sexism. Even when they know they are being treated badly, as in cases of sexual harassment and other instances of hostile sexism, young women may be so accustomed to demeaning treatment that they expect such treatment as part of normal heterosexual relationships (Witkowska and Gådin, 2005). The expectation that men will emphasize power and control and women will emphasize connection and closeness permeates the ways we think about relationships.

WOMEN'S AND MEN'S FRIENDSHIPS

Gender stereotypes that prescribe dominance, competitiveness, toughness, and leadership for men may make it difficult for them to be open with friends. By contrast, stereotypes that prescribe warmth and supportiveness as part of femininity may push women toward disclosing and listening to accounts of feelings and vulnerability. The result may be a tendency toward emotional restraint and distance among men and toward sharing of emotions among women. Researchers have indeed found girls and women higher in affiliative communication and boys and men higher in assertive communication. Some analysts have characterized the difference between male and female friendships as a divide between shared activities and shared feelings, or between "side-by-side" and "face-to-face" relationships. Men and boys tend to have more friends; women and girls tend to have fewer, more intimate friends.

However, the gender differences are small, inconsistent, and context-sensitive. A narrow focus on gender differences may obscure large within-gender variations in patterns of communication and friendship. That gender differences in friendship are affected by history and culture is evident from comparisons of men's friendships in middle-class present-day North America and other settings. For example, one researcher who studied friendship in rural Thailand noted that women were thought not to have close friends upon whom they could rely for serious help and support, but rather simply neighbors and people with whom they enjoy spending time. Men, on the other hand, were thought to have serious "friendships to the death" (Foster, 1976). In medieval Near-Eastern countries, men sometimes formalized their friendships. One formal contract of friendship between two scholars in Cairo in 1564 stated that the two men would be bound in friendship for their own lifetimes and that of their children and their children's children. They promised to pray in the same synagogue, lend each other any books they possess, and never to conceal any book from each other (Goitein, 1971). Examples such as these reveal a strikingly different perspective on male friendship from the activity oriented, emotionally restrained model described by North American researchers.

SEXUALITY IN RELATIONSHIPS

The different communication patterns developed by male and female children as they grow into adolescence may shape their experience of romantic sexual relationships in young adulthood. The impact may be not only on communication and satisfaction, but also on the power distribution in such relationships. If girls are used to self-disclosure and supportive listening, and boys are used to emotional restraint and conversational dominance, heterosexual romantic relationships appear doomed to be rocky. Women may be unsatisfied with men's listener support; men used to male–male friendships may bask in the unaccustomed warmth of a responsive female listener. Men used to jockeying for conversational control may unwittingly neglect to attend to conversational topics raised by a female partner, solidifying their culturally supported role as dominant partners in heterosexual relationships. Learned gendered patterns of communication may shape same-gender romantic relationships as well, by orienting them toward the style practiced most consistently by women or men: more mutual support for women, more power orientation for men. Lesbian couples report somewhat more equality in communication, mutual support, and decision-making than do women in heterosexual relationships; gay male couples report less equality of communication, support, and decision-making than heterosexual men (Gotta *et al.*, 2011).

WHAT DOES SEXUALITY MEAN IN RELATIONSHIPS?

Gender stereotypes and learned patterns of communication may affect the expression of sexuality in relationships. If women have learned to emphasize closeness and connection, they may be more likely than men to interpret sexuality in terms of emotion and intimacy. If men have learned to emphasize dominance and emotional restraint, it may be easier for them to think of sexuality in terms of conquest and pleasure without commitment. Indeed, a tradition that to some extent occurs across cultures and historical periods holds that sexuality carries different meanings for women and for men. Women's sexual experience and expression has traditionally been restrained and guarded, not encouraged. Men's sexual desires, on the other hand, have often been considered irresistible, uncontrollable. These attitudes provide the basis for a double standard of sexual behavior, which prescribes that women and men are judged differently for engaging in sexual activity. A woman who engages too easily or indiscriminately in sexual activity is branded with a variety of uncomplimentary labels: slut, promiscuous, loose. She is violating the gender-based expectation that she should engage in sexual relationships only when they involve love and intimacy. Such negative consequences do not accrue to a man who "sleeps around" with many women or gets a reputation as being very sexually active. That man may receive some disapproval (particularly if he is married or in a committed relationship), but he is also likely to be the target of some envy and admiration from other men, and of nothing worse than an exasperated "boys will be boys" reaction from some women.

These different standards for women and men are more exaggerated in some cultural contexts than in others. Sex, or even flirting, outside of marriage can be punishable by death for women whose families subscribe to a traditional strict code of honor. *Honor killings* claim the lives of thousands of women each year, and occur wherever the propriety of women's behavior reflects on family reputation (United Nations Population Fund, 2000). Men are less likely to risk severe punishment for heterosexual activity outside of marriage. In some contexts, however, they risk physical attack and even death for homosexual activity; in certain countries gay men face criminal charges and imprisonment.

The cultural scaffolding that props up the double standard rests on gender stereotypes, but it is more complex than the prescription that women should reserve sexual activity for intimate relationships whereas men can emphasize "the chase." Women are the ones who become pregnant and give birth. By controlling women's heterosexual activity, societies aim to ensure that children are born into stable family situations and men aim to ensure that the children they support are their own biological offspring. Another aspect is the gender hierarchy. Through controlling women's sexuality and reproduction, men establish, assert, and retain their authority over women and reinforce notions about women's emotionality and lack of suitability for leadership.

SEXUAL ORIENTATION AND SEXUAL IDENTITY

We have discussed sexuality and relationships as though they can be roughly categorized into female–male, female–female, or male–male attractions and connections. This is a frequently used shorthand for categorizing sexual relationships, but it is worth looking more closely at what these categories mean and whether they are adequate to describe sexual relationships. Such a closer look is provided by Sexual Configurations Theory (SCT; van Anders, 2015), which focuses on three dimensions of sexuality and, in so doing, allows for a multiplicity of sexual orientations and identities. This theory acknowledges numerous variations and differences in lived experiences within traditional categories of sexual orientation. It may also provide the means for a broader set of individuals to recognize themselves and their experiences in scholarship on sexuality.

Sexual Configuration Theory (SCT) focuses on three dimensions of partnered sexuality: (1) gender/sex sexuality (to whom an individual is attracted); (2) partner number sexuality (the number of partners an individual is interested in having); and (3) eroticism and nurturance (the importance of genital arousal and/or feelings of close intimacy in people's attractions). The theory allows for the questioning of many traditional assumptions and the identification of numerous possibilities. For example, within the first dimension, gender/sex sexuality, an individual may locate him- or herself as attracted mostly to women, somewhat to men, and somewhat to persons who do not identify as normative women or men. This attraction may be based on target individuals' whole identities, on physical features such as genitals or breasts, or on the individuals' behavior. On the second dimension, partner number, a person may be interested in having no partners, one partner, or two or more partners at the same time. On the third dimension, eroticism/nurturance, a person may, for example, feel closest to women, but more strongly erotically attracted to people who are gender-nonconforming. Or, she or he may feel attracted to others mainly in terms of nurturance and hardly at all in terms of eroticism.

This theory suggests that traditional categories of sexual orientation and sexual identity are too limited to fully capture people's lived experiences. It illustrates that "*all* people have located sexualities using a sexual diversity lens, regardless of their socially-derived position of sexual minority or majority [...] [and that] [...] each of us is situated in a larger social and sexual landscape" (van Anders, 2015: 1208).

CULTURE, SEXUAL SELF-SCHEMAS, AND SEXUAL SCRIPTS

Popular media are rife with presentations of sexuality—and such presentations provide some basis for individuals' ideas about how to express and label their own sexual selves. Furthermore, media messages about sexuality are gendered. Women receive conflicting directives that admirable behavior involves being "good" (i.e., restrained) and sexually assertive and sophisticated (Phillips, 2000). For example, in the United States, peers often pressure adolescent girls to engage in "sexting," but judge them harshly when they do; whereas boys receive little criticism either way (Lippman and Campbell, 2014). Portrayals of men's sexuality often emphasize action rather than feelings (Kilmartin, 2009). North American media increasingly represent sex as casual and uncommitted, embedded in a *hook-up* culture: the message is that there is no need for either women or men to tie sexual activity to emotional commitment (Garcia, Reiber, Massey, and Merriwether, 2012).

Swimming in a sea of such messages is bound to impact individuals' *sexual self-schemas*, their views of themselves as sexual beings. A self-schema is a set of cognitive generalizations about the self that help the individual to organize and make sense of incoming information. An individual whose sexual self-schema is heavily weighted with notions of desire is likely to interpret an opportunity for a sexual connection very differently to an individual whose self-schema emphasizes relationship. Not surprisingly, in light of media messages, the sexual self-schemas of women and men may differ somewhat. Both men and women describe their sexual selves using dimensions of passion, romanticism, and openness. However, one dimension that some researchers have found among men, but not among women, involves power and aggression, and includes descriptors such as aggressive, powerful, outspoken, experienced, and domineering. A dimension that some researchers have found among women but not among men involves caution and restraint, and includes descriptors such as embarrassed, conservative, cautious, and self-conscious (Andersen and Cyranowski, 1994; Andersen,

Cyranowski, and Espindle, 1999). One Canadian study found that the self-descriptions of both groups centered on three dimensions: loving/warmth, reserved/conservative, and direct/outspoken, with men scoring slightly lower than women on the loving/warmth and reserved/conservative dimensions (Hill, 2007). In describing their sexual selves, men sometimes make a distinction between physical intimacy and emotional intimacy. As one respondent commented, "If you need tenderness and human contact? Rather than talk to somebody, you prove that you're all right, and you get the attachment you need by finding a warm body" (Elder, Brooks, and Morrow, 2012: 171).

Sexual self-schemas may differ, not just between self-identified women and men but across the wide spectrum of racial, cultural, and sexual diversity. For example, one theme found in men's sexual self-schemas is confidence in appearance. In one US study, most men expressed a lack of confidence in their physical appearance, but ethnic minority men reported feeling less attractive than non–Latino White men (Elder *et al.*, 2012). Research on sexual self-schemas is sparse for non-heterosexual populations, but one example focuses on sexual self-schemas and masculinity ideologies of men who identify as bisexual (Elder, Morrow, and Brooks, 2015). This study suggests that bisexual men's sexual self-schemas are shaped in some ways by conventional masculinity socialization and in others by their attempts to carve out an identity that differs from conventional masculinity. For example, one theme that emerged from interviews with these men was the overt sexualization of women's bodies: looking at and "checking out" women and bonding with heterosexual male peers over this activity. Another theme was the men's perception that physical appearance was critically significant to gay men, and the anxiety that gay men sized them up as potential partners by scrutinizing their appearance. Still another theme was the concern that, despite being attracted to both men and women,

> there were significant cultural and political advantages of being in a relationship with a woman, including access to legal rights and avoiding sexual stigma. As a result, participants described feeling pressured to ignore their attractions to men and only consider women as long-term partners.
>
> (Elder *et al.*, 2015:985)

Clearly, there is not one single self-schema for men and one for women; context, culture, and identity are critical in shaping individuals' notions of their sexual selves.

Gender stereotypes also influence *sexual scripts*. Scripts are shared cultural understandings about how interactions will proceed—understandings that help us to organize and interpret behavior. A sexual script helps organize behaviors into a coherent story; once the first behaviors occur, the script suggests how the rest of the interaction will likely proceed (Simon and Gagnon, 1987). Scripts are based on past experience, on media representations, and on observations of other people. They tend to be mutually shared and gender-normative: in heterosexual interactions women are expected to behave in certain ways, men in others. This double standard often informs sexual scripts for heterosexual interactions: men take the initiative, women set limits; men are interested in casual sex, women are interested in relationships. When in a new situation, people often fall back on scripts to guide their behavior.

Despite the pervasiveness of these traditional (hetero)sexual scripts, most young adults surveyed report that they have engaged in casual sex (Garcia *et al.*, 2012). Some newer cultural scripts emphasize non-relational sex, hook-ups, or friends-with-benefits. The initial behaviors in the hook-up script might involve attending a certain kind of party, drinking a lot of alcohol, dancing and flirting—with the anticipation that the subsequent steps will involve casual sex with no expectations of a romantic relationship. On the face of it, these scripts interpret casual, non-relational sex as appropriate for both women and men; they prescribe sexual assertiveness for both genders. Indeed, if casual sex is prompted by autonomous motivations rather than by peer pressure or other external factors, it is not linked to poor emotional consequences for either women or men (Vrangalova, 2015). However, perhaps because of the different messages directed to women and men about sexuality, the experience of "playing by" these scripts may be gendered. Women are much more likely than men to report negative feelings and guilt after having sex with someone they had just met; and women, but not men, appear to show increased depression with the number of sexual partners they report over the past year (Garcia *et al.*, 2012). When asked about their feelings on the morning after a hook-up,

82 percent of men, but only 57 percent of women, said they were generally glad they had done it (Garcia and Reiber, 2008), and, as is shown in Figure 4.1, more women (42.9%) than men (29%) said that ideally they would have liked the hook-up to lead to a romantic relationship. Women more than men report a preference for dating over hook-ups, whereas men more than women report that they prefer hooking up (Bradshaw, Kahn, and Saville, 2010). Furthermore, women have lower rates of orgasm in sexual hook-ups than in more committed relationship contexts (Armstrong, England, and Fogarty, 2012). Although both men and women in some contexts may experience casual sex as satisfying and positive, men report more emotional and sexual satisfaction with casual sex than do women (Mark, Garcia, and Fisher, 2015).

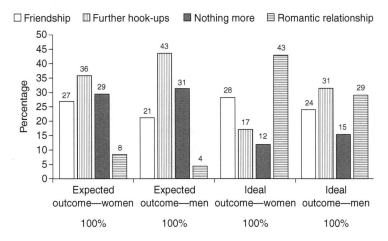

Figure 4.1 Women's and men's expected and ideal outcomes of hooking up. In a sample of more than 500 undergraduate students in the United States, women and men appeared to differ less in their expectations about the results of hooking up than in their ideals for where they would like such connections to lead. Women were more likely than men to wish that hooking up would lead to a romantic relationship; men were more likely than women to wish for further hook-ups.

Source: Based on data from Garcia and Reiber (2008).

Whereas prescriptions for masculinity may include having many sexual relationships while remaining unattached and independent, men's feelings about sex are variable and more complicated than these prescriptions. Men may subscribe to the notion that they should enjoy non-relational sex, but many also admit to desiring an emotional connection after having sex with someone several times, even if they did not originally want or plan for a relationship. When men in one sample were interviewed about hooking up, their responses included discomfort with the non-relational nature of such interactions and the articulation of possibilities for real connections and committed relationships (Epstein, Calzo, Smiler, and Ward, 2009). The men blurred the lines between hooking up and dating, sometimes using the term *hook-up* to describe situations where they had wished for a relationship that did not work out, or instances in which something that started out as casual sex turned into a dating relationship. They also described experiences of regret and vulnerability after hooking up with people in whom they were not interested. Cultural prescriptions may say that men *should* be able to have sex with a stranger without experiencing any emotional consequences, but men's reports indicate that such situations are often more complicated.

Sexual scripts for gay men and lesbians are also affected by gender stereotypes: scripts for gay men often include casual sex; those for lesbians emphasize that emotional intimacy and sexual attraction are intertwined. Indeed, researchers have found that, in comparisons among self-identified sexual orientation groups, gay men report the most sexual and emotional satisfaction in casual sex contexts, whereas lesbian women report the least (Mark *et al.*, 2015). However, as noted for heterosexual interactions, there are multiple possible scripts, and reality may not fit perfectly with any of them. Rose and Zand (2002) found that the most widely used (though not necessarily most widely preferred) script in relationship formation among lesbians was the "friendship" script. They suggest that many young women have not been exposed to a "romance" or "sexually explicit" script for relationships between women, so they may first treat and label their attraction to another woman as a friendship. The relationship gradually becomes deeper and more committed and is eventually expressed physically. In contrast, the romance script involves flirting and dating and high emotional intensity, leading quickly to an intimate bond and overt sexual contact. The sexually explicit script involves mutual physical attraction and casual sex, and is often initiated in bars or at parties. Even though the latter script is evocative of "masculine" sexuality, 63 percent of respondents in this study said they had engaged in it at least once—though none of the participants endorsed it as the one they preferred.

For young gay men, the cultural script may emphasize being sexually active, being comfortable with casual, non-relational sex, and taking sexual risks. Although many young gay men in college are well aware of this script and may incorporate it into their self-definition, many do not feel they conform to it (Wilkerson, Brooks, and Ross, 2010).

DESIRE, AROUSAL, AND SATISFACTION

In her memoir, *Infidel*, Ayann Hirsi Ali (2007) recounts the stark disconnect she experienced as a young woman between her early media-fed sexual fantasies and her first sexual intercourse. Her imagination fueled by Harlequin romance novels, she had longed to be swept off her feet by a gorgeous man. She guiltily burned with desire and relished long, passionate kisses with her boyfriend, but followed the rules of her Somali culture to delay sexual intercourse until marriage. As a young girl, she had, according to common practice in her culture, been "circumcised" (had her clitoris cut out and her labia sewn together except for a small hole for urination) to guarantee her purity, and the procedure had left her with a scar in place of a normal vaginal opening. On her wedding night, her new husband:

> gasped and sweated with the effort of forcing open my scar. It was horribly painful and took so long. I gritted my teeth and endured the pain until I became numb. Afterward, Mahmud fell heavily asleep, and I went and washed again.

Ayann's married girlfriends had told her that sex was unpleasant: that each night was a painful repetition of a scenario in which the husband would push inside the woman, move up and down until he ejaculated, then get up and take a shower—after which the woman would also take a shower and apply disinfectant to her bleeding genitals. Yet she had refused to believe that sex would be that way for her, and had stoked a passionate desire for sexual fulfillment. She dreamed of wildly erotic sexual episodes, but was instead forced into the role of a "good" virgin who lies still and feels nothing. We are not privy to what her husband thought of all this, but we do know that he was the one who was allowed to initiate and direct their sexual activity.

The double standard legitimizes men's feelings of arousal and desire, but ignores, downplays, or even condemns such feelings in women. The impact of these gendered expectations can be to encourage men and discourage women in recognizing, appreciating, and acting on their sexual feelings. Indeed, researchers have found that men show a significantly greater degree of agreement between self-reported and genital measures of sexual arousal than do women (Chivers, Seto, Lalumière, Laan, and Grimbos 2010). In other words, men's reports that they feel sexually aroused are more likely than women's reports of arousal to match up with the genital changes that signal arousal. Such findings suggest that women and men recognize, label, and interpret the physical signs of arousal differently—probably because of the very different societal messages about female and male sexuality.

SEXUAL EMPOWERMENT FOR WOMEN AND GIRLS?

One example of the different cultural conditions faced by young women and men with respect to sexual relationships appears in an interview study of lower income African American adults (Eyre, Flythe, Hoffman, and Fraser, 2012). The young women and men described their thoughts and feelings about starting a sexual and/or romantic relationship, and a few gender differences were striking. The young men spoke of how they assessed a woman as a potential romantic partner: evaluating her on her appearance, her reputation, her likelihood of being faithful, her economic prospects. They were clear that a woman who would have sex with them right away was not eligible as a serious romantic partner. The women, on the other hand, did not generally report assessing men for a romantic relationship. Thus, these young people followed a traditional cultural script in which men were proactive and women responsive—and in which women who claimed their sexuality tended to be judged harshly.

How would relationships change if women were more strongly encouraged to recognize and act on their sexual feelings? Many feminists have advocated for increased sexual empowerment for women, arguing that women should feel free to claim their sexuality: to act on their desires, seek sexual pleasure, dress and behave in sexual ways if they so choose. Indeed, Beyoncé, one of the most wildly popular and successful figures in the entertainment industry, has argued strongly, both through her song lyrics and her public statements, that women should own their sexuality, and that "You can be a businesswoman, a mother, an artist, and a feminist— whatever you want to be—and still be a sexual being. It's not mutually exclusive" (quoted in Hicklin, 2014)—and many young women claim her as a role model. If women treated their own sexual feelings as legitimate and important, and refused to be embarrassed or hemmed in by a double-standard approach to female sexuality, would the double standard fade away? Would the balance of power in heterosexual relationships change?

Such questions are particularly vexing in the context of adolescence—the time in most people's lives when sexuality emerges as a force to be reckoned with, when sexual attitudes and scripts take shape, and when individuals may be particularly emotionally vulnerable. On the one hand, it seems obvious that it would be beneficial to adolescent girls to cultivate a sense of efficacy in their sexuality—that they should be aware of and, if they choose, act on their desires, acknowledge and seek sexual pleasure. Such self-efficacy may promote self-esteem, responsible decision-making, and equality in heterosexual relationships. On the other hand, it seems equally obvious that girls may not be able to achieve real sexual empowerment in the context of a surrounding heavily sexualized and sexist media environment. Can a girl feel subjectively empowered while making choices and behaving in ways that place her under the power of others? Can free sexual expression by one girl actually help undermine sexual empowerment for other girls by contributing to the media sexualization of girls in general? Do girls who are confidently sexually expressive set a standard that is unrealistic for most of their counterparts? Such questions remind us that political and personal power are bound together. Acts of personal empowerment can contribute to cultural change, and political movements can support personal empowerment—but the personal and political approaches work in concert, and sometimes at cross purposes.

SEXUAL SATISFACTION

In the realm of sexual relationships, one dimension of empower-ment is sexual satisfaction. It seems reasonable that part of feeling sexually empowered would be feeling sexually satisfied. For women and men in mixed-sex relationships, lesbian women, and women who identify as bisexual, queer, or unlabeled, sexual satisfaction is linked with a favorable balance of sexual rewards and costs, greater equality of sexual rewards and costs between partners, and higher relationship satisfaction (Byers and Cohen, 2017).

Traditionally, women and men have differed on variables related to sexual satisfaction. For example, women more often than men report that they do not reach orgasm during sex with a partner (Michael, Gagnon, Laumann, and Kolata,, 1994). Men think more about sex than women do and often report a desire for more sex than they are getting (Baumeister, Catanese, and Vohs, 2001). How are we to interpret such findings with respect to issues of gender, power, and justice in relationships?

Sarah McClelland (2010) proposed a theory of *intimate justice* to analyze these issues by focusing on "how social and political inequities impact intimate experiences, affecting how individuals imagine, behave, and evaluate their intimate lives." She argued that to evaluate women's and men's reports of sexual satisfaction it is important also to study how entitled they feel to sexual pleasure. Someone who does not feel entitled to very much may be satisfied with very little. Cultural–political context can affect entitlement, so women and men may feel differently entitled to sexual pleasure. She also notes that it is critical to investigate what respondents mean when they describe their satisfaction as "high" or "low"—

and whether there are gender differences in these meanings. In her research, women and men described the low end of a sexual satisfaction scale very differently. Women describe the low end of the scale very negatively, using concepts such as pain, degradation, and depression. For men, the low end of the scale represents less satisfying sex, loneliness, and having an unattractive partner—men did not mention the severely negative outcomes listed by women.

McClelland's analysis situates the study of personal sexual experiences and relationships clearly within the socio-political context of power relations between groups. Her approach demonstrates why a simple catalog of female–male differences on certain sexual variables is not adequate to an understanding of why and how women and men may experience sexuality differently. Not only sexual behavior, but the entire topic of couple relationships must be placed in the context of power relations between gender groups in order to gain a clearer understanding of why and how such relationships function.

COUPLES: LONG-TERM, INTIMATE CONNECTIONS

Although we think of long-term intimate relationships as being about love and personal commitment, it is impossible to understand such relationships without recourse to less romantic notions of power, economics, and the division of labor. Traditionally, most cultures have granted authority in heterosexual couples to men. Such authority is often institutionalized, formally or informally, in the legal and religious frameworks that define marriage. Not every bride promises to love, honor, and *obey*, but there is often an implicit acceptance of male dominance in heterosexual couples.

Against this backdrop, the roles traditionally associated with male–female couples in many societies have tended to encode the notion that the man is the breadwinner and the woman is the homemaker and caregiver. This traditional division of roles does not match the actual situation of most female–male couples in Western countries. As is shown in Figure 4.2, most mothers in the United States are in the workforce. Couples in which only the husband is employed make up only 19 percent of married-couple

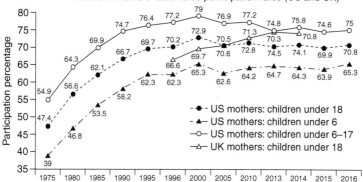

Figure 4.2 US and UK trends in mothers' labor force participation rates. In both the United States and Britain, labor force participation of mothers of young children increased significantly in the latter part of the twentieth century. Despite some small declines in recent years, the majority of mothers, even mothers of very young children, are now in the labor force.

Source: Based on data from U.S. Bureau of Labor Statistics (2017) for US data, and Office for National Statistics (2015) for UK data.

families, women comprise almost 47 percent of the labor force, and just under 70 percent of mothers of children under age 18 are in the labor force (U.S. Bureau of Labor Statistics, 2015). In 2013, among married couples where both spouses were employed, 29 percent of wives earned more than their husbands. Worldwide, women make up just over 40 percent of the labor force, and just over 50 percent of women aged 15 and older participate in the labor force (World Bank, 2016). The gap between women and men in labor force participation has shrunk to 10 percent or less in countries such as Sweden, Denmark, and France.

If there were no cultural ideology involved, when conditions changed for a couple (e.g., the man lost his job or the woman received a lucrative promotion), women and men would simply and unemotionally adjust their share of domestic work and their decision-making to reflect the change and maintain a fair division of labor. Instead, couples often adhere to traditional patterns of labor division, even in the face of changing situations—and they may find it uncomfortable to acknowledge discrepancies between their own relationships and the traditional ideal.

For example, women continue to handle more than their share of housework and childcare responsibilities (U.S. Bureau of Labor Statistics, 2016), even though many of them are employed full time. Men who earn less than their wives do not necessarily cede decision-making power or the provider role (Tichenor, 2005). Men who hold a strong ideology of traditional masculinity report poorer relationship quality with their wives if the wives earn higher incomes (Coughlin and Wade, 2012). One Swedish study noted that, in dividing household chores and childcare responsibilities, men may insist on sharper boundaries than do women—asserting that they cannot be pressured to do certain kinds of domestic tasks (Magnusson and Marecek, 2012). Clearly, then, couples are influenced by the surrounding cultural norms with respect to the gendering of roles within long-term relationships.

BASES AND STYLES OF INTERPERSONAL POWER IN RELATIONSHIPS

The amount and type of influence exerted by individuals in couples, as well as within friendships, workplace relationships, etc., reflects cultural norms and access to resources. As noted above, couple relationships involve roles that have been strongly linked to gender—and these links cannot help but affect power within these relationships.

When one person tries to influence another, the influence attempt must be based on some resource. If, for instance, a stranger were to stop you on the street and tell you to cross and walk on the other side, there would have to be a *reason* for you to comply. Perhaps the stranger is pointing a weapon at you, or promising to give you a free box of donuts if you cross the street. Perhaps she is wearing a police uniform. Perhaps you are in a culture where it is the norm to accede to such requests when made by strangers. Any of these things would provide the reason for compliance—or, as social psychologists would say, the *bases of power* underlying the influence attempt. Typical bases of power include reward ("I will do this for you if you comply"), coercion ("I will do something bad to you if you do not comply"), expertise ("My expertise tells me this is the best course of action for you"), legitimacy ("I have a right, by virtue of legitimate authority or accepted cultural norms, to demand this of you"), reference ("If you really like, love, or admire me, or value our relationship, you will do this for me"), and information ("Here are all the good, logical reasons why you should do this") (French and Raven, 1959; Raven, 1992).

The use of bases of power depends on access to particular resources, and access to resources tends to be gendered. For example, in many relationship contexts, men have control over more money than women do, so they are more able to use that as a basis for exerting influence. In long-term heterosexual couple relationships, cultural expectations with respect to masculinity and femininity can confer access to legitimate power. In a cultural context that identifies the man as the "head" of the household, men have considerable legitimacy-based power with respect to making demands for obedience from their wives and children. In a cultural context which specifies that a man has the main responsibility for providing financial support for the family, a wife has considerable legitimate moral authority when she insists that he do so—whereas a man would have little such authority in insisting that his wife provide major financial support. Agreements between individuals also confer legitimacy. For example, if a couple has agreed that they will share the housework equally, each of them has a legitimate right to insist that the other do his or her fair share. If such an agreement violates broader cultural norms, however, it will be harder to enforce on a recalcitrant partner than if it had the additional force of cultural norms.

Both cultural gender role expectations and distribution of the resources on which interpersonal power is based affect the *influence styles* used in couple relationships. For example, interpersonal influence attempts may vary in their degree of directness, from very upfront and direct to very subtle and "sneaky." Gender stereotypes suggest that a masculine influence style would be direct and "strong," whereas a feminine style would be subtle and "weak"—and there is some evidence that people expect this pattern. Yet an understanding of the bases of power allows us to look at this situation a little differently. People are likely to be more direct in their influence attempts when they are on firm ground and sure of themselves—when they control resources of legitimacy, money, physical strength, or expertise to back up their demands or requests. Thus, influence style in any individual couple relationship depends on the particular situation: a man who controls all the income may feel comfortable being very direct in demanding it be spent in a certain way; a woman who has reached an agreement with her spouse that they will share equally in the housework may be very direct in demanding that he do his share. Research supports the notion that, among heterosexual, gay male, and lesbian couples, individuals who see themselves as having more power than their partners use more direct influence tactics (Aida and Falbo, 1991). In addition, in married heterosexual couples, wives who feel they have equal power as their husbands report using more direct and fewer indirect strategies (Weigel, Bennett, and Ballard Reisch, 2006).

Still, the cultural surround that links maleness with higher status seems to have an impact. In one study of long-term same-sex and cross-sex couple relationships, researchers tried to determine what variables were associated with influence strategies. They examined the relative importance of gender, gender-role orientation, control over resources such as money, physical attractiveness, and dependence on the relationship, on the use of "strong" and "weak" influence tactics (Howard, Blumstein, and Schwartz, 1986). They found that the target partner's gender was a key factor in the type of influence used. Both women and men with male partners were more likely to use "weak" influence strategies such as manipulation and supplication. The researchers note that "The power associated with being male [...] appears to be expressed in behavior that elicits weak strategies from one's partner."

In heterosexual couples, hostile and benevolent sexism have been shown to affect conflict and resistance to influence (Overall, Sibley, and Tan, 2011). When men strongly endorsed hostile sexism, couples were less open and more hostile in their conflict interactions, and discussions were less likely to result in the desired change. On the other hand, men who expressed more agreement with benevolent sexist ideals (women are special, need to be protected) tended to behave with less hostility and were able to disarm women's resistance more successfully. Apparently, women were often willing to trade special treatment within the relationship for influence on decisions that went beyond the relationship.

FAMILIES WITH CHILDREN

Gendered expectations have an even stronger impact when children are part of the family. Pregnancy and the birth of a child can shift the balance of power within a couple. Researchers in North America have sometimes found that a woman's power in a heterosexual couple diminishes with the transition to parenthood (Koivunen, Rothaupt, and Wolfgram, 2009). Why should this be the case? Within a social environment that assigns most childcare responsibilities to women, it is women more than men whose lives change and become circumscribed by a child. It is more likely that a woman than a man will have to reduce employment commitments, thus becoming more financially dependent on a partner and less able to leave the relationship. Further, despite its necessity and importance, society does not accord high status to childrearing. A full-time mother and homemaker can feel embarrassed to say she is a "stay-at-home mom." Even mothers who maintain high-powered professional roles find themselves minimizing and concealing their childcare-related tasks—lest their co-workers or supervisors question their commitment to their jobs (Slaughter, 2012). Fathers' involvement in childcare can mitigate this situation somewhat: Fathers' active involvement and co-parenting are linked to both parents' (but especially mothers') reports of relationship quality following the birth of a first child (McCain and Brown, 2017).

In some cultural contexts, however, childbearing is of key importance for married women; the birth of a child (particularly a boy) protects or increases a woman's family status and power; infertility is associated with shame. This is especially true in settings where parents rely upon children as a source of economic support (Ali *et al.*, 2011) and where descent from ancestors is traced only through males (Obermeyer, 1992).

Women's power within the family and in society affects their children's well-being. A woman with more familial and societal power is better able to ensure adequate nutrition, education, and other forms of care for her children. Where women's status is higher, they have more access to prenatal care and to good nutrition—leading to better nutritional outcomes for their children. One study concluded that if women and men had equal status in

South Asian countries, the rate of underweight children under the age of 3 would drop by about 13 percentage points, leading to 13.4 million fewer malnourished children (Smith, Ramakrishnan, Ndiaye, Haddad, and Martorell, 2003). In Mexican families, greater bargaining power for mothers in their household is associated with fewer hours of child labor for their daughters (Reggio, 2010).

Both interpersonal power within a family, and the surrounding cultural gender stereotypes in which such power relationships are embedded, affect the division of childcare tasks. Mothers, who in almost every culture are expected to do the bulk of childcare, tend to spend far more time on such tasks than do fathers (see, e.g., Koivunen et al., 2009; Lyn and Mullan, 2011). Changes in society and in the resources available to women shift this balance toward more power for women—although never, it seems, to complete equality. Across cultures, women's political and economic power is linked to their marital power, and to a more equitable division of domestic work (Rogers, 2003). For example, over 20 years in one northern Indian village, an increase in prosperity, along with an increase in women's access to education, was correlated with a rise in the power and status of daughters-in-law with respect to mothers-in-law, and greater assertiveness of mothers in disciplining children (Minturn, Boyd, and Kapoor, 1978).

However, even in societies that emphasize gender equality, it can be hard for individual couples to overcome completely the expectation that caring for children is "women's work." Mothers feel more guilt than fathers do about their work interfering with childcare tasks (Borelli, Nelson, River, Birken, and Moss-Racusin, 2017). In the Nordic countries there is a strong cultural and policy emphasis on gender equality, and mothers and fathers have equal rights to paid parental leave. Yet mothers still use most of the available parental leave and continue to do more of the domestic and childcare work than men do—and many parents say this arrangement simply occurred "naturally" (Magnusson and Marecek, 2012). Clearly, the impact of cultural norms with respect to gender runs very deep. The effect of these stereotypic attitudes is to restrict women's choices and their power in heterosexual relationships and to increase their workload. This set of effects has consequences for women's and men's lives beyond the family. In Chapter 5 we will examine ways in which gendered expectations and the gendered division of domestic labor affect men and women in the workplace.

FOR FURTHER EXPLORATION

Chrisler, Joan C. (ed.) (2012). *Reproductive justice: A global concern* (Santa Barbara, CA: Praeger/ABC-CLIO.) This edited book includes chapters on such relationship-relevant issues as partner selection, power in relationships, pregnancy and prenatal care, birthing, and infanticide—all with a cross-cultural emphasis. In each contribution, the authors analyze the role of gender stereotypes and the gendered distribution of power on reproductive issues.

Feminist forum: Adolescent girls' sexual empowerment. *Sex Roles* (2012), *66*(11/12), 703–763. A special section of this journal issue consists of seven articles exploring and debating notions of sexual empowerment for adolescent girls. The first article, by Sharon Lamb and Zoë Peterson, opens the discussion by posing the question of whether girls *are* sexually empowered if they *feel* empowered. Subsequent articles respond to the first, creating a complex and fascinating discussion of gender, sexuality, power, and the media.

Goldberg, Abbie E. (ed.) (2010). *Lesbian and gay parents and their children: Research on the family life cycle* (Washington, DC: American Psychological Association). This collection of articles provides an overview of research on same-sex parenthood, including chapters on couple relationships, the decision to have children, the experience of raising children, and the perspectives of the children themselves.

Holland, Janet, Ramazanoglu, Caroline, Sharpe, Sue, and Thomson, Rachel (1998). *The male in the head: Young people, heterosexuality, and power* (London: The Tufnell Press). The authors analyze power in conventional heterosexual relationships by examining young women's and men's accounts of those relationships. They explore the ways in which sexual empowerment for young men is linked to their ability to access the traditional privileges of masculinity, and explore the ways in which young women try to achieve sexual empowerment by changing themselves, changing men, and taking control of their sexual encounters.

Liss, Miriam and Schiffrin, Holly H. (2014). *Balancing the big stuff. Finding happiness in work, family, and life* (Lanham, MD: Rowman & Littlefield). The authors, both psychologists, provide an overview of research on work–family balance and argue for the importance of careful prioritizing and decision-making in determining what balance works best in particular families. They also outline the social issues, such as parental leave and affordable childcare, that must be attended to in order to promote work–family balance.

Tolman, Deborah L. (2002). *Dilemmas of desire: Teenage girls talk about sexuality* (Cambridge, MA: Harvard University Press). The author, a psychologist, reports on her interviews with suburban and urban adolescent girls aged between 15 and 18 in two US high schools about their feelings, thoughts, and actions concerning sexuality.

REFERENCES

Aida, Y. and Falbo, T. (1991). Relationships between marital satisfaction, resources, and power strategies. *Sex Roles*, *24*, 43–56. doi: 10.1007/BF00288702.

Ali, A.H. (2007). *Infidel*. New York: Free Press.

Ali, S., Sophie, R., Imam, A.M., Khan, F.I., Ali, S.F., Shaikh, A., and Farid-ul-Hasnain, S. (2011). Knowledge, perceptions and myths regarding infertility among selected adult population in Pakistan: A cross-sectional study. *BMC Public Health*, *11*, 760. doi: 10.1186/1471-2458-11-760. www.biomedcentral.com/1471-2458/11/760.

Andersen, B.L. and Cyranowski, J.M. (1994). Women's sexual self-schema. *Journal of Personality and Social Psychology*, *67*, 1079–1100. doi: 10.1037/0022 3514.67.6.1079.

Andersen, B.L., Cyranowski, J.M., and Espindle, D. (1999). Men's sexual self-schema. *Journal of Personality and Social Psychology*, *76*, 645–661. doi: 10.1037/0022-3514.76.4.645.

Armstrong, E.A., England, P., and Fogarty, A.C.K. (2012). Accounting for women's orgasm and sexual enjoyment in college hookups and relationships. *American Sociological Review, 77*, 435–462. doi: 10.1177/0003122412445802.

Baumeister, R.F., Catanese, K.R., and Vohs, K.D. (2001). Is there a gender difference in strength of sex drive? Theoretical views, conceptual distinctions, and a review of relevant evidence. *Personality and Social Psychology Review, 5*, 242–273.

Borelli, J.L., Nelson, S.K., River, L.M., Birken, S.A., and Moss-Racusin, C. (2017). Gender differences in work–family guilt in parents of young children. *Sex Roles, 76*, 356–368. doi:10.1007/s11199-016-0579-0.

Bradshaw, C., Kahn, A.S., and Saville, B.K. (2010). To hook up or date: which gender benefits? *Sex Roles, 62*, 661–669. doi: 10.1007/s11199-010-9765-7.

Byers, E.S. and Cohen, J.N. (2017). Validation of the Interpersonal Exchange Model of sexual satisfaction with women in a same-sex relationship. *Psychology of Women Quarterly, 4*, 32–45. doi: 10.1177/0361684316679655.

Chivers, M.L., Seto, M.C., Lalumière, M.L., Laan, E., and Grimbos, T. (2010). Agreement of self-reported and genital measures of sexual arousal in men and women: A meta-analysis. *Archives of Sexual Behavior, 39*, 5–56. doi: 10.1007/s10508-009-9556-9.

Coughlin, P. and Wade, J.C. (2012). Masculinity ideology, income disparity, and romantic relationship quality among men with higher earning female partners. *Sex Roles, 67*, 311–322. doi: 10.1007/s11199-012-0187-6.

Elder, W.B., Brooks, G.R., and Morrow, S.L. (2012). Sexual self-schemas of heterosexual men. *Psychology of Men and Masculinity, 13*, 166–179. doi: 10.1037/a0024835.

Elder, W.B., Morrow, S.L., and Brooks, G.R. (2015). Sexual self-schemas of bisexual men: A qualitative investigation. *The Counseling Psychologist, 43*, 970–1007. doi: 10.1177/0011000015608242.

Epstein, M., Calzo, J.P., Smiler, A.P., and Ward, L. (2009). "Anything from making out to having sex": Men's negotiations of hooking up and friends with benefits scripts. *Journal of Sex Research, 46*, 414–424. doi: 10.1080/00224490902775801.

Eyre, S.L., Flythe, M., Hoffman, V., and Fraser, A.E. (2012). Primary relationship scripts among lower-income, African American young adults. *Family Process, 51*, 234–249.

Fishman, P.M. (1978). Interaction: The work women do. *Social Problems, 25*, 397–406. doi: 10.1525/sp.1978.25.4.03a00050.

Foster, B.L. (1976). Friendship in rural Thailand. *Ethnology, 15*, 251–267.

French, J.R. and Raven, B. (1959). The bases of social power. In D. Cartwright (ed.), *Studies in social power* (pp. 150–167). Oxford: University of Michigan Press.

Garcia, J.R. and Reiber, C. (2008). Hook-up behavior: A biopsychosocial perspective. *The Journal of Social, Evolutionary, and Cultural Psychology, 2*, 192–208.

Garcia, J.R., Reiber, C., Massey, S.G., and Merriwether, A.M. (2012). Sexual hookup culture: A review. *Review of General Psychology, 16*, 161–176. doi: 10.1037/a0027911.

Goitein, S.D. (1971). Formal friendship in the medieval near east. *Proceedings of the American Philosophical Society, 115*, 484–489.

Gotta, G., Green, R., Rothblum, E., Solomon, S., Balsam, K., and Schwartz, P. (2011). Heterosexual, lesbian, and gay male relationships: A comparison of couples in 1975 and 2000. *Family Process, 50*, 353–376. doi: 10.1111/j.1545-5300.2011.01365.x.

Hicklin, A. (2014). Beyoncé liberated. Behind the scenes of the world's most powerful brand. *Out.com*, April 8. www.out.com/entertainment/music/2014/04/08/beyonc%C3%A9-liberated.

Hill, D.B. (2007). Differences and similarities in men's and women's sexual self-schemas. *Journal of Sex Research, 44*, 135–144. doi:10.1080/00224490701263611.

Howard, J.A., Blumstein, P., and Schwartz, P. (1986). Sex, power, and influence tactics in intimate relationships. *Journal of Personality and Social Psychology, 51*, 102–109. doi: 10.1037/0022-3514.51.1.102.

Itakura, H. and Tsui, A.B.M. (2004). Gender and conversational dominance in Japanese conversation. *Language in Society, 33*, 223–248. doi: 10.10170S0047404504332033.

Kilmartin, C. (2009). *The masculine self* (4th edn). Cornwall-on-Hudson, NY: Sloan Publishing.

Koivunen, J.M., Rothaupt, J.W., and Wolfgram, S.M. (2009). Gender dynamics and role adjustment during the transition to parenthood: Current perspectives. *The Family Journal, 17*, 323–328. doi: 10.1177/1066480709347360.

Lippman, J.R. and Campbell, S.W. (2014). Damned if you do, damned if you don't […] if you're a girl: Relational and normative contexts of adolescent sexting in the United States. *Journal of Children and Media, 8*, 371–386. doi: 10.1080/17482798.2014.923.

Lyn, C. and Mullan, K. (2011). How mothers and fathers share childcare: A cross-national time–use comparison. *American Sociological Review, 76*, 834–861. doi: 10.1177/0003122411427673.

Magnusson, E. and Marecek, J. (2012). *Gender and culture in psychology: Theories and practices.* New York: Cambridge University Press.

Mark, K.P., Garcia, J.R., and Fisher, H.E. (2015). Perceived emotional and sexual satisfaction across sexual relationship contexts: Gender and sexual orientation differences and similarities. *The Canadian Journal of Human Sexuality*, *24*, 120–130. doi:10.3138/cjhs.242-A8.

McCain, L. and Brown, S.L. (2017). The roles of fathers' involvement and coparenting in relationship quality among cohabiting and married parents. *Sex Roles*, *76*, 334–345. doi: 10.1007/s11199-016-0612-3.

McClelland, S.I. (2010). Intimate justice: A critical analysis of sexual satisfaction. *Social and Personality Compass*, *4*(9), 663–680. doi: 10.1111/j.1751-9004.2010.00293.x.

Michael, R.T., Gagnon, J.H., Laumann, E.O., and Kolata, G. (1994). *Sex in America*. Boston, MA: Little, Brown.

Minturn, L., Boyd, D., and Kapoor, S. (1978). Increased maternal power status changes in socialization in a restudy of Rajput mothers of Khalapur, India. *Journal of Cross-cultural Psychology*, *9*, 483–498. doi: 10.1177/002202217894007.

Obermeyer, C.M. (1992). Islam, women, and politics: The demography of Arab countries. *Population and Development Review*, *18*, 33–60.

Office for National Statistics (2015). Compendium: Participation rates in the UK labor market: 2014. Reference tables. www.ons.gov.uk/employmentandlabourmarket/peopleinwork/employmentandemployeetypes/compendium/participationratesintheuklabourmarket/2015-03-19/participationratesintheuklabourmarket2014referencetables.

Overall, N.C., Sibley, C.G., and Tan, R. (2011). The costs and benefits of sexism: Resistance to influence during relationship conflict. *Journal of Personality and Social Psychology*, *101*, 271–290. doi: 10.1037/a0022727.

Phillips, L.M. (2000). *Flirting with danger*. New York: New York University Press.

Raven, B.H. (1992). A power/interaction model of interpersonal influence: French and Raven thirty years later. *Journal of Social Behavior and Personality*, *7*, 217–244.

Reggio, I. (2010). The influence of the mother's power on her child's labor in Mexico. *IDEAS*. http://ideas.repec.org/p/cte/werepe/we101305.html.

Rogers, A.A. (2003). Power in marriage: A multidisciplinary and cross-cultural investigation. Unpublished doctoral dissertation, Southern Illinois University. *Dissertation Abstracts International*: Section B: The Sciences and Engineering, *63* (7-B).

Rose, S.M. and Zand, D. (2002). Lesbian dating and courtship from young adulthood to midlife. *Journal of Lesbian Studies*, *6*, 85–109. doi: 10.1300/J155v06n01_09.

Simon, W. and Gagnon, J. (1987). A sexual scripts approach. In J. Greer and W. O'Donohue (eds), *Theories of human sexuality* (pp. 363–383). New York: Plenum Press.

Slaughter, A. (2012). Why women still can't have it all. *The Atlantic*, July/August. www.theatlantic.com/magazine/archive/2012/07/why-women-still-cant-have-it-all/309020/.

Smith, L.C., Ramakrishnan, U., Ndiaye, A., Haddad, L., and Martorell, R. (2003). *The importance of women's status for child nutrition in developing countries*. Washington, DC: International Food Policy Research Institute. www.theaahm.org/fileadmin/user_upload/aahm/docs/rr131.pdf.

Spender, D. (1989). *The writing or the sex?* New York: Pergamon Press.

Tichenor, V. (2005). Maintaining men's dominance: Negotiating identity and power when she earns more. *Sex Roles, 53*, 191–205. doi: 10.1007/s11199-005-5678-2.

United Nations Population Fund (2000). *State of the world population 2000*. www.unfpa.org/public/cache/offonce/home/publications/pid/3453;jsessionid=4C3A8C52B424B99A07B517B2 A2BDA089.

U.S. Bureau of Labor Statistics (2015). *Women in the labor force: A databook*. www.bls.gov/opub/reports/womens-databook/archive/women-in-the-labor-force-a-databook-2015.pdf.

U.S. Bureau of Labor Statistics (2016). News release, June 24: *American Time Use Survey—2015 results*. www.bls.gov/news.release/pdf/atus.pdf.

U.S. Bureau of Labor Statistics (2017). *Women in the labor force: A databook* (table 7). www.bls.gov/opub/reports/womens-databook/2017/home.htm.

van Anders, S.M. (2015). Beyond sexual orientation: Integrating gender/sex and diverse sexualities via Sexual Configurations Theory. *Archives of Sexual Behavior, 44*, 1177–1213. doi: 10.1007/s10508-015-0490-8.

Vrangalova, Z. (2015). Does casual sex harm college students' well-being? A longitudinal investigation of the role of motivation. *Archives of Sexual Behavior, 44*, 945–959. doi: 10.1007/s10508-013-0255-1.

Weigel, D.J., Bennett, K.K., and Ballard-Reisch, D.S. (2006). Influence strategies in marriage: Self and partner links between equity, strategy use, and marital satisfaction and commitment. *Journal of Family Communication, 6*, 77–95. doi: 10.1207/s15327698jfc0601_5.

Wilkerson, J.M., Brooks, A.K., and Ross, M.W. (2010). Sociosexual identity development and sexual risk taking of acculturating collegiate gay and bisexual men. *Journal of College Student Development, 51*, 279–296. doi: 10.1353/csd.0.0131.

Witkowska, E. and Gådin, K.G. (2005). Have you been sexually harassed in school? What female high school students regard as harassment. *International Journal of Adolescent Medicine and Health, 17*, 391–406. doi: 10.1515/IJAMH.2005.17.4.391.

World Bank (2016). *Labor force participation*. DataBank. http://data.worldbank.org/indicator/SL.TLF.CACT.FE.ZS.

5

THE GENDERED WORKPLACE

In 2017, a number of "firsts" occurred for women in the world of work. The United States assigned the first group of female infantry to a marine battalion, and the Navy revealed plans to assign the first female enlisted SEALS to units. In Afghanistan, the country's first all-female orchestra won the 2017 Freemuse award, acknowledging their courage and their status as role models. The neurosurgical department at the Johns Hopkins School of Medicine accepted its first black female resident, Nancy Abu-Bonsrah. Cressida Dick became the first woman appointed head of the Metropolitan Police, Britain's largest police force. St. Paul's Cathedral in London appointed its first female chorister, Carris Jones.

Although fewer, there were some firsts for men in 2017 as well. Manny Gutierrez became the first male spokesmodel for cosmetic giant Maybelline. Pharrell Williams signed on as the first male model to appear on a handbag campaign for Chanel. Wooyoung became the first male cover model for Japan's 'Shel'tter' magazine. Lewys Ball became the first male spokesperson for make-up company Rimmel London. And, in a move that may come to affect the socialization and aspirations of boys, toy company American Girl introduced its first ever full-sized male doll (Logan Everett, a drummer).

The fact that it is still possible to find stories about the "first woman" and "first man" to hold particular jobs is a reminder of how work has been gendered. Around the world, women and men work in different jobs. This chapter begins with an examination of these patterns of occupational segregation and theories about the underlying reasons for them. The discussion includes consideration of both male-dominated and female-dominated workplaces, and the impact of being a gender token in either situation. Included are a variety of issues, such as discrimination, gendered family roles, and beliefs that women and men differ in certain abilities. There follows an examination of the gender pay gap, which is traceable in part to occupational segregation. Next, we discuss employment discrimination, along with attempts to ameliorate it through *affirmative action*. Finally, since family roles are strongly implicated in workplace gender inequalities, the chapter touches on the evolution and impact of the "family-friendly" workplace.

OCCUPATIONAL SEGREGATION: WOMEN AND MEN IN DIFFERENT JOBS

There has been a global trend toward greater access for women to education and labor force participation. Since 1970, women's share of the labor force has steadily increased in almost all regions of the world, although that increase has slowed in recent years. Women now make up at least 47 percent of the labor force in many countries, including the Scandinavian countries, the United States, Canada, New Zealand, Portugal, and France.

However, there is persistent gender segregation in the workplace—and, as we have seen, the division of labor in the home also remains strongly gendered. Even a casual examination of the world of work shows, for instance, that most clerical and service workers are women; most construction and skilled manual workers are men; most professional football, soccer, hockey, basketball, and cricket players are men; most childcare workers, healthcare aides, and nurses are women; men are more likely than women to be political leaders, engineers, chief executives of companies, and university presidents. Occupational segregation by gender is significant and obvious in most countries (Jarman, Blackburn, and Racko, 2012).

Occupational segregation by gender is both vertical (i.e., women tend to be clustered at the low-status, low-paid end of almost every type of work) and horizontal (i.e., women and men at similar status levels are divided into different types of work). Vertical segregation is slowly diminishing in the most economically developed countries as more women move into managerial and professional positions. For example, women now make up more than one-third of physicians and 16 percent of medical school deans (American Association of Medical Colleges, 2015); 36 percent of lawyers, and more than 31 percent of law school deans (American Bar Association, 2017) in the United States. This is a major shift from a generation ago, when those professions and their leadership were solidly dominated by men. However, horizontal gender segregation remains stubbornly intact in most situations (Charles, 2011). Figure 5.1 illustrates occupational gender segregation in in the UK and the USA.

The persistence of occupational gender segregation probably stems from a complex interplay between societal and personal gender stereotypes, discrimination by powerholders against outgroups, habit, and social inertia—and the repeated lifetime impact of all these upon individuals' choices and behaviors. Let us first consider how expected social roles reproduce themselves.

WHY OCCUPATIONAL SEGREGATION? THE IMPACT OF SOCIAL ROLES

Social psychologist Alice Eagly (1987) proposed *social roles theory* to explain the persistence of the segregation of women and men into different jobs. This theory describes a positive feedback loop in which certain jobs that require gender-stereotyped qualities tend to be filled by members of the gender group presumed to have those qualities—and then the dominance of one gender group in such jobs reinforces the gender stereotyping of both the job and its incumbents. For example, being a childcare worker is assumed to require warmth, a nurturing orientation, and a love of children—all qualities that are stereotyped as feminine. Not surprisingly, then, women will be thought more likely to have these qualities and better suited to this job than men. Someone hiring for this job will likely expect to hire a woman. Women will be more likely than

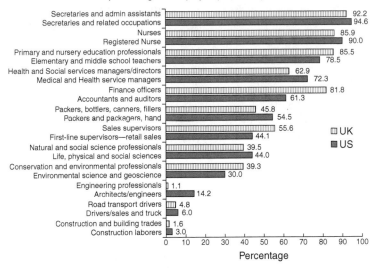

Figure 5.1 Occupational segregation by gender in two Western countries, 2016–2017. In both Britain and the United States, as in other countries, occupational segregation by gender is quite dramatic. At the extremes, secretarial and clerical workers are far more likely to be women than men; engineers and construction workers are far more likely to be men than women.

Sources: Based on data from U.S. Bureau of Labor Statistics (2017), and Office for National Statistics (2017).

men to apply for this job because both genders have learned the societal expectation that women are appropriate for such work. So, over and over again, women will be more likely than men to be hired as childcare workers. Once in the job, childcare workers use and further develop the nurturing skills necessary to do the job successfully. Observers see childcare workers behaving in warm, nurturing ways, and most of the childcare workers they see behaving in these ways are women. This observation reinforces the idea that women are warm and nurturing and that they (not men) are the appropriate people to fill such jobs. The whole process reinforces gender stereotypes and produces a cycle that is difficult to break: women are selected (and self-select) as childcare workers because they are stereotyped as having the warm, nurturing qualities needed for that job. The job develops and rewards those qualities. Observers, seeing mostly women childcare workers behaving in warm, nurturing ways, strengthen their opinion that women tend to be warm and nurturing.

The cycle described here encourages the persistence of both explicit and implicit gender stereotypes associated with occupational roles. As noted in Chapter 1, the repeated association of women with certain qualities, settings, and behaviors, and men with others, helps create implicit stereotypes that are virtually automatic in their activation. When we think childcare worker, we think woman; when we think engineer, we think man. This happens even though we well know that men can be terrific childcare workers and women can be excellent engineers. Individuals with weaker implicit gender stereotypes may be more ready to pursue counter-stereotypic occupational paths, or to accept gender non-traditional incumbents in gender-stereotyped jobs. For example, a study of French university students revealed that the implicit association of mathematical and reasoning abilities with masculinity was weaker among female engineering students than among female humanities students, or among male engineering or humanities students (Smeding, 2012).

A social roles approach illustrates how deep and pervasive societal gender stereotypes can bias individuals' evaluations of themselves and others, and can maintain barriers and rules about femininity and masculinity to which people feel they must conform. What makes it so difficult to break out of this pattern of occupational segregation is the thoroughly ingrained nature of beliefs related to gender. In many situations, everyone knows they are not supposed to make occupational decisions on the basis of gender—but they do it anyway, often without realizing it. For example, many people have learned to associate high-prestige positions as orchestra musicians with men. When auditions for orchestral positions were carried out behind a screen so that the musical performance could be heard but the musician could not be seen (and his or her gender could not be known), female musicians were more often called back than when auditions were carried out in the normal way (Goldin and Rouse, 2000).

Even when making decisions about their own abilities and performance, individuals may unwittingly apply gender-related cultural standards and norms. In one study, students were told (falsely) that men typically perform better on a test of "contrast sensitivity." Male students rated their performance more highly and were more likely than female students to say that they aspired to work in a job requiring that ability (Correll, 2004). Simply being given this one-time gender-biased feedback about an ability they had probably never considered before affected students' occupational aspirations. Imagine the effect of being told over and over again that, for example, men are better than women at math and science.

Publicly stating stereotype-consistent educational or occupational choices indicates conformity to approved gender roles. For instance, if an interest in poetry or dance is considered feminine, a young man can emphasize his masculinity—to himself and to his peers—by declaring his dislike of those fields. Indeed, one study of graduate business students found that single women reined in their stated ambitions and aspirations for salary when (and only when) they believed other students would see their responses (Bursztyn, Fujiwara, and Pallais, 2016). The researchers suggested that, by declining to appear ambitious, the women were conforming to what they perceived as acceptable career-related responses for their gender.

Given strong cultural messages about what jobs are appropriate and comfortable for each gender, it is not surprising if women and men develop different preferences and make different decisions with respect to their occupational paths. These culturally shaped preferences may play a major role in maintaining horizontal occupational segregation—particularly in societies that emphasize the value of individual choice and that have the economic resources to accommodate such choices. In societies where young people are admonished to pursue their own choices and follow their passions, some forms of occupational gender segregation may be especially resistant to change (Charles, 2011). This is not because women and men "naturally" want and enjoy different kinds of work, but because the emphasis on personal choice and self-expression provides so much scope for translating internalized gender norms into occupational decisions. In such contexts, Charles says, "self-expression often results in 'expression of gendered selves'." Young people exhorted to choose a subject they love as a college major are unlikely to zero in on a field they have learned to think of as gender-inappropriate, especially if they are not economically constrained to do so. Thus, implicit, explicit stereotyping, and self-stereotyping conspire to produce the persistent cycle described by social role theory.

DIFFERENT ABILITIES?

The notion that women and men differ in the abilities they bring to their work has a significant history. Up until the nineteenth century, scientists posited that women's brains were smaller than men's, and, when that notion was disproven, that the most important parts of the brain were larger in men than in women. As late as the early twentieth century, women were thought to have far less ability than men for higher learning, and the mental effort associated with university-level education was thought damaging and debilitating to women (Rosenberg, 1982). This belief served to justify barring women from higher education.

Now, however, women are a strong, even majority presence in higher education. Women in the United States are 33 percent more likely than men to complete a Bachelor's degree (U.S. Department of Labor, 2016). Globally, the ratio of women to men enrolled in post-secondary education is just over 1.04 to 1.0, although there is considerable variation across countries (UNESCO, 2015). Even in countries where women have historically been underrepresented in higher education, women's enrollments have been steadily increasing. The argument that women "cannot handle" higher education no longer has any credibility.

However, there is still a significant difference between women and men in their college fields of study. Among college graduates, the percentage of education majors who are women in most countries is greater than 70 percent, but women make up only 41 percent of science majors and 28 percent of engineering, manufacturing, and construction majors (OECD, 2015). Debate about the reasons for these differences has been fierce. Some researchers have emphasized the possibility that women and men differ in some of the fundamental abilities linked to performance in math, science, and language. Indeed, researchers have found some small but reliable average gender differences in performance, with women tending to score a little better on tests of certain specific verbal skills and men tending to score a little better on tests of certain mathematical and spatial skills (Halpern, 2012). How much do such performance differences represent different levels of ability? How much do they reflect the different social–environmental conditions under which women and men are trying to perform? What barriers do girls and boys face, in terms of encouragement or discrimination, before they even get into a situation in which they are trying to demonstrate their abilities?

Some researchers have focused on the social forces that push girls and boys, and later women and men, in different career directions. These forces do not appear to be insignificant. One study analyzed natural interactions between mothers and their preschool-aged children. Mothers talked significantly more about numbers to boys than to girls—perhaps promoting more early familiarity and liking for mathematical concepts among boys (Chang, Sandhofer, and Brown, 2011). Parents and teachers may hold and communicate different expectations for girls' and boys' competence in mathematics. As early as second grade, US children view math as a masculine domain, and boys in this age group identify more strongly with math than do girls (Cvencek, Meltzoff, and Greenwald, 2011). Italian children show a similar pattern (Muzzatti and Agnoli, 2007). In Singapore, boys identify more strongly with math than girls do, despite the fact that girls excel in math; and children's stereotyping of math as a masculine domain increases with age (Cvencek, Meltzoff, and Kapur, 2014). Even in kindergarten, Chilean children expect that girls (but not boys) will find math harder, perform worse at it, and enjoy it less than language (del Rio and Strasser, 2013). In France, fifth-grade children report an awareness of the math–male association, but apply it more to adults than to children; however, they apply the reading–female stereotype to both adults and children (Martinot, Bagès, and Désert, 2012). As noted in Chapter 3, when individuals are aware that their group is stereotyped in terms of particular abilities, this awareness can impact their performance—a phenomenon known as stereotype threat.

Differential treatment continues into adulthood. In a field study, researchers found that male and female applicants for a lab manager position were evaluated and treated differently by the science faculty from research-intensive universities in the United States—even though their application materials were identical (Moss-Racusin, Dovidio, Brescoll, Graham, and Handelsman, 2012). Both male and female faculty respondents rated female applicants as less competent and hireable, and offered significantly lower starting salaries and less mentoring to them than to identical male applicants. Apparently, even accomplished scientists in research-oriented universities expect that women will perform more poorly than men in science careers. Such differential expectations are likely to contribute much more strongly to occupational gender segregation than are small average gender differences in abilities.

THE GENDER PAY GAP

There is a persistent and pervasive gap between women's and men's earnings worldwide. Figure 5.2 illustrates that gap in several Western countries. So stubborn is the gap that, even in Iceland, a country usually found near the top of indices of gender equality, employed women earned 14 percent less than men in 2015 (Statistics Iceland, 2016). Frustrated by the lack of progress in closing the gap, Iceland became the first country to propose legislation to force employers to prove that they are paying women and men equally (Alderman, 2017).

Even controlling for college major, occupation, number of hours worked per week, and economic sector, American women earn less than men just one year after college graduation (Corbett and Hill, 2012). The U.S. Census Bureau (C. Ryan, 2012), examining earnings by field of degree, showed men out-earning women in all degree fields among the population aged 25 and older; men earn more than women in almost every occupation (U.S. Census Bureau, 2015). In Canada, men's age-adjusted earnings are higher than women's across all fields of study (Statistics Canada, 2016). Among women and men with college degrees in the same field, a gender pay gap is evident within the first five years after graduation (Chamberlain and Jayaraman, 2017). The gap exists within every racial and ethnic group, though it is largest within those groups (non-Hispanic white and Asian) in which men tend to earn the most. Research even suggests that when individuals transition from male to female gender expression they are likely to experience a drop in earnings, whereas those who transition from female to male may experience no change or a slight increase (Grant, Mottet, and Tanis, 2011).

Around the world, the gender pay gap disadvantages women: according to the *Global Gender Gap Report* from the World Economic Forum (2016), no country in the world has reached gender parity in pay, and only five countries—France, Chile, Peru, Hungary, and Brazil—have a pay gap smaller than 20 percent between women and men performing similar work. They estimate that it could take 170 years to wipe out the gender disparities in pay and economic opportunities worldwide. To add insult to injury, women—already earning less—must often pay more than men for items such as clothing and personal care products marketed according to gender. One study of this so-called "pink tax" showed that products marketed for women (e.g., shirts, jeans, razors) cost about 7 percent more than similar products for men (New York City Department of Consumer Affairs, 2015).

Gender differences in education or specialty cannot completely explain the gender pay gap. Even in the Nordic countries where women make up the majority of the high-skilled workforce, women earn less than men (World Economic Forum, 2016). The gap is also not fully accounted for by differences in the number of hours per week or weeks per year that men and women work, or by women's greater likelihood than men to leave work temporarily to care for children (Lips, 2013; Roth, 2006).

One important factor is the type of work that women and men do: men are more likely than women to hold jobs that are well paid and/or that are governed by formal regulations about minimum wage, overtime pay, or union-scale wages. For example, consider domestic work: work performed in or for private households, such as housecleaning, cooking, childcare, and in-home care for the sick or elderly. In the United States, women comprise more than 83 percent of maids, housekeeping cleaners, and personal care aides (U.S. Department of Labor, 2014); women comprise 83 percent of domestic workers worldwide (International Labour

Figure 5.2 Women's percentage of men's gross median earnings. The gap between women's and men's earnings has narrowed relatively slowly since the 1990s, and in no country have women's earnings reached parity with men's.

Source: Based on data from OECD (2017).

Organization, 2012). The women doing this work in developed nations are often immigrants from poorer countries. Their work arrangements are often informally and privately determined, and the work they do, while essential, is undervalued. These jobs usually fall outside the scope of labor laws, so work arrangements are often unregulated and wages are typically low. At the other end of the income spectrum, in well-paid top management, computing, and engineering occupations, men tend to predominate (U.S. Department of Labor, 2014). Simply getting more women into high-end jobs apparently does not solve the problem. As women move into male-dominated fields in significant numbers, the pay tends to drop—because employers devalue work done by women (Levanon, England, and Allison, 2009).

In developed countries, greater horizontal segregation (i.e., greater division of women and men into different kinds—not levels—of jobs) may be associated both with less disadvantage for women in terms of empowerment and with a smaller gender pay gap. For example, in Sweden, a country with a reputation for gender equality where women do well on such measures of empowerment as seats in Parliament and earned income share, the workforce is highly gender segregated. When women and men are highly segregated into different occupations, there is less opportunity for gender discrimination *within* occupations. If women are the majority in an occupation, women have a greater chance of reaching the highest levels of that occupation because there are more women than men available for promotion. As we will see below, however, men are disproportionately successful in reaching leadership positions in female-dominated occupations—so an occupation would have to be completely filled by women in order to ensure that women would occupy all the senior positions! Still, these findings show that occupational segregation and the pay gap have a complex relationship.

CHANGING PATTERNS AND SCOPE OF EMPLOYMENT DISCRIMINATION

EMPLOYMENT DISCRIMINATION: A BRIEF HISTORY

Employment discrimination based on sex was once an entrenched and accepted practice. Although women have always worked, the notion that they should work for pay was considered scandalous in some circles. A 1918 article in the *Australian Medical Gazette* listed all the harms done when young women spend their days earning money in factories, shops, and offices in a "butterfly and parasitic existence," instead of preparing themselves for childbearing and domesticity. It concludes by recommending the enactment of legislation "which will prohibit the employment of girls and women in any walk of life which is not unquestionably women's work, until they shall have passed through an apprenticeship in household work" (quoted in D'Aprano, 2001: xxii). In certain jobs, there was a long and strict prohibition against women; both verifiable stories and fanciful legends abound of women who, through the centuries, pretended to be men in order to take on roles as soldiers, priests, and monks, even pope. In North America, Australia, and elsewhere, until well into the twentieth century, newspapers categorized "help wanted" ads for women and men as a matter of course. It was considered reasonable (and legal) to reject a job applicant by saying, "I don't want a woman (or a man) for this position." The legality of sex discrimination in hiring was undercut in the UK with the Sex Discrimination Act of 1975, and in the USA with a 1961 presidential executive order prohibiting workplace discrimination based on personal characteristics, the establishment of the Committee on Equal Employment Opportunity, and Title VII of the Civil Rights Act of 1964. In Canada, the Canadian Human Rights Act of 1977 outlawed sex discrimination in employment, and similar legislation now exists in most other countries. Such laws did not wipe out sex discrimination in hiring, but they made blatant discrimination more difficult.

When women *were* hired, they were routinely paid less than men, with the justification that they could not do the work as well as men, that men, but not women, had families to support, and that paying women the same wages as men would be ruinous for the economy. Women's need to support a family was not a justification for employment or fair pay. Rather, when female employees were known to have families, the situation often served as an excuse to bar them from certain jobs—or from being employed at all. For example, beginning in the late 1880s, Australian law provided that married women would not be eligible for employment in the Public Service, and women workers who did marry would be forced to leave their employment. Up until the 1970s in the United States, pregnant schoolteachers were often forced to take unpaid maternity leave, on the grounds that continuing to teach would be dangerous to the woman and her unborn child and that the pregnancy would be distracting to the students. Women were also barred from certain manufacturing jobs because of their *potential* to become pregnant, since exposure to certain chemicals or working conditions might be dangerous to a fetus (Legal Information Institute, 2012). Pregnancy discrimination was recognized as a form of sex discrimination through court cases, leading in the USA to the passage of the Pregnancy Discrimination Act of 1978. This Act prohibits discrimination based on pregnancy, childbirth, or related medical conditions. Courts in the European Union, Canada, the UK, and other countries have made rulings consistent with the idea that pregnancy discrimination is a type of sex discrimination and is illegal. However, pregnancy discrimination complaints continue to be filed at high rates (e.g., Zillman, 2014).

Legislation mandating equal employment and/or equal pay exists in many countries. In Britain, the Equal Pay Act passed in 1970, with its implementation slowed for five years to allow employers to adjust. In Australia, the National Security (Female Minimum Rates) Regulation of 1943 raised the basic female wage from 54 percent to 75 percent of men's wages; the Equal Pay Act passed in 1972. In the United States, the Equal Pay Act of 1963 made it illegal to pay a woman less than a man for performing the same or substantially similar job. In New Zealand, the Government Service Equal Pay Act of 1960 eliminated separate pay scales for women and men in public service jobs; pay equity legislation extended to the wider workforce in 1972. The 1979 Norwegian Gender Equality Act stipulated that women and men in the same enterprise would earn equal pay for the same work or work of equal value. Legislation has moved women and men toward equal pay, but the gender pay gap remains a stubbornly persistent problem worldwide.

Beyond hiring and pay, employment discrimination based on gender has also affected promotion and advancement. In a landmark case in the United States, Ann Hopkins, a broker for the financial firm Price Waterhouse, was denied partnership even though she had generated more money for the firm than others who were made partners. The reasons given included that she needed to dress and act in more feminine ways and that she would benefit from a "charm school" course. Reasoning that these points were evidence of thinly disguised gender discrimination, Hopkins sued the company and ultimately won her case in 1989. After considering expert testimony from psychologists about gender stereotyping, the judge agreed that Hopkins was being unfairly held to a standard (to be feminine and charming) that men were not expected to meet. The case showed that discrimination is particularly likely when evaluation criteria are ambiguous and members of a previously excluded group are moving into new employment roles (Fiske, Bersoff, Borgida, Deaux, and

Heilman, 1991). Furthermore, such discrimination often goes unrecognized, even by its perpetrators. As noted in Chapter 1, our reactions to others are often affected by implicit stereotypes; we do not even know we are reacting in a biased way.

SEXUAL HARASSMENT

One form of gender-based discrimination at work is sexual harassment: unwelcome sexual advances that intimidate or discomfit an individual and/or the creation of a hostile work environment through sexual innuendos, teasing, touching, etc., that unreasonably interferes with an individual's workplace experience and performance. Such behavior was once considered the stuff of workplace humor rather than a serious problem. Television comedies featured secretaries being chased around their desks by lecherous male bosses—all in supposed good fun! The problem was not even publicly named as sexual harassment until the 1970s (Brownmiller, 1999). However, far from being a joke, sexual harassment can impact victims in serious ways, causing feelings such as helplessness, lower self-esteem, shame, anxiety, and depression (Yoon, Funk, and Kropf, 2010), and symptoms such as sleeplessness, nausea, suppressed immunity, and increased inflammation (Chan *et al.*, 2008). Individuals being sexually harassed are also likely to be tardy or absent from work, withdraw socially, value their occupation less, and show an overall decline in job performance (Chan *et al.*, 2008).

Sexual harassment at work is acknowledged as a common problem around the world, but because the behavior often goes unreported, reliable numbers are difficult to ascertain. A government survey of more than 9600 women in Japan revealed that more than one-third of those working full time reported being sexually harassed at work (McCurry, 2016). In an online survey by *Cosmopolitan* magazine, about one in three female respondents reported being sexually harassed at work (Vaglanos, 2015). In Australia, 33 percent of women and 9 percent of men reported experiencing sexual harassment at work during their lifetime (Australian Human Rights Commission, 2012). More than half of British women workers surveyed reported some form of harassment at work, with one woman in eight reporting unwanted sexual touching or attempts to kiss them; among respondents aged 16 to 24, the proportion reporting sexual harassment was 64 percent (Trades Union Congress, 2016).

In the United Sates, sexual harassment is classified as sex discrimination and prohibited under Title VII of the Civil Rights Act of 1964. The Equal Employment Opportunity Commission (EEOC) files civil suits against employers based on employee complaints. In 2016, more than 12,800 sex-based harassment and more than 6,700 sexual harassment complaints were filed with the EEOC. In one example, Carrols Corporation, a large Burger King franchisee, paid $2.5 million to settle a sexual harassment lawsuit brought by the EEOC. The suit charged that female employees, many of them teenagers, had been targets of harassment—ranging from obscene comments and jokes to unwanted touching, stalking, and even rape—by managers, and that women who complained were subject to retaliation (U.S. Equal Employment Opportunity Commission, 2013). In Britain, workplace sexual harassment complaints go to an employment tribunal, which can order the harasser and/or employer to pay compensation, improve working conditions, reinstate a complainant's job, or other remedies. However, there are significant fees associated with pursuing a claim (at the time of writing £1200); this can serve as a deterrent to many complainants. In countries such as France, China, Kenya, Lithuania, and Spain, sexual harassment is a criminal offense and can be punishable by fines and/or jail time (UN Women, 2012). In India, legislation passed in 2013 broadened the definition of workplace sexual harassment and the responsibilities of organizations to deal with it—resulting in an increase in the number of reports (Dutta, 2017).

GLASS CEILINGS AND GLASS ESCALATORS: IS THE IMPACT OF BEING A TOKEN DIFFERENT FOR WOMEN AND FOR MEN?

For a male- or female-dominated occupation to tilt in the direction of becoming more gender-balanced, someone from the underrepresented gender has to be first. The individual who makes a foray into a job dominated by colleagues of the other gender, thus becoming a *gender token*, faces a number of issues, first noted by

Kanter (1977). This person will necessarily stand out among her or his co-workers—which can be either a good or a bad thing. Standing out can make a person more self-conscious and anxious, and thus more prone to make mistakes. Indeed, this outcome is exactly what researchers found when they examined the performance of female and male tokens in small groups in the laboratory (Lord and Saenz, 1985). Not only did the tokens not perform at their best, but also their mistakes were more likely to be noticed and remembered than those of other group members. This may be one reason for the negative emotions often reported by people in token positions. For example, policewomen whose numbers made up less than 15 percent of their department's officers reported less job satisfaction, more job-related depression, and lower self-esteem than did their counterparts in departments with more than 15 percent of women (Kimmel and Gormley, 2003).

A gender token faces more than simply being perceived as unusual. He or she must also contend with specific gender stereotypes and power relationships that undermine the perception of his or her suitability for and/or competence at the job. Because of the content of gender stereotypes, their impact may be different for men and for women in token positions. Male tokens may find it easier than female tokens to connect with (often male) supervisors, and thus may be taken more seriously (see, e.g., Floge and Merrill, 1986; Yoder and Sinnett, 1985). A possible explanation for this phenomenon is the stereotypic expectation of greater male than female competence. Token women also seem less likely to find support from female supervisors, perhaps because of the implied competition for a restricted number of slots for women in male-dominated work settings and/or the desire of female supervisors to avoid being associated with other women (almost by definition a lower status group) (K.M. Ryan *et al.*, 2012).

A token may find it difficult to find routine support and friendship from workplace colleagues. Here, too, women and men in such positions may differ in their experience. One US study revealed that whereas women in male-dominated occupations perceived relatively low levels of support from co-workers, men in female-dominated occupations perceived relatively high levels of support (Taylor, 2010). On this dimension, being in a numerical minority was apparently a disadvantage for women but an advantage for men.

Particularly in managerial and professional occupations, women become increasingly rare—and so seem more and more like tokens—at higher levels of advancement. There are quite a few women in middle management, but very few female senior managers, CEOs of top companies, or female members of corporate boards (Fortune Knowledge Group, 2016; Grant Thornton, 2017). Some describe this situation as a *glass ceiling*: it feels as though women smash against an invisible and impermeable barrier when they try to move up past a certain level. Globally, the percentage of women in senior business leadership roles increased only 1 percent (from 24 to 25 percent) between 2016 and 2017 (Grant Thornton, 2017). An examination of the presence (or absence) of women on corporate boards around the world shows that, although women's representation on corporate boards is increasing (now at 12 to 15 percent globally), there is still a lot of room for progress (Catalyst, 2016). Even in countries that have made significant efforts to advance women, women are still underrepresented in certain top positions. Denmark, for example, has the sixth-highest number of women on boards (almost 22 percent), but not a single board in Denmark has a women chair (Deloitte, 2017). In Canada, just over 13 percent of board seats are held by women, and 5.5 percent of boards are chaired by women; The United Kingdom has 15.6 percent of board seats held by women, and just under 4 percent of boards are chaired by women (Deloitte, 2017).

The "glass ceiling" imagery suggests that women make relatively smooth progress in their careers until they approach the upper levels of advancement and then are suddenly and inexplicably stopped by something they cannot see. Some analysts have taken issue with this view of the barriers women face, arguing that the shortage of women at the top is not caused by a sudden collision with a glass ceiling, but by the cumulative effect of a series of barriers and obstacles that winnow down the number of women at each step of advancement. As we will see in Chapter 6, a different way of looking at the issue may be that women pursuing career advancement are traversing a labyrinth, with lots of dead-ends and blind alleys, or an inexorably narrowing pipeline, with many leaks along the way.

In contrast to the extra barriers faced by women who are tokens, men who are tokens in female-dominated professions appear to experience a *glass escalator*: a constellation of subtle mechanisms and pressures that enhance men's advancement in women's professions (Williams, 1992; Cognard-Black, 2004). The escalator effect stems from stereotypes about men's abilities, skills, and leadership styles— stereotypes that affect men's behavior and others' perceptions of their behavior and potential. The effect is often to facilitate men's advancement and privilege them for leadership opportunities, even in professions such as nursing or social work where they form a numerical minority. This advantage in upward mobility appears to accrue most easily to white men, and is less likely to be available to men from minorities who work in feminized occupations— perhaps, in part, because minority men are less likely to receive support from majority women (Wingfield, 2009).

MOTHERHOOD PENALTIES AND FATHERHOOD PREMIUMS

Parenthood can be an employment-related disadvantage for women but an advantage for men. A *motherhood penalty* is one of the major contributors to the gender wage gap. One study showed that the cumulative earnings of non-mothers in the United States were 64 percent of men's, whereas mothers earned between 52 and 57 percent of men's earnings, depending on how many children they had (Sigle-Rushton and Waldfogel, 2007). Having two to four children can decrease a woman's wages by 4 to 8 percent, according to one researcher (Glauber, 2007). Others have found a 7 percent reduction in wages per child (Budig and England, 2001). Men with children do not experience a decrease in wages. In fact, for men, particularly those who are white married professionals in "traditional" households, having children results in an increase in wages—a *fatherhood premium* (Glauber, 2008; Hodges and Budig, 2010). The fatherhood premium is greatest for men at the top of the income distribution and the motherhood penalty is largest among low-income women—those who can least afford it (Budig, 2014). The gap engendered by both is smaller in countries where policies such as maternal and paternal leave and publicly funded childcare make it easier for mothers to remain in the labor force (Budig, Misra, and Boeckmann, 2016).

It seems obvious that, among parents, the gendered division of labor with respect to childcare responsibilities must contribute to a motherhood wage penalty. In the United States, for example, most women work full time, yet women still engage in more hours of childcare activities than men (U.S. Bureau of Labor Statistics, 2015). This heavy share of domestic responsibility could lead women to work fewer hours outside the home, to choose more flexible, part-time work with lower pay, or have lower productivity rates while at work. That interpretation fits well with a *human capital model* of the gender pay gap: the idea that women, especially mothers, simply invest less than men do in their employment, and thus harvest fewer rewards.

The human capital approach contains the assumption that women's choices about how much time and energy to invest in employment or family are free, not forced. However, mothers are constrained in these choices. For example, between 2001 and 2003 just under 40 percent of US women who were pregnant with their first child had to take unpaid time off work (Johnson, 2008). Although just over half of first-time mothers have access to at least some paid maternity leave, this flexibility is available mainly to educated women. One US study showed that, among first-time mothers with less than a high school education, only 18.5 percent were given paid maternity leave; 50 percent quit their jobs and 10.9 percent lost their jobs (Laughlin, 2011). Inadequate leave policies and lack of childcare resources for mothers may cause them to feel that they must decide between work and family. Working fewer hours, taking time off for children, or completely stepping out of the workforce to care for young children comes with an economic cost, resulting in lower earnings for mothers—but it is not a cost they freely choose.

What about the wage premium that fathers receive? This effect could be due to men's increased effort at work when they know they have a child to support. Indeed, men do tend to increase their effort at work when they become fathers. However, the fatherhood premium is still evident even after researchers adjust for fathers' longer hours, work effort, and other factors (Glauber, 2008). It appears that fatherhood, especially among men who fit society's ideas about ideal or normative upper-class masculinity (i.e., hetero-sexual, white, well educated, married) is regarded by employers as a positive quality—representative perhaps of responsibility, loyalty, and dependability (Hodges and Budig, 2010). Fathers benefit from positive stereotypes while mothers suffer from structural discrimina-tion based on traditional assumptions about parental roles.

AFFIRMATIVE ACTION AS A SOLUTION?

U.S. Supreme Court Justice Sonia Sotomayor (2013), the first Latina American on the Court, recounts the reaction from the school nurse at her high school when Sotomayor received word from Princeton University that she was being considered for admis-sion to that prestigious institution. The nurse asked her why she, and not the number one and number two students in the gradu-ating class, was on the list for consideration. Sotomayor had not heard the term "affirmative action" at that time, but she realized from the tone of the question that the nurse felt there was some-thing unfair going on. Now an unabashed supporter of the prin-ciple of affirmative action, Sotomayor calls it something that opened doors for her and changed the course of her life. She argues that it is important to have some structures in place to counter peo-ple's tendency to unthinkingly prefer, recommend, admit, hire, and promote individuals who are like themselves. Yet the whole idea of affirmative action remains controversial—so controversial that some advocates of the basic principle have sought to avoid the term alto-gether. When authoring a ground-breaking report about the need to fight employment discrimination, Canadian judge Rosalie Abella (1984) consciously chose to go beyond the framework of individual rights implied in the affirmative action concept. Instead, she wrote about *employment equity* strategies to counter unintentional systemic discrimination that produced barriers to women and minorities.

Affirmative action encompasses a variety of proactive strategies to increase the access of women and minorities to educational and employment opportunities. In the workplace, such strategies include expanding recruitment efforts to ensure they reach underrepresented groups, offering special training opportunities to targeted groups, and educating supervisors about their potential biases. In some countries, affirmative action strategies may include targets or aspirational or mandatory quotas for the proportion of women or minorities in certain positions. For example, a German law requires companies to have 30 percent of corporate board seats filled by women. This law aligns them with other European countries—Spain, France, Iceland, Italy, and Belgium—in setting mandatory boardroom quotas (Smale and Miller, 2015).

Affirmative action stirs strong debates. Some people feel it is not fair to consider the gender or race of an applicant for a job or a spot in an educational program. They argue that affirmative action may result in discriminating against traditional applicants while unfairly giving opportunities to less qualified women or minorities. Proponents of the other side argue that many decades of disadvantage to women and minorities cannot be undone without deliberate action to include them in arenas where they have historically faced barriers— and that critics of affirmative action ignore other instances of preferential treatment such as legacy admissions to colleges, or hiring based on personal networks. Some research suggests that affirmative action may, in some circumstances, undermine the self-confidence of its beneficiaries and promote the stereotype that they could not succeed on their own (e.g., Heilman and Alcott, 2001). However, under "real-world" conditions, when an individual knows that she or he is qualified, such concerns appear to be minimal. Affirmative action tends to be resisted most strongly by those who benefit from the status quo (Gu, McFerran, Aquino, and Kim, 2014); however, after decades of discrimination, it appears unlikely that a truly "equal opportunity" workplace can be created without such strategies (Crosby, Iyer, and Sincharoen, 2006).

MOVING TOWARD FAMILY-FRIENDLY WORKPLACES

We have noted that parenthood is linked to different workplace outcomes for women and for men. Are there ways to level the playing field for female and male workers trying to balance paid employment and family responsibilities? Employers have offered strategies such as part-time work, flexible hours, telecommuting, job sharing, and parental leave as ways to help parents allocate their time and energy efficiently across work and family domains. Yet there are clear costs to employees who choose "family-friendly" flexibility options offered by employers. Many employees are aware that if they take advantage of flexible work arrangements, their commitment to the job may be questioned and they may suffer negative career consequences. Women are particularly trapped by this situation: they may be judged as wavering in their career commitment if they take maternity leave or reduce their hours, and as bad parents if they combine demonstrably serious work commitment with family. Workers deciding whether to avail themselves of these opportunities must consider the possibility that they will be judged according to both gender stereotypes and norms that women should put family first, and an "ideal worker" norm that prescribes prioritizing work over all other responsibilities.

The family-friendly options available to workers reflect societal assumptions and norms about gender roles and parenting. In countries where there are strong traditional attitudes toward motherhood, extended maternity leave and part-time work options are likely to be offered to employed mothers—and women may feel strongly pressured to accept such benefits, despite potential harm to their careers (Den Dulk, 2005). If societal norms promoting the assignment of caregiving tasks primarily to women are not challenged and undermined, "family-friendly" workplace reforms can solidify the gendered division of household labor by making it possible for women to continue to carry the major share of household work and putting little pressure on men to do more (Daly, 2011).

Research suggests that professionals, both women and men, who deliberately reduce their load at work to accommodate family responsibilities can sometimes achieve both career success and satisfaction with family roles—though they may receive fewer promotions than their colleagues (Hall, Lee, Kossek, and Las Heras, 2012). More research is needed to understand the long-term consequences of various ways of combining work and family, and to find the most sustainable ways of doing so. Clearly, stereotypes and norms about gender and parenting are key to determining what kinds of arrangements are tried and how well they work.

FOR FURTHER EXPLORATION

Babcock, Linda and Laschever, Sara (2003). *Women don't ask: Negotiation and the gender divide* (Princeton, NJ: Princeton University Press). Using a wide variety of research findings, the authors provide an excellent overview of the many ways in which socialized gender role expectations affect women's and men's sense of entitlement and their readiness to negotiate for what they want in the workplace and other settings. Using real-world examples, they also provide a convincing summary of the many impacts of gender differences in negotiation—along with some practical advice.

Broadbridge, Adelina M. and Fielden, Sandra L. (eds) (2015). *Handbook of gendered careers in management. Getting in, getting on, getting out* (Cheltenham: Edward Elgar). A comprehensive series of chapters examines issues such as beliefs about the glass ceiling, work–family interface, leadership, challenges of global careers, and retirement from a gender perspective.

Crosby, Faye J. (2004). *Affirmative action is dead: Long live affirmative action* (New Haven, CT: Yale University Press). The author draws from research in psychology, law, political science, education, and sociology to describe affirmative action, analyze the often ambivalent public reactions to it, and delineate the arguments for and against it.

D'Aprano, Zelda (2001). *Kath Williams: The unions and the fight for equal pay* (Melbourne, Australia: Spiniflex Press). The author provides a fascinating social history of the struggle for equal pay in Australia, while introducing the reader to some of the main characters in this fight.

Kessler-Harris, Alice (2001). *In pursuit of equity: Women, men, and the quest for economic citizenship in 20th-century America* (New York: Oxford University Press). A pre-eminent labor historian provides an overview of the history of the development of women's participation in paid work in the United States, including careful consideration of the role of marriage, discrimination, and equal pay.

REFERENCES

Abella, R.S. (1984). *Report of the Commission on Equality in Employment* (Vol. 1). Ottawa, Canada: Minister of Supply and Services.

Alderman, L. (2017). Equal pay for men and women? Iceland wants employers to prove it. *The New York Times*, March 28.www.nytimes.com/2017/03/28/business/economy/iceland-women-equal-pay.html?nl=todayshsheadlines&emc=edit_th_20170329&_r=1.

American Association of Medical Colleges (2015). *The state of women in academic medicine: The pipeline and pathways to leadership, 2013–2014.* www.aamc.org/members/gwims/statistics/.

American Bar Association (2017). *A current glance at women in the law (January 2017).* www.Americanbar.org/content/dam/aba/marketing/women/current_glance_statistics_january2017.authcheckdam.pdf.

Australian Human Rights Commission (2012). *Working without fear: Results of the sexual harassment national telephone survey 2012.* www.humanrights.gov.au/sites/default/files/content/sexualharassment/survey/SHSR_2012%20Web%20Version%20Final.pdf.

Brownmiller, S. (1999). *In our time: Memoir of a revolution.* New York: Dell Publishing.

Budig, M.J. (2014). The fatherhood bonus & the motherhood penalty. Parenthood and the gender gap in pay. *Third Way.* http://content.thirdway.org/publications/853/NEXT_-_Fatherhood_Motherhood.pdf.

Budig, M. and England, P. (2001). The wage penalty for motherhood. *American Sociological Review, 66*, 204–225.

Budig, M.J., Misra, J., and Boeckmann, I. (2016). Work–family policy trade-offs for mothers? Unpacking the cross-national variation in motherhood earnings penalties. *Work and Occupations, 43*, 119–177. doi: 10.1177/0730888415615385.

Bursztyn, L., Fujiwara, T., and Pallais, A. (2016). *'Acting wife': Marriage market incentives and labor market investments.* University of Chicago. http://home.uchicago.edu/~bursztyn/Bursztyn_Fujiwara_Pallais_Dec2016.pdf.

Catalyst (2016). Knowledge Center. *Women on corporate boards globally.* www.catalyst.org/knowledge/women-corporate-boards-globally.

Chamberlain, A. and Jayaraman, J. (2017). *The pipeline problem: How college majors contribute to the gender pay gap.* Glassdoor, April. https://research-content.glassdoor.com/app/uploads/sites/2/2017/04/FULL-STUDY-PDF-Gender-Pay-Gap2FCollege-Major.pdf.

Chan, D.K-S., Lam, C.B., Chow, S.Y., and Cheung, S.F. (2008). Examining the job-related, psychological and physical outcomes of workplace sexual harassment: A meta-analytic review. *Psychology of Women Quarterly, 32*, 362–376.

Chang, A., Sandhofer, C.M., and Brown, C.S. (2011). Gender biases in early number exposure to preschool-aged children. *Journal of Language and Social Psychology*, *30*, 440–450. doi: 10.1177/0261927X11416207.

Charles, M. (2011). A world of difference: International trends in women's economic status. *Annual Review of Sociology*, *37*, 355–371. doi: 10.1146/annurev. soc.012809.102548.

Cognard-Black, A.J. (2004). Will they stay, or will they go? Sex-atypical work among token men who teach. *The Sociological Quarterly*, *45*, 113–139. doi: 10.1111/j.1533-8525.2004.tb02400.x.

Corbett, C. and Hill, C. (2012). *Graduating to a pay gap: The earnings of women and men one year after college graduation*. Washington, DC: American Association of University Women.

Correll, S.J. (2004). Constraints into preferences: Gender, status, and emerging career aspirations. *American Sociological Review*, *69*, 93–113. doi: 10.1177/000312240406900106.

Crosby, F.J., Iyer, A., and Sincharoen, S. (2006). Understanding affirmative action. *Annual Review of Psychology*, *57*, 585–611. doi: 10.1146/annurev. psych.57.102904.190029.

Cvencek, D., Meltzoff, A.N., and Greenwald, A.G. (2011). Math-gender stereotypes in elementary school children. *Child Development*, *82*, 766–779. doi: 10.1111/j.1467-8624.2010.01529.x.

Cvencek, D., Meltzoff, A.N., and Kapur, M. (2014). Cognitive consistency and math–gender stereotypes in Singaporean children. *Journal of Experimental Child Psychology*, *117*, 73–91. doi:10.1016/j.jecp. 2013.07.018.

Daly, M. (2011). What adult worker model? A critical look at recent social policy reform in Europe from a gender and family perspective. *Social Politics: International Studies in Gender, State and Society*, *18*, 1–23. doi: 10.1093/sp/jxr002.

D'Aprano, Z. (2001). *Kath Williams: The unions and the fight for equal pay*. Melbourne, Australia: Spinifex Press.

del Río, M.F. and Strasser, K. (2013). Preschool children's beliefs about gender differences in academic skills. *Sex Roles*, *68*, 231–238. doi: http://dx.doi. org/10.1007/s11199-012-0195-6.

Deloitte (2017). *Women in the boardroom. A global perspective* (4th edn). www2. deloitte.com/women-in-the-boardroom.

Den Dulk, L. (2005). Workplace work–family arrangements: A study and explanatory framework of differences between organizational provisions in different welfare states. In S.A.Y. Poelmans (ed.), *Work and family: An international research perspective* (pp. 211–238). Mahwah, NJ: Lawrence Erlbaum.

Dutta, K. (2017, March 17). Saluting the Vishaka judgment, 20 years on. REdiff News, March 17. www.rediff.com/news/column/saluting-the-vishaka-judgment-20-years-on/20170317.htm.

Eagly, A.H. (1987). *Sex differences in social behavior: A social role interpretation.* Hillsdale, NJ: Erlbaum.

Fiske, S.T., Bersoff, D.N., Borgida, E., Deaux, K., and Heilman, M.E. (1991). Social science on trial: Use of sex stereotyping research in *Price Waterhouse v. Hopkins. American Psychologist, 46,* 1049–1060. doi: 10.1037/0003-066X.46.10.1049.

Floge, L. and Merrill, D.M. (1986). Tokenism reconsidered: Male nurses and female physicians in a hospital setting. *Social Forces, 64,* 925–947. doi: 10.2307/2578787.

Fortune Knowledge Group (2016). *Women in the C-Suite: Developing senior leaders.* https://fortunefkg.com/women-in-the-c-suite-developing-senior-leaders/#tab-id-1.

Glauber, R. (2007). Marriage and the motherhood wage penalty among African Americans, Hispanics, and Whites. *Journal of Marriage and Family, 69,* 951–961.

Glauber, R. (2008). Race and gender in families and at work: The fatherhood wage premium. *Gender and Society, 22,* 8–30.

Goldin, C. and Rouse, C. (2000). Orchestrating impartiality: The impact of "blind" auditions on female musicians. *American Economic Review, 90,* 715–741.

Grant, J.M., Mottet, L.A., and Tanis, J. (2011). *Injustice at every turn: A report of the National Transgender Discrimination Survey.* www.thetaskforce.org/static_html/downloads/reports/reports/ntds_full.pdf.

Grant Thornton (2017). *International Business Report: Women in business 2017: New perspectives on risk and reward.* www.grantthornton.global/en/insights/articles/women-in-business-2017/.

Gu, J., McFerran, B., Aquino, K., and Kim, T.G. (2014). What makes affirmative action-based hiring decisions seem (un)fair? A test of an ideological explanation for fairness judgments. *Journal of Organizational Behavior, 35,* 722–745. doi:/10.1002/job.1927.

Hall, D.T., Lee, M.D., Kossek, E.E., and Las Heras, M. (2012). Pursuing career success while sustaining personal and family well being: A study of reduced-load professionals over time. *Journal of Social Issues, 68,* 742–766.

Halpern, D.F. (2012). *Sex differences in cognitive abilities* (4th edn). New York: Psychology Press.

Heilman, M.E. and Alcott, V.B. (2001). What I think you think of me: Women's reactions to being viewed as beneficiaries of preferential selection. *Journal of Applied Psychology, 86,* 574–582.

Hodges, M.J. and Budig, M.J. (2010). Who gets the daddy bonus? Organizational hegemonic masculinity and the impact of fatherhood on earnings. *Gender and Society, 24,* 717–745. doi: 10.1177/0891243210386729.

International Labour Organization (2012). *Domestic workers.* www.ilo.org/global/topics/domestic-workers/lang-en/index.htm.

Jarman, J., Blackburn, R.M., and Racko, G. (2012). The dimensions of occupational gender segregation in industrial countries. *Sociology, 46,* 1003–1019. doi: 10.1177/0038038511435063.

Johnson, T.D. (2008). *Maternity leave and employment patterns: 2001–2003* (Report No. P70–113). www.census.gov/prod/2008pubs/p70-113.pdf.

Kanter, R.M. (1977). *Men and women of the corporation.* New York: Basic Books.

Kimmel, J.T. and Gormley, P.E. (2003). Tokenism and job satisfaction for policewomen. *American Journal of Criminal Justice, 28,* 73–88. doi:/10.1007/BF02885753.

Laughlin, L. (2011). Maternity leave and employment patterns: 2006–2008. *Current Population Report,* pp. 70–128. Washington, DC: U.S. Census Bureau. www.census.gov/prod/2011pubs/p70-128.pdf.

Legal Information Institute, Cornell University Law School (2012). 89–1215. International Union, United Automobile, Aerospace and Agricultural Implement Workers of America, UAW *et al.* v. Johnson Controls, Inc. www.law.cornell.edu/supct/html/89-1215.ZS.html.

Levanon, A., England, P., and Allison, P. (2009). Occupational feminization and pay: Assessing causal dynamics using 1950–2000 U.S. Census data. *Social Forces, 88,* 865–891. doi: 10.1353/sof.0.0264.

Lips, H.M. (2013). The gender pay gap: Challenging the rationalizations: Perceived equity, discrimination, and the limits of human capital models. *Sex Roles, 68,* 169–185. doi: 10.007/s11199-012-0165-z.

Lord, C.G. and Saenz, D.S. (1985). Memory deficits and memory surfeits: Differential cognitive consequences of tokenism for tokens and observers. *Journal of Personality and Social Psychology, 49,* 918–926. doi: 10.1037/0022-3514.49.4.918.

Martinot, D., Bagès, C., and Désert, M. (2012). French children's awareness of gender stereotypes about mathematics and reading: When girls improve their reputation in math. *Sex Roles, 66,* 210–219. doi: 10.1007/s11199-011-0032-3.

McCurry, J. (2016). Nearly a third of Japan's women "sexually harassed at work". *Guardian,* March 2. www.theguardian.com/world/2016/mar/02/japan-women-sexually-harassed-at-work-report-finds.

Moss-Racusin, C.A., Dovidio, J.F., Brescoll, V.L., Graham, M.J., and Handelsman, J. (2012). Science faculty's subtle gender biases favor male students. *PNAS, 109,* 16474–16479. doi: 10.1073/pnas.1211286109.

Muzzatti, B. and Agnoli, F. (2007). Gender and mathematics: Attitudes and stereotype threat susceptibility in Italian children. *Developmental Psychology, 43,* 747–759. doi: 10.1037/0012-1649.43.3.747.

New York City Department of Consumer Affairs (2015). *From cradle to cane: The cost of being a female consumer*. New York: Author. www1.nyc.gov/assets/dca/downloads/pdf/partners/Study-of-Gender-Pricing-in-NYC.pdf.

OECD (2015). *Education indicators in focus*. March. www.oecd.org/education/EDIF-2015-No-30-ENG.pdf.

OECD (2017). Gender wage gap (indicator). doi: 10.1787/7cee77aa-en. https://data.oecd.org/earnwage/gender-wage-gap.htm.

Office for National Statistics (2017). EMP04: Employment by occupation. April to June 2017. www.ons.gov.uk/employmentandlabourmarket/peopleinwork/employmentandemployeetypes/datasets/employmentbyoccupationemp04.

Rosenberg, R. (1982). *Beyond separate spheres: Intellectual origins of modern feminism*. New Haven, CT: Yale University Press.

Roth, L.M. (2006). *Selling women short: Gender and money on Wall Street*. Princeton, NJ: Princeton University Press.

Ryan, C. (2012). Field of degree and earning by selected employment characteristics: 2011. www.census.gov/prod/2012pubs/acsbr11-10.pdf.

Ryan, K.M., King, E.B., Adis, C., Gulick, L.M.V., Peddie, C., and Hargraves, R. (2012). Exploring the asymmetrical effects of gender tokenism on supervisor–subordinate relationships. *Journal of Applied Social Psychology*, *42*, S1, E56–E102. doi: 10.1111/j.1559-1816.2012.01025.x.

Sigle-Rushton, W. and Waldfogel, J. (2007). Motherhood and women's earnings in anglo-American, continental European, and Nordic countries. *Feminist Economics, 13*, 55–91.

Smale, A. and Miller, C.C. (2015). Germany sets gender quota in boardroom. *The New York Times*, March 6. www.nytimes.com/2015/03/07/world/europe/german-law-requires-more-women-on-corporate-boards.html.

Smeding, A. (2012). Women in Science, Technology, Engineering, and Mathematics (STEM): An investigation of their implicit gender stereotypes and stereotypes' connectedness to math performance. *Sex Roles, 67*, 617–629. doi: 10.1007/s11199-012-0209-4.

Sotomayor, S. (2013). *My beloved world: A memoir*. New York: Random House.

Statistics Canada (2016). *Table 1: Mean age-adjusted earnings of men and women, by field of study, 2010*. www.statcan.gc.ca/pub/11-626-x/2016056/tbl/tbl01-eng.htm.

Statistics Iceland (2016). *Women's income from work was less than 30% of men's in 2015*. October 24. www.statice.is/publications/news-archive/wages-and-income/unadjusted-gpg-2015/.

Taylor, C.J. (2010). Occupational sex composition and the gendered availability of workplace support. *Gender and Society, 24*, 189–212. doi: 10.1177/0891243209359912.

Trades Union Congress (2016). *Still just a bit of banter? Sexual harassment in the workplace in 2016*. London: Author. www.tuc.org.uk/sites/default/files/SexualHarassmentreport2016.pdf.

UN Women (2012). Overview and workplace sexual harassment as a crime. www.endvawnow.org/en/articles/530-overview-and-workplace-sexual-harassment-as-a-crime.html.

UNESCO (2015). *EFA Global Monitoring Report. Gender and EFA 2000–2015: Achievements and challenges*. http://unesdoc.unesco.org/images/0023/002348/234809E.pdf.

U.S. Bureau of Labor Statistics (2015). *American Time Use Survey*. www.bls.gov/tus/.

U.S. Bureau of Labor Statistics (2017). Labor force statistics from the Current Population Survey. Table 11. www.bls.gov/cps/cpsaat11.htm.

U.S. Census Bureau (2015). Table 1: Full-time, year-round workers and median earning in the past 12 months by sex and detail occupation, 2015. www.census.gov/people/io/publications/table_packages.html.

U.S. Department of Labor, Women's Bureau (2014). Highest and lowest paid occupations. www.dol.gov/wb/stats/highest_lowest_paying-occupations_2014.htm.

U.S. Department of Labor, Bureau of Labor Statistics (2016). *America's young adults at 29: Labor market activity, education and partner status: Results from a longitudinal study*. Economic News Release, April 8. www.bls.gov/news.release/nlsyth.nr0.htm.

U.S. Equal Employment Opportunity Commission (2013).: *Carrols Corp. to pay $2.5 million to settle EEOC sexual harassment and retaliation lawsuit*. Press release, January 9. www.eeoc.gov/eeoc/newsroom/release/1-9-13.cfm.

Vaglanos, A. (2015). 1 in 3 women has been sexually harassed at work, according to survey. *The Huffington Post*, February 19. www.huffingtonpost.com/2015/02/19/1-in-3-women-sexually-harassed-work-cosmopolitan_n_6713814.html.

Williams, C. (1992). The glass escalator: Hidden advantages for men in the "female" professions. *Social Problems*, *39*, 253–267.

Wingfield, A.H. (2009). Racializing the glass escalator. Reconsidering men's experiences with women's work. *Gender and Society, 23*, 5–26. doi: 10.1177/089124320832305.

World Economic Forum (2016). *The global gender gap report 2016*. Geneva, Switzerland: Author. www3.weforum.org/docs/GGGR16/WEF_Global_Gender_Gap_Report_2016.pdf.

Yoder, J.D. and Sinnett, L.M. (1985). Is it all in the numbers? A case study of tokenism. *Psychology of Women Quarterly, 9*, 413–418. doi: 10.1111/j.1471-6402.1985.tb00890.x.

Yoon, E., Funk, R., and Kropf, N. (2010). Sexual harassment experiences and their psychological correlates among a diverse sample of college women. *Affilia: Journal of Women and Social Work, 25*(1), 8–18.

Zillman, C. (2014). Yes, pregnancy discrimination at work is still a huge problem. *Fortune*, July 15. http://fortune.com/2014/07/15/pregnancy-discrimination/.

6

GENDER, LEADERSHIP, AND PUBLIC LIFE

In a blistering speech before Parliament in late 2012, Australian Prime Minister Julia Gillard called out opposition leader Tony Abbot's repeated use of blatant sexism to try to undermine her leadership (Little, 2012). Noting his previous public comments that it might not be a bad thing that there were fewer women than men in leadership positions, and that women might be less adapted by temperament or physiology for command, his condescending references to the housewives of Australia, and his willingness to be photographed standing next to signs that labeled Gillard personally as a "witch" or a "man's bitch," Gillard asserted that, if the opposition leader wanted to "know what misogyny looks like in modern Australia, he [...] needs a mirror."

It is difficult to think of a man in a prominent leadership position who has had to chide women in any similar way for using sexism to undermine his leadership. As we have seen in earlier chapters, masculinity, and not femininity, is stereotypically linked to public leadership—so people do not derogate a male leader just because he is a man. Indeed, in the 2016 US presidential election, then-candidate Donald Trump claimed repeatedly that his opponent, Hillary Clinton, simply did not look "presidential" – an underhanded but unmistakable allusion to the perception that, as a woman, she did not fit the long-accepted presidential requirement of maleness.

However, gender stereotypes can also damage men who are leaders. A man in a position of public leadership who displays qualities viewed as too feminine risks criticism and loss of respect for being too "soft"—unless his masculine credentials as tough, decisive, and hard are firmly in place. Once he demonstrates sufficient masculinity, a male leader is permitted to display some compassion and vulnerability at appropriate moments—such as the press conference where US General Norman Schwartzkopf shed some tears when talking about the troops killed during the Gulf War of 1990 to 1991. People admire male leaders who can deploy compassion and care in rationed doses without losing their commanding edge. Still, one of the most devastating attacks on a male politician is that he is "soft" on something: on crime, on communism, on terrorism, on corruption.

GENDER AND POLITICAL LEADERSHIP: GLOBAL TRENDS AND SOME EXAMPLES

The World Economic Forum compares women and men within countries on their health, educational, economic, and political outcomes. In 2016 the Forum reported that, whereas global gender gaps in health and educational outcomes were closing relatively rapidly, only 59 percent of the economic outcomes gap and 23 percent of the political outcomes gap had been closed (World Economic Forum, 2016). Clearly, political leadership is a domain where gender equality is lagging. Despite progress over recent decades, women still make up less than 24 percent of the Members of Parliament in the countries of the world (Inter-Parliamentary Union, 2018). As Figure 6.1 shows, women are underrepresented, relative to their numbers, in parliaments around the world. As of 2018, only three countries, Rwanda, Cuba, and Bolivia, had women as more than half of their parliamentary representatives (Inter-Parliamentary Union, 2018). In 2018, just over 6.3 percent of the world's heads of state or heads of government are women—a drop since 2014.

Women political leaders must often negotiate stereotypes. Dilma Rousseff, who took over as President of Brazil in 2011 (and was

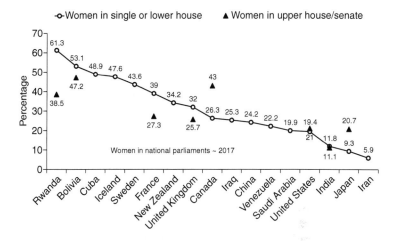

Figure 6.1 Representation of women in national parliaments and upper houses or senates. Women are underrepresented in the legislative bodies that govern nations. Although women form a majority of the world's population, in only two countries (Rwanda and Bolivia) are women a majority among elected parliamentary representatives.

Source: Based on data from Inter-Parliamentary Union (2017).

forced out in 2016), was the first woman to hold this position. She was dubbed the "mother of the nation" during her election campaign. She was also called the Iron Lady (a nickname that has, in the past, been given to many women political leaders, including Margaret Thatcher of Britain, Golda Meier of Israel, Benazir Bhutto of Pakistan, and Yulia Tymoshenko of Ukraine). As a candidate, current British Prime Minister Theresa May drew media questions about motherhood, cooking, and whether or not she should wear high heels—and has also been labeled an Iron Lady.

In Africa, two female heads of state, Ellen Johnson-Sirleaf (President of Liberia) and Joyce Banda (President of Malawi from 2012 to 2014) (both also dubbed "iron ladies"), committed themselves to advancing women's rights on that continent. Both presided over a strengthening of the voices of women in government, increases in the proportion of girls in school, and initiatives on maternal health and safety. Each came by her dedication to these issues through life experiences that mirror those of many other women: Banda survived an abusive marriage and once worked as a market vendor—a job held by many African women (Opolade, 2012). Sirleaf was married at the age of 17 (and later divorced), and is mother of four and grandmother of eight.

Female political leaders often struggle to bridge the perception that, because they are powerful, they cannot be "real" women. Some emphasize the conjunction of femininity with power by taking on a maternal persona—as in Dilma Rousseff's "mother of the nation" title. That title has also been applied to other female political leaders, including Gro Brundtland, former prime minister of Norway, Fatima Jinnah, one-time candidate for the presidency of Pakistan, and Winnie Mandela, well-known activist of South Africa). For many powerful women, however, labels such as "iron lady"—implying not only toughness, but perhaps a cold and unfeeling style—seem unavoidable. German Chancellor Angela Merkel has been called the Iron Frau; US Secretary of State Madeline Albright was labeled the Titanium Lady; and critics of Jane Byrne, the first female mayor of Chicago, mocked her by calling her Attila the Hen. Rather than fight such labels, some women leaders—such as Ellen Johnson-Sirleaf and her female cabinet members, known collectively as Liberia's "iron ladies," have adopted them as badges of honor (*Iron Ladies of Liberia*, 2008). A few leaders have managed to project an image that spans the gap between "masculine" toughness and "feminine" softness: media coverage of former U.S. House of Representatives Speaker and current Minority Leader Nancy Pelosi describes her both as having a "spine of steel" and a "heart of gold" (Dabbous and Ladley, 2010).

Despite the visibility of some high-profile female political leaders, the rate of progress for women in politics has been slow. In the 15 years between 2002 and 2017, the percentage of women among elected representatives in lower houses of congress or parliaments rose only from 13.8 to 19.3 in the United States, from 17.9 to 30 in the United Kingdom, from 20.6 to 26.3 in Canada, and from 29.2 to 34.2 in New Zealand. In some countries (e.g., Micronesia, Qatar, Yemen), the number of women in national legislative bodies remained at zero during this time, while in others (e.g., Haiti, Iran, Lebanon, Nigeria, Botswana) the numbers are below 10 percent (Inter-Parliamentary Union, 2017). Important and interconnected barriers to women's political progress include being ignored or stereotyped by the media, lack of access to campaign financing, and a cultural tendency to treat women as second-class citizens (Llanos, 2011).

Yet, in a few countries, women have made dramatic gains. During the same 15 years, women's representation in Cuba's legislative body rose from 27.6 percent to 48.9 percent, their representation in Bolivia's lower house increased from 18.5 percent to 53.1 percent, and their representation in Rwanda's Parliament increased from 25.7 percent to 61.3 percent (Inter-Parliamentary Union, 2017).

What explains the uncommon success of countries such as Cuba, Bolivia, and Rwanda in increasing the representation of women? The key seems to be that gender equality has not been left to chance. Explicit efforts have been made to overcome traditional anti-woman biases and to support the entry of women into politics. In both Cuba and Rwanda, new systems of government were crafted by men and women who fought together to replace older ones. Analysts argue that in Cuba, women's rights were broadly incorporated into the changes that grew out of the revolution, so that women's access to resources such as health and literacy increased. A commitment to women's rights as a "revolution within a revolution" was implemented through policy changes that encouraged and supported the advancement of women. The Cuban government built a database of candidates with equal numbers of men and women, and implemented a platform of goals and strategies to support women's leadership (Oxfam, 2012). In Rwanda, the 2003 constitution prescribes that women and men have equal access to elective offices, and specifies that at least 30 percent of the posts in decision-making bodies must be held by women (Constitution of the Republic of Rwanda, 2003). In addition, the tragic genocidal conflict in Rwanda left many women as widows or sole supporters of their families, making it necessary for women to take on leadership positions (Bikorimana, 2012). In Bolivia too, a new constitution mandates equal representation of women and men candidates at all levels. However, that constitution also contains language recognizing traditional customs and practices of indigenous communities, some of which do not accept women leaders. In all three countries, the situation for women is still far from perfect. Women in Cuba refer to a "gender paradox:" their country has a strong legal commitment to gender equality but also a deep-rooted tradition of patriarchal attitudes and structures (Torregrosa, 2012). In Rwanda, some people complain of "positive discrimination" toward women. However, because they are tasked with domestic responsibilities that interfere with their access to higher education, women are still underrepresented in secondary schools and universities (Bikorimana, 2012). In Bolivia, patriarchal attitudes still have a chilling effect on women's political participation. Female politicians are often targets of harassment, bullying, and violence—so much so that only 9 percent of women elected leaders stand for office a second time (BBC, 2014). Legislation to counter gender-based harassment and political violence was passed in 2012, but enforcement has proven difficult (UN Women, 2013). Clearly, gender equality in access to political leadership does not just happen, even in the presence of goodwill and a general belief that equality is a good thing. Rather, equality requires a comprehensive, proactive, and determined set of strategies—perhaps affirmative action strategies, as in Cuba, and/or quotas, as in Rwanda and Bolivia, along with a culture committed to supporting and enforcing equality.

The persistence of a perceived disconnect between femininity and political power is one reason for the extraordinary measures sometimes required to speed up women's integration into high-level political leadership roles. Research has shown that respondents react negatively to female, but not male, politicians who are seen as interested in seeking power (Okimoto and Brescoll, 2010). Respondents who viewed a female politician as having power-seeking intentions said they were less likely to vote for her; however, the likelihood of voting for a male politician was unrelated to his perceived power-seeking intentions. Furthermore, when a female politician was described as ambitious and having a strong will to power, respondents viewed her as less competent and deficient in communality (low in supportiveness and caring)—and reported feeling emotions toward her that indicated moral outrage: anger, contempt, disgust. When a male politician was similarly described as ambitious and power-oriented, he was seen as having more desirable agentic qualities (assertiveness, strength, toughness), but was not viewed as lower in communality or competence and did not stir reactions of moral outrage. These findings suggest that women who aspire to high political leadership are viewed not just as unusual and as violating expectations, but rather as stepping out of line—of breaking the rules. These women are transgressing prescriptive stereotypes with respect to femininity, whereas men who aspire to political leadership are fulfilling prescriptive stereotypes with respect to masculinity. Depending on the context, for women, such transgressions produce reactions ranging from mild public disapproval, to scathing media criticism, to threats and violence.

GENDER AND ORGANIZATIONAL LEADERSHIP: GLOBAL TRENDS AND SOME EXAMPLES

As with formal political leadership, formal organizational or corporate leadership has not been easily accessible for women. As of 2015, the average representation of women on the corporate boards of Europe's largest listed companies was 25 percent, up from 13.9 percent in 2011 (European Women on Boards, 2016); in 2016, 96 percent of the CEOs of the *Euro 350* companies and 95 percent of the CEOs of *Fortune 500* companies were men (Sabic, 2016). In the Asia-Pacific, the numbers for female representation on corporate boards were even lower: 4.5 percent for South Korea, 8.6 percent for India, and 2.7 percent for Japan (Catalyst, 2017). Figure 6.2 shows women's underrepresentation in corporate governance. As noted in Chapter 5, European countries have responded to the shortage of women in such positions by setting an aspirational quota for member countries: at least 40 percent of non-executive directors of corporate boards should be women by 2020 (BBC, 2012). Countries such as Norway, which have already implemented such quotas, have found that the increased representation of women at director level has increased the likelihood of women's appointment to top leadership roles such as corporate CEOs or board chairs (Wang and Kelan, 2012).

Among the most powerful women in the business world are Mary Barra, CEO and Chair of General Motors, Ginni Rometty,

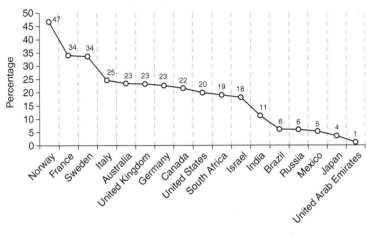

Figure 6.2 Representation of women on corporate boards by selected countries. Women are underrepresented on the boards of major corporations around the world. In Norway, where quotas have been in place for some years, women's presence on boards is significantly higher than in many other countries.

Source: Based on data from Catalyst (2017), and European Women on Boards (2016).

the first woman CEO of IBM, Ana Botín, Executive Chair of Banco Santander, Europe's largest bank, and Sheryl Sandberg, COO of Facebook. Among the "top 50" women in business listed by *Fortune* magazine (Fortune, 2016), each of these women worked her way up over many years to head an extremely male-dominated institution. Their success demonstrates the possibility for women of breaking into the very highest corporate levels, but the very existence of the list illustrates the novelty of women at the top.

"UNCOUNTED" LEADERS: ACTIVIST WOMEN

Women are underrepresented in formal organizational leadership positions, but there is no basis for the idea that women are less interested than men in leadership. Women and men do not differ on measures of power motivation (Winter, 1988). Research shows a small tendency for men to score higher than women on certain dimensions of the motivation to manage in hierarchic organizations (desire to engage in competition with peers; desire to behave in an active, assertive way; desire to impose wishes upon subordinates; and desire to stand out from the group) (Eagly, Karau, Miner, and Johnson, 1994). These dimensions are congruent with the masculine definition of leadership in top-down organizations, where men tend to predominate in administrative positions, and managers have considerably more power than do subordinates. Women score higher on two other dimensions of leadership in such organizations: desire to have positive relationships with superiors, and desire to meet day-to-day managerial role requirements. However, many of the most accomplished female leaders have *not* worked in traditional male-dominated hierarchic organizations, but have directed their energy into forming and nurturing grassroots activist groups seeking social change.

Because they have not worked under formal labels such as CEO, board chairperson, senator, or president, the contributions of women leaders may be uncounted and overlooked. Women such as Susan B. Anthony, Elizabeth Cady Stanton, Emmeline and Sylvia Pankhurst, Mary Ann Shadd, and Emily Howard Stowe—warriors in the fight for women's suffrage—were effective and critically important leaders who made world-changing contributions. Many women have devoted their leadership drive and skills to advancing women's rights. Their names are often forgotten, but their impact may well go beyond that achieved by individuals who hold more traditional leadership positions. We may think, for example, of Meena Keshwar Kamal, founder of the Revolutionary Women of Afghanistan (RAWA), defying restrictions on education of women and girls by developing and supporting a secret network of underground schools. We can list Nawal Saadawi of Egypt, Maryam Rajavi of Iran, Salwa Charfi of Tunisia, or Ghada Jamsheer of Bahrain—all outspoken activists for women's rights in their countries, in often risky defiance of cultural and religious restrictions (Halila, 2008). And then there are Tawakkol Karman of Yemen and Malala Yousafzai of Pakistan, the two youngest-ever recipients of the Nobel Peace Prize, each speaking passionately at rallies and organizing demonstrations in support of peace and women's and girls' rights. Most of the barriers to women's leadership are linked to the socio-cultural environment, and do not represent essential differences between women and men.

GENDER STEREOTYPES AND THE EVALUATION OF FEMALE AND MALE LEADERS

Decades ago, research documented that the image of formal leadership was entwined with masculinity. When people thought of managers, they thought of men (Schein, 1973; Schein, Mueller, Lituchy, and Liu, 1996). When respondents thought of powerful people, they envisioned men (Lips, 2001). When asked if they would vote for a female political candidate for president, they expressed uneasiness (Smith, Paul, and Paul, 2007). Although there are more women in high-profile leadership positions these days, the stereotype of leaders continues to reek of masculinity (Cuadrado, García-Ael, and Molero, 2015; Koenig, Eagly, Mitchell, and Ristikari, 2011). In fact, researchers have explained the dearth of women in leadership by citing a clear *lack of fit* (Heilman, 1983) or *role incongruity* (Eagly and Karau, 2002) between the requirements of stereotypical femininity (niceness, care, compassion, consideration) and the qualities expected of leaders (goal-orientation, decisiveness, determination). In particular, the stereotype that women are more emotional than men has undermined their attempts to fit leadership roles (Brescoll, 2016). The attempt to fulfill the contradictory requirements of both roles can put women in a double bind.

A DOUBLE BIND FOR WOMEN

Women leaders struggle within a double bind. In 2007, the American research firm Catalyst surveyed more than 1200 executives in the United States and Europe about their views of women and men in leadership roles. The report, appropriately entitled *Damned if you do, doomed if you don't*, revealed that when women behaved in ways consistent with feminine gender stereotypes by, for example, showing concern for others' perspectives, they were viewed as less competent. On the other hand, if they behaved in more masculine ways (acting assertively or displaying ambition), they were judged unfeminine and overly tough (Catalyst, 2007). Women leaders consistently faced higher standards than men, and tended to be viewed either as too soft or too tough—rarely just right. Women leaders had to settle for either being seen as competent or being well liked, but rarely found themselves both liked *and* admired as competent.

Many studies show that women in professional roles are penalized for the behaviors or attributes that are ignored, tolerated, or even praised when exhibited by men. Women reap more disapproval than men do when they are not "nice" or display poor social skills (Rudman and Glick, 1999). Women who express anger over a colleague's mistake are seen as being emotional and out of control; men who express the same sentiments in the same situation gain stature (Brescoll and Uhlmann, 2008). Powerful women, but not powerful men, incur disapproval and backlash if they talk more than others (Brescoll, 2011). On the other hand, women also incur disapproval if they are not assertive enough. Acting tentatively in a leadership role reduces the likeability and influence of women but not of men (Bongiorno, Bain, and David, 2014). In general, female leaders are less likely than male leaders to be viewed as legitimate by subordinates. Disrespect from subordinates leads to negative responses by leaders, which reinforces subordinates' disrespect. Thus, female leaders can become trapped in a self-reinforcing cycle of illegitimacy (Vial, Napier, and Brescoll, 2016).

Female executives who dress in what others regard as a provocative way suffer a large drop in perceived competence—a drop not experienced by women in lower status jobs (Glick, Larsen, Johnson, and Branstiter, 2005). There is no evidence that male executives incur a loss of respect or status if they dress provocatively—but that may be because, for men, power is sexy and so dressing provocatively doesn't even come up. Both attractive women and attractive men sometimes benefit from a "beauty premium" in earnings (Adreoni and Petrie, 2008), but attractive men seem to benefit more than attractive women, and only women are sometimes penalized for being *too* attractive (Bennett, 2010). Women in low-status and/or "feminine" positions are penalized for not being attractive, but women in (or applying for) high-status and/or "masculine" positions who appear too beautiful or sexy are sometimes subject to what some have labeled the "beauty is beastly" effect (Heilman and Stopeck, 1985). According to this idea, attractiveness is detrimental for female applicants for leadership positions because attractiveness is associated with femininity—and femininity is seen as incongruent with the requirements for these jobs. In other words, beauty makes women appear unfit for the position. In one study, participants were shown photos of attractive and unattractive women and men, and were asked to sort them according to suitability for particular jobs (Johnson, Podratz, Dipboye, and Gibbons, 2010). Attractive women were discriminated against for masculine jobs where physical appearance was unimportant.

Another study examined the impact of attractiveness upon evaluations of female and male leaders with different leadership styles (Braun, Peus, and Frey, 2012). The differential impact of attractiveness upon reactions to female and male leaders was pronounced for transformational leaders (leaders who used charismatic behavior to inspire and motivate followers), but not for leaders using a more traditional, transactional style (i.e., who focused on task completion, rewards, and punishments). Attractive women using a transformational leadership style elicited less trust and loyalty from followers than did unattractive women using a similar style. For male transformational leaders, attractiveness made no difference. In the case of female leaders, attractiveness appeared to strengthen followers' perceptions of a lack of fit between the leaders' femininity and the strong, influential behavior required of a transformational leader.

Although the qualities believed to be important for leaders vary across cultures, women's strengths seem to be consistently underestimated. A study of managers from ten Western European countries and the United States revealed, across cultures, a relatively consistent tendency to view women leaders as more supportive and men as more oriented to problem-solving. The strength of these stereotypes about women's and men's leadership capabilities varied by culture, but what is especially disheartening for women is that, at least in some countries, they were believed to have fewer of whatever qualities were deemed important—particularly by men. In Nordic cultures where the ideal leader was expected to be a delegator, men were seen as better delegators; in Anglo cultures where the ideal leader was expected to be good at inspiring others, men were seen as more effective than women on this dimension (Catalyst, 2006).

The most successful women leaders may be those who are good at being chameleons: who can project assertiveness and confidence, but who can also, depending on the circumstances, "turn those traits on or off" (O'Neill and O'Reilly, 2011). In fact, among managers in this study, women who had masculine traits and were good at tailoring their behavior to the social environment received three times as many promotions as did masculine women who tended *not* to adapt their behavior, 1.5 times more promotions than masculine men, and twice as many as feminine men. For the men with feminine traits, being a chameleon apparently conferred no advantage.

Men may be leery of female leaders because culturally perceived masculinity is fragile—and men's own status can be affected by being subordinate to someone who violates gender stereotypes (Brescoll, Uhlmann, Moss-Racusin, and Sarnell, 2012). Researchers found that male subordinates of either a female supervisor in a masculine domain (a female construction-site supervisor) or a male supervisor in a feminine domain (a male human resources supervisor) were paid less and attributed lower status than men whose supervisors were in gender-congruent domains. The status loss for these men appeared to be caused by the perception that they lacked masculinity; the situation could be remedied by providing information that bolstered the men's perceived masculinity (that they enjoyed watching football, eating steak and ribs, and driving fast cars). Women's status or pay was unrelated to working for a gender-atypical supervisor. In this kind of situation, then, gender stereotypes can harm men as well as women.

LEADERSHIP, SELF, AND IDENTITY

Given the gendered stereotypes about leadership, it would not be surprising if women and men had different perceptions, expectations, aspirations, hopes, and fears about holding leadership positions. One way to think about these perceptions is in terms of *possible selves*: individuals' particular visions and fantasies of what they could be or become in the future (Markus and Nurius, 1986). Everyone has a set of many possible selves, created from their social experience and from exposure to models and images portrayed in the media. These different possible selves may include visions both positive (e.g., a successful businessperson) and negative (e.g., a failed political candidate). They are not necessarily aspirational goals but rather possibilities that a person can imagine for the self.

Gender differences in leadership-related possible selves among young women and men may reveal ways in which they have absorbed cultural messages about gender, power, and leadership. Several studies have examined these issues among university students—a population from which many leaders are likely to spring. Lips (2000) asked a sample of US students to imagine themselves as persons with power, to rate how possible and how positive it would be for them to occupy that role, and then to describe what they would be like in their imagined powerful role. Next, the students envisioned themselves in three specific powerful roles: corporate CEO, political leader, and director of a scientific research center, and responded to the same questions. Women rated the possibility of occupying both their imagined powerful role and the political leader role lower than did men. Furthermore, women were more likely than men to anticipate that powerful roles, particularly the political leader role, could entail relationship problems. The relationship concerns they expressed included being disrespected by subordinates, being categorized according to their femininity rather than to their position, and figuring out how to have time and energy left over for relationships outside of work.

Attempts to integrate power with cultural femininity may differ across cultures. In a similar study that included students from Puerto Rico as well as the US mainland (Lips, 2001), women respondents were significantly more likely than men to anticipate relationship problems in powerful roles, and women in both samples listed the political leader role as the least possible role. Female respondents were more likely than males to mention appearance as a way of managing perceived contradictions between femininity and power, emphasizing that they would look attractive, even though powerful, or that they would convey power by looking elegant and stylish. Women in both samples expected relationship issues to crop up in powerful roles. However, only the women in the US mainland sample connected this expectation to lower ratings of possibility and positivity of occupying powerful roles. This may reflect a greater insistence by mainland US culture than by Puerto Rican culture that femininity involves being generally accommodating and nonabrasive, even with strangers. Cultural differences in perceptions of acceptable ways to mix femininity and power are also suggested in another study (Killeen, Lopez-Zafra, and Eagly, 2006), in which researchers asked undergraduate students in the USA and Spain to envision themselves in a leadership role and then to indicate how positive and possible the role would be. Here again, men perceived the powerful role as more possible for themselves than did women, but only in the Spanish sample did men rate powerful roles as more positive for themselves than did women. Men were more likely than women to report that holding a powerful role would facilitate close relationships with spouse, children, and friends and relationships with men or women in general—echoing earlier findings that powerful roles present fewer relationship concerns for men than for women. Taken together, these findings suggest that women's ambivalence about holding powerful positions transcends cultural boundaries, although the ambivalence may connect to somewhat different issues in different cultural contexts. They also suggest that one factor slowing down women's entry into leader roles may be women's weaker sense that these roles are possible for them—particularly in combination with close relationships.

May encouraging someone to construct a "leadership identity" change that person's sense of possibility as a leader? This is the notion behind leadership development programs aimed at women in educational and corporate organizations. Building an identity as a leader, like the construction of other identities, involves a series of interactive processes in which a person engages in certain actions, and others react and provide feedback that informs the person's self-view. The recognition and affirmation of one's exercise of leadership creates a positive spiral, strengthening one's identity as a leader and increasing the motivation to look for new opportunities and take the risks associated with adopting a leadership role. Thus, women are often encouraged to try out leadership behaviors and to seek out opportunities for advancement, under the assumption that they can thus build confidence in capacity for leadership. However, for a woman in most cultures, developing an identity as a leader and integrating that identity as a core part of her self-concept takes place in contexts where leadership is implicitly defined as masculine and feminine authority is met with suspicion (Ely, Insead, and Kolb, 2011). Attempts to develop women's leadership identities and skills must integrate an awareness of the subtle biases and barriers that greet women as they work to advance. One way of thinking about this set of obstacles is to imagine a labyrinth, with many dead-ends and blind alleys.

THE LABYRINTH

Social psychologists Alice Eagly and Linda Carli (2007) chose a labyrinth metaphor to describe the situation which women face in their quest for leadership positions. A labyrinth is full of twists, turns, and impenetrable walls, but there is a viable route to the center. It is an appropriate image, Eagly and Carli argue, because it incorporates the notion of multiple obstacles—from start to finish—rather than a single, impervious barrier (glass ceiling) at the end. Women seeking leadership roles encounter multiple obstacles: prejudice; wage discrimination (often beginning at entry-level jobs); slower promotions to supervisory and administrative positions at all levels; less favorable evaluations; resistance to women's leadership and influence; and demands of family life that fall disproportionately upon women, particularly by giving them less time for professional networking. All of these barriers are chronic; they can appear repeatedly as women advance through their careers, and their effects are cumulative. They are also often so subtle that they go unrecognized—leaving women to feel frustrated and powerless because they cannot seem to translate their ability and motivation into the leadership roles to which they aspire. If a woman does not recognize the ways in which this context may be holding her back, she is likely to internalize a sense of inadequacy instead of an identity as a leader. Eagly and Carli argue that organizations can adopt strategies that increase leadership opportunities for women: reducing the subjectivity of performance evaluation, changing the norm that employees must put in long hours at work to be seen as productive, and providing mentoring relationships that support networking. They also suggest establishing family-friendly human resources practices and encouraging male employees to participate in those benefits. The latter suggestion is a reminder that making the leadership situation better for women can also improve things for men. As Ely and colleagues (2011) note, some of the subtle biases that hold women back are also likely to interfere with the recognition of talented men who do not fit easily into existing organizational norms and structures. Subtle biases may permeate an organization's routine practices, and may not be the result of intentional actions and decisions. Working to eliminate those biases opens doors for a variety of talented individuals.

ARE THERE "FEMALE" AND "MALE" LEADERSHIP STYLES?

Several women world leaders participating in an international panel on development were quick to voice opinions about the differences between men and women as leaders. Helen Clark, former prime minister of New Zealand, said that women look at leadership differently than men: that women are more likely to look at leadership as an opportunity for service, perhaps because women are often so directly involved in caring for children or frail relatives (Saine, 2012). President Ellen Johnson Sirleaf of Liberia noted that it makes a real difference to have women in leadership roles, and President Joyce Banda of Malawi commented that "Leadership is a love affair [...] you must fall in love with the people and the people must fall in love with you" (Saine, 2012: par. 5).

We have seen that women and men in leadership roles are sometimes evaluated differently, depending on their leadership style—suggesting that people may believe that different styles are appropriate for women and for men. But is there any evidence that women and men actually lead differently? Researchers attempting to answer this question have focused on two broad leadership styles: *transformational* and *transactional*. *Transformational leadership* includes four aspects: stimulating followers to think innovatively, motivating followers to contribute to a shared vision, showing consideration and support for followers' concerns and development, and modeling one's own ideals, values, and beliefs. *Transactional leadership*, by contrast, is a style that focuses more narrowly on reaching set goals, completing tasks, assigning rewards and punishments based on performance, and detecting errors (Bass and Avolio, 1994).

Transformational leadership is often the favored contemporary approach. Women in leadership positions show a small but consistent tendency toward a more transformational style than men (Eagly, Johannesen-Schmidt, and van Engen, 2003). The difference appears greatest for the dimension of transformational leadership that encompasses supportive, encouraging treatment of subordinates. Women also differ from men on one dimension of transactional leadership that is strongly linked to leadership effectiveness: rewarding subordinates based on performance. Observers seem to recognize accurately these differences between women and men as leaders (Vinkenburg, van Engen, Eagly, and Johannesen-Schmidt, 2011). It would seem reasonable to assume that these differences may give women a "leadership advantage"—and indeed, a number of commentators in the popular press have speculated that women have the qualities to be better leaders than men. In light of the relative shortage of women leaders in politics and business, this assertion is puzzling.

To unravel the puzzle, it is important to remember that leadership effectiveness is dependent on the context: the type of task being undertaken and the characteristics and attitudes of those being led (Chemers, 1997). We have noted that one difficulty for women leaders lies in a perceived lack of fit or role incongruity between the qualities perceived as necessary for leadership and those stereotyped as desirably feminine. This incongruity can appear especially stark in jobs that are male-dominated or appear to require a large element of masculine toughness—the very leadership roles in which women tend to be scarce and most embattled. To straddle this perceived divide, women leaders must emphasize both their competence *and* their warmth, their decisiveness *and* their supportiveness, their sensitivity *and* their strength. Given this double set of requirements and the necessity to perform a delicate balancing act between them, it would be surprising if women did not approach leadership somewhat differently than men. Because it may help with some elements of this balancing act, the transformational style may be advantageous for female leaders. Transformational leadership incorporates behaviors that are supportive, considerate, and encouraging—all qualities congruent with expectations for women—so this style may present less incongruity for women than did older notions of leadership. Indeed, observers rate individualized consideration as more important for women's than for men's promotion, underlining the necessity for women to "demonstrate both sensitivity and strength, whereas male leaders only need to prove they are strong" (Vinkenburg *et al.*, 2011).

Even if women manage to carry this double burden, however, cultural change can be slow. Particularly in the most masculine stereotyped leader roles, women may continue to be judged against old-fashioned notions of hierarchical leadership, even though today's organizations are likely to be team-based and consensus-oriented. Furthermore, as we have seen, there is a tendency to view men as possessing more of whatever leadership qualities are culturally valued. Both of these factors put the brakes on any tendency for women to gain a leadership advantage through a transformational style. As Eagly and Carli (2007) note, however, organizations can now claim credit for innovation and progressive change when they increase the number of women in leadership roles, and this cultural change continues to be a force toward gender equity.

LEADERS AS ROLE MODELS FOR WOMEN AND MEN

Not surprisingly, people form important aspects of their views of leadership through exposure to leaders. Where most high-profile leaders are men, and where ideals of leadership involve a mainly top-down, directive style, that vision of traditionally masculine, authoritative leadership can be self-perpetuating. The situation may sap women's belief in themselves as possible leaders and may undermine the confidence of both women and men in their leadership abilities if they are not comfortable with that leadership style.

It seems logical that presenting people with role models of leaders who do not fit traditional gendered leadership stereotypes would help women and non-traditional men to articulate possible selves as leaders. Indeed, exposure to women and men in gender-counter-stereotypic roles helps to break down gender stereotypes and can improve persistence in gender-non-traditional fields (e.g., Herrmann *et al.*, 2016; Miller, Eagly, and Linn, 2015). Paradoxically, however, women often seem threatened rather than encouraged when presented with models of highly successful female leaders. Researchers in one study exposed women to successful female leaders, male leaders, or no leaders before they performed a leadership task. The women exposed to the female leaders actually reported lower self-evaluations, more feelings of inferiority, and lower leadership aspirations than did women in the other two groups (Hoyt and Simon, 2011). In another study, exposing women to a description of a very successful female CEO lowered their self-ratings of competence (Parks-Stamm, Heilman, and Hearns, 2008). In a similar vein, women presented with examples of women in powerful positions such as business professor, surgeon, or president of a company's financial division responded by associating themselves less with leadership and showing less interest in masculine jobs (Rudman and Phelan, 2010). Women who read about a successful woman in a masculine stereotyped professional role rated that role as less attainable than did women who were not exposed to the successful woman (Lawson and Lips, 2014). The only conditions under which seeing successful female role models seems to bolster women's confidence in their capacity to achieve such positions are when the role models are explicitly presented as being similar to the respondent (e.g., Asgari, Dasgupta, and Stout, 2012; Lockwood, 2006).

Why should it be so difficult to use successful female role models to inspire other women to aspire to leadership positions? Perhaps women tend to see those role models as very different from themselves—and thus not as appropriate models. Influenced by stereotypes that assert a lack of fit between leadership and femininity, women may view successful female leaders as unfeminine—and thus be repelled rather than attracted by the possibility of becoming like those leaders. Alternatively, women may simply feel that, because they are so exceptional, these successful women are very unusually talented and brave—or very unusually thick-skinned, driven, and unlikable—and may exaggerate the contrast between themselves and the role models. Indeed, when there are few women in senior positions within a company, the women in that company report less likelihood of identifying with senior women or seeking their advice. In an organization in which senior women are scarce, that very scarcity may make these women appear unfit as role models (Ely *et al.*, 2011).

Even if presenting women with role models does not always increase their confidence in their abilities, might it enhance their leadership-related performance? In one study, researchers placed participants in a virtual reality environment and instructed them to deliver a persuasive public speech (Latu, Mast, Lammers, and Bombari, 2013). The virtual environment depicted a room with a responsive 12-person audience, in which a picture of either a successful powerful woman (Angela Merkel or Hillary Clinton), a successful powerful man (Bill Clinton), or no picture was displayed. Researchers measured the length and quality of the speeches and the participants' self-evaluations of their performance. In the presence of either no picture or a picture of Bill Clinton, men spoke longer than women; however, this gender gap disappeared when participants spoke in a virtual room with a picture of Angela Merkel or Hillary Clinton—because women in those conditions spoke longer. Women's speeches were also higher in quality in the female role model conditions, and the women in these conditions evaluated their own performance more positively. Thus, women seemed to be empowered by their exposure to female role models.

This study helps us understand why, despite the discouraging results reported at the beginning of this section, female role models may be important in facilitating the movement of more women into leadership positions. In this study, women did not simply compare themselves in some abstract way to Angela Merkel and Hillary Clinton—and thus, perhaps, trigger feelings that they could never measure up to these outstanding women. Rather, they had the opportunity to perform a challenging, leadership-related task while being presented with these inspiring models. After performing the task successfully, they were able to judge themselves based on having accomplished the task. Rather than contrasting themselves with these exemplary women, perhaps they were able to align themselves psychologically with them, drawing inspiration and empowerment. These findings suggest that the most effective way to use female role models to encourage more women into leadership is to combine exposure to role models with chances for women to tackle leadership tasks.

This study, along with a number of others, showed no effect of gender of role model on male participants. This may be because there are so many more visible male than visible female leaders in our social environment—thus men have many more available same-gender leader role models and simply take male leadership for granted.

THE IMPACT OF LEADERSHIP POSITIONS UPON THE MEN AND WOMEN WHO HOLD THEM

When Hillary Clinton prepared to step down from her post as US Secretary of State, after four years in which she logged some 1700 meetings with world leaders, 956,733 airplane miles, and visits to 112 different countries, she said she would like to "catch up on about 20 years of sleep deprivation" and see if she could get "untired" (Hillary Clinton on life after being Secretary of State, 2013). Veteran US Congressman David Obey, preparing to retire from office in 2010 after 21 terms, commented that "quite frankly, I am bone tired" (Ruffini, 2010: par. 2). Similarly, US Representative Barney Frank, preparing to step down, said, "after 45 years, I'm tired" (Lavender, 2012: par. 2). Clearly, one likely impact of serving in a demanding leadership position is exhaustion. That effect may or may not be linked to gender—but our knowledge about the different conditions that surround male and female leaders suggests that gender-related expectations can make a difference to the way leadership is experienced.

In a ground-breaking study, Erika Apfelbaum (1993) interviewed Norwegian and French women in high leadership positions. The specific contexts provided by Norway and France for these women's leadership made profound differences to their experiences. For French women in the late twentieth century, leadership felt burdensome, difficult, and conflict-laden. By contrast, the Norwegian women enjoyed being leaders and spoke positively about their roles. Apfelbaum attributed these differences, in part, to the differing histories of the two countries. Even in the early 1990s, Norway had a long history of gender equality and there were already a substantial number of women in high political office, whereas France was not used to women in leadership positions and had relatively few. The Norwegian women felt solidly grounded in their legitimacy as leaders; the French women felt embattled. Most of the Norwegian women were married, and said they had few problems balancing marriage with a demanding career; most of the French women were single, and reported difficulties in achieving a satisfactory balance between their personal relationships and their high-powered roles. These findings are a reminder that women are likely to pay a high price for leadership, not in every situation, but in contexts where women leaders are unusual and the culture does not support women as legitimate leaders. Male leaders seem less likely to suffer such difficulties in institutional environments where male leaders are rare—perhaps because male leadership, even when unusual, is seen as legitimate (Cognard-Black, 2004). In the absence of societies where female leadership is much more strongly expected than male leadership, it is not possible to examine the impact upon men of a situation parallel to the situation that existed for French women in the early 1990s. However, it would be possible to examine how the experience of female leaders in Norway and France has changed as the cultural context has shifted since the 1990s. In Norway, gender equality in politics has remained strong. In 2017, women held almost 40 percent of the seats in the Norwegian legislature—almost the same percentage as 20 years ago. The country has had two female prime ministers: Gro Harlem Brundtland and Erna Solberg. In France, a shift toward increased political gender equality has been quite dramatic, but that country still lags behind Norway. Two women (Ségolène Royal and Marine Le Pen) have made credible runs for the presidency; women hold just under 26 percent of seats in the National Assembly (up from 6.4 percent 20 years ago) and over 27 percent of seats in the Senate (up from 5.6 percent 20 years ago) of the French Parliament (Inter-Parliamentary Union, 2017). These changes have likely improved the leadership experience for French women.

FOR FURTHER EXPLORATION

Chin, Jean Lau, Lott, Bernice, Rice, Joy K. and Sanchez-Hucles, Janis (eds) (2007). *Women and leadership: Transforming visions and diverse voices* (Malden, MA: Blackwell Publishing). This collection adopts a feminist perspective and contains chapters on topics that include communication styles, women as academic and corporate leaders, the impact of diverse cultural contexts, collaborative leadership, and developing transformational leaders, along with chapters dedicated to leadership among Latinas, Black, Asian American, and American Indian women, women with disabilities, and lesbian women.

Ducat, Stephen J. (2004). *The wimp factor: Gender gaps, holy wars, and the politics of anxious masculinity* (Boston, MA: Beacon Press). The author analyzes the history of Western culture from the point of view of gender attitudes. With a particular focus on American politics and foreign policy, he argues that much of the nation's foreign and domestic policy is driven by the desire to demonstrate "masculine" self-reliance and dominance, and to reject "feminine" approaches of care and nurturing.

Eagly, Alice H. and Carli, Linda L. (2007). *Through the labyrinth: The truth about how women become leaders* (Boston, MA: Harvard Business School Publishing). Two social psychologists examine the research to determine why it remains so difficult to get women into leadership positions. They argue that the glass ceiling image is less appropriate than a labyrinth metaphor to describe the barriers women face in their careers as they try to negotiate the paths to power.

Rajasekar, J. and Beh, L. (eds) (2013*). Culture and gender in leadership: Perspectives from the Middle East and Asia* (London: Palgrave Macmillan UK). The editors offer a varied set of articles focused on how gender and culture shape leadership opportunities and expression in countries such as Korea, Afghanistan, United Arab Emirates, China, and India.

Rhode, Deborah L. (ed.) (2017). *Women and leadership* (New York: Oxford University Press). With an up-to-date introduction and a compilation of classic articles on women in leadership, the editor, a legal scholar at Stanford University and former chair of the American Bar Association's Commission on Women in the Profession, provides thought-provoking sections on women leaders in politics, management, law, academia, and on boards.

REFERENCES

Adreoni, J. and Petrie, R. (2008). Beauty, gender and stereotypes: Evidence from laboratory experiments. *Journal of Economic Psychology, 29*, 73–93.

Apfelbaum, E. (1993). Norwegian and French women in high leadership positions: The importance of cultural contexts upon gendered relations. *Psychology of Women Quarterly, 17*, 409–429. doi: 10.1111/j.1471-6402.1993. tb00653.x.

Asgari, S., Dasgupta, N., and Stout, J.G. (2012). When do counterstereotypic ingroup members inspire versus deflate? The effect of successful professional women on young women's leadership self-concept. *Personality and Social Psychology Bulletin, 38*, 370–383. doi: 10.1177/0146167211431968.

Bass, B.M. and Avolio, B.J. (1994). *Improving organizational effectiveness through transformational leadership.* Thousand Oaks, CA: Sage.

BBC (2012). EU defends women-on-boards plans. BBC News, November 14. www.bbc.co.uk/news/business-20322317.

BBC (2014). Bolivian women battle against culture of harassment. BBC News, March 12. www.bbc.com/news/world-latin-america-26446066.

Bennett, J. (2010). The beauty advantage. *Newsweek*, July 19. www.thedaily beast.com/newsweek/2010/07/19/the-beautyadvantage.html.

Bikorimana, D. (2012). Rwanda: The land of gender equality? *Think Africa Press*, May 15. http://thinkafricapress.com/rwanda/womengender equality.

Bongiorno, R., Bain, P.G., and David, B. (2014). If you're going to be a leader, at least act like it! Prejudice towards women who are tentative in leader roles. *British Journal of Social Psychology, 53*, 217–234. doi: http://dx.doi.org/10.1111/bjso.12032.

Braun, S., Peus, C., and Frey, D. (2012). Is beauty beastly? Gender-specific effects of leader attractiveness and leadership style on followers' trust and loyalty. *Zeitschrift für Psychologie, 220*, 98–108. doi: 10.1027/2151-2604/a000101.

Brescoll, V.L. (2011). Who takes the floor and why: Gender, power, and volubility in organizations. *Administrative Science Quarterly, 56*, 622–641. doi: 10.1177/0001839212439994.

Brescoll, V.L. (2016). Leading with their hearts? How gender stereotypes of emotion lead to biased evaluations of female leaders. *The Leadership Quarterly*, *27*, 415–428. doi: 10.1016/j.leaqua.2016.02.005.

Brescoll, V.L. and Uhlmann, E.L. (2008). Can an angry woman get ahead? Status conferral, gender, and expression of emotion in the workplace. *Psychological Science*, *19*, 268–275. doi: 10.1111/j.1467-9280.2008.02079.x.

Brescoll, V.L., Uhlmann, E.L., Moss-Racusin, C., and Sarnell, L. (2012). Masculinity, status, and subordination: Why working for a gender stereotype violator causes men to lose status. *Journal of Experimental Social Psychology*, *48*, 354–357. doi: 10.1016/j.jesp. 2011.06.005.

Catalyst (2006). *Different cultures, similar perceptions: Stereotyping of Western European business leaders*. New York: Catalyst. www.catalyst.org/knowledge/different-cultures-similar-perceptions-stereotypingwestern-european-business-leaders.

Catalyst (2007). *The double-bind dilemma for women in leadership: Damned if you do, doomed if you don't*. New York: Catalyst. www.catalyst.org/knowledge/double-bind-dilemma-women-leadership-damnedif-you-do-doomed-if-you-dont-0.

Catalyst (2017). Quick take: Women on corporate boards globally. New York: Catalyst, January 4. www.catalyst.org/knowledge/women-corporate-boards-globally.

Chemers, M.M. (1997). *An integrative theory of leadership*. Mahwah, NJ: Erlbaum.

Cognard-Black, A.J. (2004). Will they stay, or will they go? Sex-atypical work among token men who teach. *The Sociological Quarterly*, *45*, 113–139. doi: 10.1111/j.1533-8525.2004.tb02400.x.

Constitution of the Republic of Rwanda (2003). www.rwandahope.com/constitution.pdf.

Cuadrado, I., García-Ael, C., and Molero, F. (2015). Gender-typing of leadership: Evaluations of real and ideal managers. *Scandinavian Journal of Psychology*, *56*, 236–244. doi: 10.1111/sjop. 12187.

Dabbous, Y. and Ladley, A. (2010). A spine of steel and a heart of gold: Newspaper coverage of the first female Speaker of the House. *Journal of Gender Studies*, *19*, 181–94. doi: 10.1080/09589231003695971.

Eagly, A.H. and Carli, L.L. (2007). *Through the labyrinth: The truth about how women become leaders*. Boston, MA: Harvard Business School Publishing.

Eagly, A.H. and Karau, S.J. (2002). Role congruity theory of prejudice toward female leaders. *Psychological Review*, *109*, 573–598. doi: 10.1037/0033-295X.109.3.573.

Eagly, A.H., Johannesen-Schmidt, M.C., and van Engen, M.L. (2003). Transformational, transactional, and laissez-faire leadership styles: A meta-analysis comparing women and men. *Psychological Bulletin, 129*, 569–591. doi: 10.1037/0033-2909.129.4.569.

Eagly, A.H., Karau, S.J., Miner, J.B., and Johnson, B.T. (1994). Gender and motivation to manage in hierarchic organizations: A meta-analysis. *The Leadership Quarterly, 5*(2), 135–159. doi: 10.1016/1048-9843(94)90025-6.

Ely, R.J., Insead, H.I., and Kolb, D.M. (2011). Taking gender into account: Theory and design for women's leadership development programs. *Academy of Management Learning and Education, 10*, 474–493.

European Women on Boards (2016). *Gender Diversity on European boards*. April. http://european.ewob-network.eu/wp-content/uploads/2016/04/EWoB-quant-report-WEB-spreads.pdf.

Fortune (2016). Most powerful women. http://fortune.com/most-powerful-women/.

Glick, P., Larsen, S., Johnson, C. and Branstiter, H. (2005). Evaluations of sexy women in low- and high-status jobs. *Psychology of Women Quarterly 29*, 389–95. doi: 10.1111/j.1471-6402.2005.00238.x.

Halila, S. (2008). The new female Muslim thinkers or DWEMS (Daring Women as Enlightened Muslim Scholars). *The International Journal of the Humanities, 6*. http://thehumanities.com/publications/journal/.

Heilman, M.E. (1983). Sex bias in work settings: The lack of fit model. *Research in Organizational Behavior, 5*, 269–298.

Heilman, M.E. and Stopeck, M.H. (1985). Being attractive, advantage or disadvantage? Performance-based evaluations and recommended personnel actions as a function of appearance, sex, and job type. *Organizational Behavior and Human Decision Processes, 35*, 202–215.

Herrmann, S.D., Adelman, R.M., Bodford, J.E., Graudejus, O., Okun, M.A., and Kwan, V.S.Y. (2016). The effects of a female role model on academic performance and persistence of women in STEM courses. *Basic and Applied Social Psychology, 38*, 258–268. doi: 10.1080/01973533.2016.1209757.

Hillary Clinton on life after being Secretary of State: "I hope to get to sleep in" (2013). *The Huffington Post*, January 30. www.huffingtonpost.com/2013/01/30/hillary-clinton-sleep-deprivation_n_2581005.html?ir=Healthy+Living.

Hoyt, C.L. and Simon, S. (2011). Female leaders: Injurious or inspiring role models for women? *Psychology of Women Quarterly, 35*, 143–157. doi: 10.1177/0361684310385216.

Inter-Parliamentary Union (2018). Women in national parliaments. Situation as of April 1st 2018. http://archive.ipu.org/wmn-e/classif.htm.

Iron Ladies of Liberia (2008). Independent Lens. Public Broadcasting System. www.pbs.org/independentlens/ironladies/film.html.

Johnson, S.K., Podratz, D.E., Dipboye, R.L., and Gibbons, E. (2010). Physical attractiveness biases in ratings of employment suitability: Tracking down the "beauty is beastly" effect. *The Journal of Social Psychology, 150*, 301–318. doi: 10.1080/00224540903365414.

Killeen, L.A., Lopez-Zafra, E., and Eagly, A.H. (2006). Envisioning oneself as a leader: Comparisons of women and men in Spain and the United States. *Psychology of Women Quarterly, 30*, 312–322.

Koenig, A.M., Eagly, A.H., Mitchell, A.A., and Ristikari, T. (2011). Are leader stereotypes masculine? A meta-analysis of three research paradigms. *Psychological Bulletin, 137*, 616–642. doi: 10.1037/a0023557.

Latu, I.M., Mast, M.S., Lammers, J., and Bombari, D. (2013). Successful female leaders empower women's behavior in leadership tasks. *Journal of Experimental Social Psychology* (published online before print). doi: 10.1016/j.jesp.2013.01.003.

Lavender, P. (2012). Barney Frank: Retirement will be welcomed because "I'm tired." *Huffington Post*, December 26. www.huffingtonpost.com/2012/12/26/barney-frank-retirement-_n_2364927.html.

Lawson, K.M. and Lips, H.L. (2014). The role of self-perceived agency and job attainability in women's impressions of successful women. *Journal of Applied Psychology, 44*, 433–441. doi: 10.1111/jasp. 12236.

Lips, H.M. (2000). College students' visions of power and possibility as moderated by gender. *Psychology of Women Quarterly, 24*, 39–43. doi: 10.1111/j.1471-6402.2000.tb01020.x.

Lips, H.M. (2001). Envisioning positions of leadership: The expectations of university students in Virginia and Puerto Rico. *Journal of Social Issues, 57*, 799–813. doi: 10.1111/0022-4537.00242.

Little, A. (2012, October 10). Australian Prime Minister schools misogynist in awesome rant. *Ms.blog*, October 10. http://msmagazine.com/blog/2012/10/10/australian-prime-minister-schools-misogynist-inawesome-rant/.

Llanos, B. (2011). *Unseeing eyes: Media coverage and gender in Latin American elections*. International Institute for Democracy and Electoral Assistance. www.idea.int/publications/unseeing-eyes/index.cfm.

Lockwood, P. (2006). "Someone like me can be successful": Do college students need same gender role models? *Psychology of Women Quarterly, 30*, 36–46. doi: 10.1111/j.1471-6402.2006.00260.x.

Markus, H. and Nurius, P. (1986). Possible selves. *American Psychologist, 41*, 954–969. doi: 10.1037/0003-066X.41.9.954.

Miller, D.I., Eagly, A.H., and Linn, M.C. (2015). Women's representation in science predicts national gender-science stereotypes: Evidence from 66 nations. *Journal of Educational Psychology, 107*, 631–644. doi: 10.1037/edu0000005.

Okimoto, T.G. and Brescoll, V.L. (2010). The price of power: Power seeking and backlash against female politicians. *Personality and Social Psychology Bulletin, 36*, 923–936. doi: 10.1177/0146167210371949.

O'Neill, O.A. and O'Reilly, C. (2011). Overcoming the backlash effect: Self-monitoring and women's promotions. *Journal of Occupational and Organizational Psychology, 84*, 825–832. doi: 10.1111/j.2044-8325.2010.02008.x.

Opolade, D. (2012). The fairer leaders. *The New York Times*, July 10. http://latitude.blogs.nytimes.com/2012/07/10/african-states-aheadof-the-west-in-female-political-representation/.

Oxfam (2012). *50 years later: Women and social change in Cuba*. www.oxfam.ca/sites/default/files/imce/women-social-change-cuba.pdf.

Parks-Stamm, E.J., Heilman, M.E., and Hearns, K.A. (2008). Motivated to penalize: women's strategic rejection of successful women. *Personality and Social Psychology Bulletin, 34*, 237–247. doi: 10.1177/0146167207310027.

Rudman, L.A. and Glick, P. (1999). Feminized management and backlash toward agentic women: The hidden costs to women of a kinder, gentler image of middle managers. *Journal of Personality and Social Psychology, 77*, 1004–1010. doi: 10.1037/0022-3514.77.5.1004.

Rudman, L.A. and Phelan, J.E. (2010). The effect of priming gender roles on women's implicit gender beliefs and career aspirations. *Social Psychology, 41*, 192–202. doi: 10.1027/1864-9335/a000027.

Ruffini, C. (2010). David Obey, "Bone tired," to retire from Congress. *CBS News*, May 5. www.cbsnews.com/8301-503544_162-20004248-503544.html.

Sabic, P. (2016). How times have changed? Transatlantic CEO gender gap analysis of the S&P Euro 350 and S&P 500. *S&P Global. Market Intelligence.* www.spcapitaliq-corporations.com/cms/wp-content/uploads/2016/09/How-Times-Have-Changed.-CEO-Gender-Gap-Analysis-SPEuro350_SP-500-sept-2016.pdf?t=1475006696.

Saine, C. (2012). Africa's female presidents say they offer different kind of leadership. *Voice of America*, June 11. www.voanews.com/content/africas-female-presidents-say-they-offer-different-kindleadership/1206098.html.

Schein, V.E. (1973). The relationship between sex role stereotypes and requisite management characteristics. *Journal of Applied Psychology, 57*, 95–100. doi: 10.1037/h0037128.

Schein, V.E., Mueller, R., Lituchy, T., and Liu, J. (1996). Think manager—think male: A global phenomenon? *Journal of Organizational Behavior, 17*, 33–41. doi: 10.1002/(SICI)1099-1379(199601)17:1<33::AID-JOB778>3.0.CO;2-F.

Smith, J.L., Paul, D., and Paul, R. (2007). No place for a woman: Evidence for gender bias in evaluations of presidential candidates. *Basic and Applied Social Psychology, 29*, 225–233. doi: 10.1080/01973530701503069.

Torregrosa, L.L. (2012, May 1). Cuba may be the most feminist country in Latin America. *International Herald Tribune*, May 1. http://rendezvous. blogs.nytimes.com/2012/05/01/cuba-may-be-the-most-feminist-countryin-latin-america/.

UN Women (2013). *Bolivia. Gender-based political violence.* Advancing gender equality: Promising practices. Case studies from the Millennium Development Goals Achievement Fund.www.unwomen.org/mdgf/C/Bolivia_C. html.

Vial, A.C., Napier, J.L., and Brescoll, V.L. (2016). A bed of thorns: Female leaders and the self-reinforcing cycle of illegitimacy. *The Leadership Quarterly, 27*, 400–414. doi: 10.1016/j.leaqua.2015.12.004.

Vinkenburg, C.J., van Engen, M.L., Eagly, A.H., and Johannesen-Schmidt, M.C. (2011). An exploration of stereotypical beliefs about leadership styles: Is transformational leadership a route to women's promotion? *The Leadership Quarterly, 22*, 10–21. http://dx.doi.org/10.1016/j.leaqua.2010.12.003.

Wang, M. and Kelan, E. (2012). The gender quota and female leadership: effects of the Norwegian gender quota on board chairs and ceos. *Journal of Business Ethics*, December 14, no pagination specified. doi: 10.1007/s10551-012-1546-5.

Winter, D.G. (1988). The power motive in women—and men. *Journal of Personality and Social Psychology, 54*, 510–519.

World Economic Forum (2016). *The global gender gap report.* Geneva, Switzerland: Author. www3.weforum.org/docs/GGGR16/WEF_Global_Gender_Gap_Report_2016.pdf.

7

GLOBAL PATTERNS OF GENDER-RELATED VIOLENCE

In January 2013, the U.S. Defense Department announced that it would lift the ban against American women serving in combat positions, and in 2015, all US military combat positions were opened to women. Although women make up more than 14 percent of that nation's active duty military, and many female soldiers have been injured or killed during the wars in Iraq and Afghanistan, women had been excluded from the 230,000 positions that officially involve direct combat. In certain other countries (e.g., Canada, Australia, New Zealand), women already serve in combat roles (Barnes and Nissenbaum, 2013).

Resistance to women in combat has a long history. Women, it has been argued, cannot meet the physical standards for combat roles. Women are not tough enough for the dangers of combat or the rigors, discomfort, and dirt of the battlefield. Women taken by the enemy in war risk being raped. The presence of women will endanger male military personnel because, in battle, the men will take special risks to protect the women—and the women will not be able to protect the men. Common themes in these arguments are a visceral discomfort with the notion of women engaging in active, potentially lethal, physical aggression, and a feeling that women need protection. These ideas are rooted in the descriptive and prescriptive stereotypes of femininity outlined in earlier chapters: women are supposed to be gentle, nurturing, compassionate, caring, accommodating—not tough, aggressive, decisive, or willing to take physical risks.

These stereotypes feed the notion that women need special protection—an idea linked to benevolent sexism—and that society is providing that protection by keeping them out of combat roles. However, even when not officially in combat, military women are often subjected to violence. This point became starkly clear to the US public early in the Iraq War, when Pfc Lori Piestewa, who was not in a combat role but driving a transport truck, was killed when her unit was ambushed (Legon, 2003). Furthermore, military women need not even be deployed in order to face violence. In the same week as the combat rule change was announced, congressional hearings were investigating a pervasive pattern of sexual assault of recruits and trainees at a Texas Air Force base. The "enemy" who perpetrated the assaults in this case were the women's instructors during basic training (Bernard, 2013). Sexual assault appears to be a continuing and pervasive problem in all branches of the US military (Lamothe, 2017), underlining the irony of the claim that women are somehow being protected by being kept out of combat roles.

Considerations of women, men, and violence produce strong emotional reactions, in part because they activate powerful prescriptive stereotypes of femininity and masculinity. We have learned to think about aggression and violence as gendered.

INTERPERSONAL VIOLENCE IS GENDERED

Violence is associated with men and with masculinity: men are most often both the perpetrators and victims of the assaults and homicides that end up in the public record (Federal Bureau of Investigation, 2015). Researchers who study aggression in laboratory situations or through self- or peer-report find a greater likelihood of male than female direct and physical aggression among children (Lansford et al., 2012), adolescents (Card, Stucky, Sawalani, and Little, 2008), and adults (Archer, 2004). Males have also been found to be higher in verbal aggression, though by a smaller margin

(Archer, 2004). Gender differences in aggression are consistent but modest, and most often appear where the provocation for aggression is low and where the norms of the situation favor male more than female aggression (Eagly and Steffen, 1986; Giancola et al., 2002; Hyde, 1984). Gender differences in *relational aggression* (aggression that harms another by damaging her or his social status and/or relationships) are not so consistent (Lansford et al., 2012). Relational aggression fits more neatly with femininity stereotypes and is more socially acceptable for women than physical aggression.

It is tempting to suppose that this type of aggression is more characteristic of women than of men, but both women and men, girls and boys, engage in relational aggression, depending on the circumstances (Loflin and Barry, 2016).

It may well be the case that women and men do not differ in how aggressive they are, but rather in the kinds of aggression they display. Men are no more likely than women to get angry, but they choose forms of aggression that are riskier or more costly, such as physical aggression, use of weapons, or direct confrontation (Archer, 2004). There is abundant evidence that women can and do behave aggressively, and that they have as much potential as men to be aggressive (Richardson, 2005; White and Kowalski, 1994). However, both women's and men's display of aggression is likely shaped by social norms, the power distribution in a given situation, and the potential costs of various behavioral options.

Men, in particular, often find themselves in situations where they are expected to behave aggressively. As part of the masculine role in many cultures, men are supposed to be the protectors and defenders of their families, their communities, their nations. They are more likely than women to be placed in roles, such as police and military occupations, that require aggression. Yet even when men conform to the requirements of these roles by doing what they must, they can pay a significant cost. For example, Timothy Kudo (2013), US Marine Corps veteran of the war in Afghanistan, writes that he carries with him "every day" the unshakeable memories of the incidents in which he ordered people to be killed. Noting that the Department of Veterans Affairs has labeled this problem as a *moral injury*, Kudo comments: "This isn't the kind of injury you recover from with rest, physical therapy and pain medication."

For men the cost of *not* behaving aggressively in some situations may be humiliation and a devastating loss of status or self-esteem. Perhaps for this reason, one significant trigger for overt aggressive behavior by men appears to be challenges to their masculinity—men may sometimes behave in physically aggressive ways to restore masculine status that has been threatened (Bosson, Vandello, Burnaford, Weaver, and Wasti, 2009). One Canadian study showed, for instance, that when men have lower economic or educational status than their female partners, they are more likely to be emotionally abusive (Kaukinen, 2004).

One problem with understanding violence from a gender perspective, then, is that violence is interpreted differently when perpetrated by women and by men. A man behaving violently may be seen as acting out his masculinity, but a woman behaving violently is defying or undermining perceptions of her femininity. Furthermore, because women are viewed as weaker than men, their aggression—particularly against men—may not be taken seriously. Such considerations must inform the analysis of gendered patterns of violence.

Masculinity in certain situations involves claiming status in a hierarchy and power over others. In particular, masculinity often implies superiority to, and power over, women. Perhaps, then, it is not surprising that acts of interpersonal violence by men are often directed at the women with whom they are in intimate relationships—and that acts of interpersonal violence by women are often directed, frequently in self-defense, at male partners.

INTIMATE PARTNER VIOLENCE

Like other forms of violence, family violence is not gender neutral. As Figures 7.1 and 7.2 show, women are more likely than men to be targets of abuse from intimate partners. Although both women and men can be perpetrators or victims of domestic violence, women are far more likely than men to suffer serious injury, to live in terror of a spouse, or to have to flee their homes for their own or their children's safety (Office for National Statistics, 2016a; Smith *et al.*, 2017). This pattern holds true all over the world (World Health Organization, 2012). However, as we will see, this

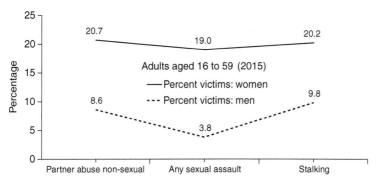

Lifetime prevalence of intimate violence (since age 16) in England and Wales

Figure 7.1 Prevalence of intimate partner violence in England and Wales among adults. Both women and men may suffer at the hands of an intimate partner, but crime statistics show that women are more likely than men to be targets of all types of abuse from partners.

Source: Based on data from Office for National Statistics (2016b).

does not mean that women do not perpetrate intimate partner violence. It also does not mean that intimate partner violence can always be considered within neat categories based on gender binaries: male-on-female, female-on-male, female-on-female, male-on-male. Although most of the available statistics do fit these binary categories, researchers have usually not given respondents the option to declare their gender as something other than female or male (e.g., transgender, genderqueer). Individuals experience and manifest gender in a multitude of ways, and intimate partner violence can occur in any partnership.

Violence in intimate partnerships can be physical (such as hitting, kicking, choking), sexual (such as rape, coercion of specific sexual acts), or psychological (such as insults, screaming, isolating the individual from friends or family). All can have devastating consequences, and they often occur in concert (Black *et al.*, 2011).

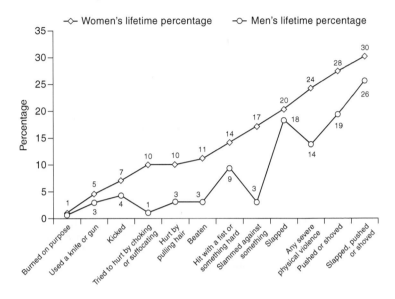

Figure 7.2 US lifetime prevalence of types of physical violence by an intimate partner. Both women and men may be victims of severe physical violence, such as being beaten, kicked, or choked by an intimate partner. Over a lifetime, the percentage of women reporting such violence is higher than men for almost every form of physical violence.

Source: Based on data from Black *et al*. (2011).

INTIMATE PARTNER VIOLENCE AGAINST WOMEN

MALE PARTNER VIOLENCE AGAINST WOMEN

The statistics on abuse of women by male intimate partners are staggering. The World Health Organization (Garcia-Moreno, Jansen, Ellsberg, Heise, and Watts , 2005) found that, across ten countries (Bangladesh, Brazil, Ethiopia, Japan, Peru, Namibia, Samoa, Serbia and Montenegro, Thailand and the United Republic of Tanzania), the proportion of women who reported ever experiencing physical or sexual violence from a partner ranged from a low of 15 percent to a high of 71 percent. When asked only about their experience of the previous year, the proportion of women reporting partner violence still ranged from 4 to 54 percent. Women who had ever experienced severe physical violence at the hands of a partner (being hit with a fist, kicked, dragged, threatened or harmed with a weapon) ranged from 4 to 49 percent. In the United States, almost one in every four women has experienced severe physical violence from an intimate partner during her lifetime (Black *et al.*, 2011).

Since the violence takes place in the context of an ongoing relationship, acts of domestic violence tend not to be one-time events but rather become long-term patterns. The WHO study found that most women who experienced intimate partner violence once experienced it repeatedly—a finding that is consistent with other investigations of domestic violence (Frieze, 2005). There are many different patterns of violence within couples (Frieze, 2005, 2008; Williams and Frieze, 2005); two that have been identified have been labeled "intimate terrorism," involving one-sided abusive violence, and "common couple violence," involving fairly low-level mutual violence that rarely results in injury (Johnson and Ferraro, 2000). Women in the first group, being terrorized by a partner, may find it impossible to leave the situation. They may have no safe place to go, be economically dependent on their partner, or be so demoralized by the violence and the accompanying verbal abuse that their self-confidence in their ability to live independently is shattered (Arias and Pape, 2015). However, if they stay in the situation, and even if they fear for their lives, many abused women develop strategies for survival and coping with the abuse—often including fighting back verbally and/or physically (Miller and Meloy, 2006). When a woman does leave, the danger of the situation often escalates as an outraged husband or partner tracks her down and vents his anger in a violent, or even lethal, attack (Brownridge, 2006).

We have already seen that men do not seem to be essentially more angry or aggressive than women. What, then, is the explanation for so much male violence directed at female partners? One important explanation may lie in cultural gender arrangements. As noted above, men can use violence to act out masculinity—particularly as masculinity implies power over women. Furthermore, societal arrangements and norms sometimes give men formal or informal authority over their wives and daughters, thus providing perceived legitimacy to the use of force against them—and giving women little recourse when they are targets of violence by a spouse. One survey of women in Iraq found that 63 percent agreed that a husband is justified in beating his wife (Linos, Khawaja, and Kaplan, 2012). Research in India showed that women's risk of intimate violence was linked to tolerance of violence against women in their communities (Boyle, Georgiades, Cullen, and Racine, 2009). A Canadian study revealed that men who are more accepting of a patriarchal ideology are more likely to be violent toward their wives (Lenton, 1995). Thus culturally supported gender ideology provides some plausible explanations for the pervasiveness of male violence against female intimate partners. However, if enacting masculinity and exerting male authority were the only causes of intimate partner violence, intimate partner violence against women by female partners would be extremely rare. This does not seem to be the case.

FEMALE PARTNER VIOLENCE AGAINST WOMEN

Intimate partner violence does not occur only in heterosexual couples. One recent study of sexual minority young adults shows that violence within intimate partners is common and individuals at greatest risk for such violence are those who identify as female, male-to-female transgender, and Black/African American young adults (Reuter, Newcomb, Whitton, and Mustanski, 2017). A national survey in the United States revealed that nearly one in three respondents who self-identified as lesbian had, at least once in her lifetime, experienced severe physical violence from an intimate partner. More than two-thirds of these respondents reported that the perpetrator of the violence was female (Walters, Chen, and Breiding, 2013). This survey indicated that violence is as common in lesbian and gay intimate partnerships as in heterosexual couples. However, because there is little acknowledgement of female-on-female intimate partner violence, and few sources of support for survivors, many women who have experienced violence within lesbian relationships report feeling silenced and isolated (Walters, 2011). The invisibility of intimate partner violence in lesbian couples may be linked to gender stereotypes that women are not physically aggressive or violent.

Like violence in intimate heterosexual relationships, violence in lesbian couples may be associated with factors specific to the relationship, such as power imbalances or dependency. However, the phenomenon also reflects a cultural context of stereotyping and discrimination based on sexual orientation. For women in lesbian relationships, the stresses associated with being in a sexual minority can be associated with both lower relationship quality and intimate partner violence. Women in lesbian couples who have most strongly internalized the surrounding culture's negative attitudes about lesbians are most likely to experience poor relationship quality and, in turn, to perpetrate or be victimized by violence in that relationship (Balsam and Szymanski, 2005).

INTIMATE PARTNER VIOLENCE AGAINST MEN

VIOLENCE AGAINST MEN BY FEMALE PARTNERS

About one in every seven men in the United States reports experiencing in his lifetime severe physical violence (slammed against something, hit with a fist or something hard, or beaten) by an intimate partner; about 2 percent report experiencing this type of violence during the previous year (Black *et al.*, 2011). Among heterosexual men, more than 99 percent of those who say they have experienced intimate partner violence report that the perpetrator was female (Walters *et al.*, 2013). Global statistics on the abuse of men by female intimate partners are less available than comparable statistics for female targets of abuse by men.

On surveys of violence in intimate heterosexual relationships in Western countries, women are as likely, or more likely, than men to report being violent, and slightly more men than women say they have been targets of one-sided severe violence (Archer, 2000; Williams and Frieze, 2005). These findings run counter to most people's expectations, and indicate that intimate partner violence is a more complex phenomenon than men battering women. One possible explanation for women's higher reports of perpetrating violence is that women may be more likely than men to fight back against partner violence—because some male victims may feel it is illegitimate to be physically aggressive against a woman. Another possible explanation is the presence of a reporting bias: because male violence against women is not socially acceptable, men may be more reluctant than women to admit committing violent acts against an intimate partner of the other gender.

Male victims of severe intimate partner violence may have little recourse for help and support. There are fewer services available to male victims, and men are less likely than women to report their victimization or call upon law enforcement for assistance (Nowinski and Bowen, 2012). Since gender stereotypes portray men as tougher than women, it can be very difficult for a man to admit being abused by a female partner, and it can be difficult for others to believe that he is unable to stop the abuse.

VIOLENCE AGAINST MEN BY MALE PARTNERS

Among gay men in the United States, the reported lifetime prevalence of severe physical violence by an intimate partner is 16.4 percent (Walters *et al.*, 2013). More than 90 percent of these men reported only male perpetrators. The violence may be precipitated by stress in the relationship and, as in other types of couples, gender stereotypes and ideology may play a role. For example, in one study of gay male couples in Cuba, economic hardship appeared to lead to feelings of threatened masculinity, which led in turn to violence as a reassertion of masculinity (Santaya and Walters, 2011).

Overall, it appears that, at least in the countries where both male- and female-initiated violence in different kinds of intimate couples have been studied, intimate partner violence occurs in heterosexual and same-gender couples with approximately similar frequency, and that women as well as men perpetrate violence, even severe violence, on intimate partners. However, this does not imply that gender is irrelevant to understanding intimate partner violence. It is not clear that the same violent behaviors have the same meaning or impact for women and men in intimate relationships, or that all the most appropriate questions are being asked of women and men in surveys of intimate partner violence. For example, it may mean something different to a man than to a woman to push or be pushed by a partner. And if a woman's clothes are destroyed by her partner, she may perhaps experience that as more violent than a slap—but destruction of clothing may not even be included in the list of violent acts used in the measures of violence (McHugh, Livingston, and Ford, 2005). A difference in the underlying meaning may help explain the robust and consistent finding that women victimized by violence in an intimate relationship experience more negative psychosocial outcomes, such as distress and marital dissatisfaction, than do men (Williams and Frieze, 2005).

INTIMATE PARTNER VIOLENCE AGAINST TRANSGENDER PERSONS

Research on intimate partner violence involving transgender individuals, although scarce, indicates that they may experience higher rates of such violence than cisgender people—perhaps lifetime rates as high as 50 percent (Yerke and DeFeo, 2016). Furthermore, transgender persons who are victimized by their partners may face particular difficulties in finding help. If they seek police assistance, they are more likely than other violence victims to encounter discrimination, harassment, or even assault. If they go to a domestic violence shelter, they may be turned away because they are not "real" women. Medical professionals may discriminate against them. Thus, transgender people in abusive relationships are likely to have access to even fewer avenues of help and escape than others in violent relationships.

Intimate partner violence exploits the vulnerabilities of the victim, so it is not surprising that emotional abuse based on transgender prejudice is a common type of intimate partner abuse reported by transgender respondents (Yerke and DeFeo, 2016). This abuse may include threatening to disclose the person's gender identity or birth-assigned sex, withholding of resources for hormone treatments and surgeries or for items related to gender expression such as wigs and clothing, and negative comments about physical features (e.g., breasts, genitals) that mark the transgender person as not a "real" woman or man. Physical violence also often targets these aspects of the transgender person's body. Perhaps more than any other category of intimate partner violence, this violence centers on feelings about gender—making an individual's gender identity a source of vulnerability and pain.

STALKING

Stalking is a pattern of threats or harassment, often involving unwanted contact or obvious surveillance. Examples of stalking include repeated harassing phone calls or emails, following or spying on the target person, or leaving items for the target to find. About one out of every six women and one out of every nineteen men in the United States reports being stalked during their lifetime (Black et al., 2011). Most stalking is done by people who know the target person. For more than two-thirds of female victims and just over 41 percent of male victims, the perpetrator is a current or former intimate partner. Women are much more likely to be stalked by men than by women; men are likely to be targeted about equally by male and female stalkers. Stalking is a "gendered" crime because of the consistent pattern of female victims outnumbering male victims—particularly when the definition of stalking is limited to behaviors that instill fear and/or that involve credible threats (Lyndon et al., 2012). A substantial number of female and male college students report being stalked; on the other hand, many students do not self-identify as stalking victims, even when targeted by behaviors that meet criteria for stalking (McNamara and Marsil, 2012). Cyberstalking, the use of computer-mediated communication to harass the victim, was reported by more than 40 percent of students surveyed on one US college campus; it was experienced disproportionately by women and by racial and sexual minority students (Reyns, Henson, and Fisher, 2012). Women experience more severe psychological, physical, and social consequences from stalking than do men, in large part because women's fear responses to stalking tend to be higher than men's (Sheridan and Lyndon, 2012). Yet, as with other forms of violence, stalking is not always treated seriously by law enforcement, or it elicits responses based on gender stereotypes.

RAPE AND SEXUAL ASSAULT

In December 2012, the brutal gang rape of a 23-year-old woman on a bus in Delhi triggered mass protests in India and shock around the world. The young woman, who later died of her injuries, was a student who had been to see a film at a local shopping mall. Returning home, she and a male friend were attacked by a group of men on a bus, where both were beaten with an iron bar and she was raped repeatedly. It was reported that the six men who abused her said they would teach this woman a lesson for going out at night with a man. Protestors demanded action from the government to punish these and other rapists, and argued that crimes of sexual assault against women were too often ignored or trivialized. Commentators suggested that many women were afraid to report sexual assaults because police officers were unsympathetic, and some claimed that the preference for sons in India had nourished a sense of male privilege and entitlement that undermines respect for women (Nelson, 2012).

Whereas many rapes do not involve this much brutality or a gang of strangers, this tragic incident and its aftermath brings into focus many key gender-related issues about sexual assault. First, it is far more likely to happen to women than to men, and to be perpetrated by men. Second, it is a crime that is sometimes not taken seriously by lawmakers, law enforcement officers, and communities—and for this reason it often goes both under-punished and under-reported. Third, reasons for the trivialization of sexual assault include rape-supportive attitudes, such as the belief that female victims deserve or even want to be raped, as indicated by their behavior. Finally, all of the previous issues are rooted in patriarchal notions that men are entitled to judge and dictate behavior to women, to mete out punishment when women do not conform to such dictates, and to have access to sex with women when and how they deem appropriate (Gavey, 2005; Jewkes, 2012).

The World Health Organization (Garcia-Moreno *et al.*, 2005) found that rates of sexual violence against women ranged from 6 to 59 percent within intimate partnerships and from about 1 to 12 percent by non-partner perpetrators across ten countries studied. In two-thirds of the places where data were collected, over 5 percent of the women said that their first experience of sexual intercourse had been forced. Globally, it is estimated that 7.2 percent of women have experienced sexual violence from someone who is not their partner, and 30 percent of ever-partnered women have experienced physical and/or sexual violence by their partners (World Health Organization, 2013). Researchers have reported that 28 to 37 percent of adult men in South Africa, 24 percent of men in India, and between 10 and 15 percent of men in Bangladesh have committed rape (Jewkes, 2012). According to a national survey, 18.3 percent of women and 1.4 percent of men in the United States have been raped at some time during their lives (Black *et al.*, 2011). More than half of the women said they were raped by an intimate partner, and more than 40 percent reported being raped by an acquaintance. Of the men who were raped, more than half said the perpetrator was an acquaintance, and just over 15 percent said the perpetrator was a stranger. For more than 30 percent of female victims the first rape occurred before the age of 18; for just over 12 percent it occurred before the age of 10. More than 27 percent of male victims were first raped before the age of 10.

A review of 75 US studies of sexual assault against individuals who identify as gay, lesbian, or bisexual found that the prevalence of lifetime sexual assault among lesbian or bisexual women ranged from 15.6 to 85 percent; the prevalence of lifetime sexual assault among gay or bisexual men ranged from 11.8 to 54 percent (Rothman, Exner, and Baughman, 2011). For transgender people, the rates may be even higher. Researchers have estimated that between 50 and 66 percent of transgender people experience sexual assault during their lifetime; 15 to 20 percent of these assaults were perpetrated by police officers or healthcare professionals (Office for Victims of Crime, 2014). Also, sexual assaults often form a component of anti-transgender hate crimes.

Perpetrators of sexual violence are often intimate partners, family members, or acquaintances of the victims; one result is that a victim's sense of security and trust in interpersonal relationships is likely to be profoundly shaken by rape. It is also evident that, although many men have been victims of rape, this type of violence is far more likely to be experienced by women than by men in their lifetime. There are a number of reasons why this is so, but one reason is likely the way societies think of and talk about heterosexual activity (Gavey, 2005). As noted in Chapter 4, there is a pervasive double standard applied to male and female heterosexuality, with men designated as aggressors and initiators, and women designated as gatekeepers and limiters. Men are supposed to press for sex and women are supposed to resist—and all of this is simply part of a ritual that usually ends in sex. In such a framework, the line between seduction and rape becomes blurred. Rape is, by definition, forcing sex on another person. Yet some men who report that they have forced or coerced a woman into having sex also say they have not committed rape (Koss, 1988; Lisak and Miller, 2002); and some women who report that they have been forced or coerced into having sex say they have not been raped (Kahn, Jackson, Kully, Badger, and Halvorsen, 2003). Furthermore, some respondents apparently believe that a man is justified in forcing a woman to have sexual intercourse if she has had sex with him before (Shotland and Goodstein, 1992) or if she behaves in certain ways, such as allowing him to pay for a meal or entertainment, teasing, or "leading him on," and then changing her mind (Bostwick and DeLucia, 1992; Emmers-Sommer and Allen, 1999). If men are thought to need and desire sexual activity more than do women, and women do not feel entitled to resist sexual activity unless they have been clear and forceful about that resistance from the start, the stage is set for a high frequency of rapes of women by men.

The situation is even more conducive to rape in cultural contexts where women are explicitly designated as men's property or subject to their husbands' authority. Rape in the context of marriage was long considered an oxymoron in many societies, since a husband was deemed to be entitled to have sex with his wife whether or not she was willing. The United Nations *Declaration on the Elimination of Violence Against Women*, published in 1993, established marital rape as a violation of human rights (United Nations, 1993). Rape within marriage is now a crime in many countries (United Nations, 2015) and this criminalization would also apply to same-sex marriages in countries where such unions are recognized. India's Supreme Court ruled in October 2017 that a man who has sex with his underage wife is committing rape—striking down a law permitting men to have sex with girls as young as 15 providing it is within the context of marriage (Safi, 2017). Despite official recognition of spousal rape as illegal, however, women and men in many developing countries continue to believe that a husband is justified in forcing an unwilling wife to have sex. Women who are married at a young age and who have few resources in terms of education, experience, or finances are at particular risk (United Nations, 2015). Child marriage is still common in many parts of the world; even in the United States there is no minimum age for a girl to marry in more than half of all states (Kristof, 2017).

RAPE AS A WEAPON OF WAR

There is a long and painful tradition of using rape to demoralize and humiliate opponents in war. There is, of course, a gender aspect to this practice: historically, most soldiers have been male, and women have been left behind while men go out to fight. By ravaging women "belonging" to the enemy, troops systematically demonstrate their dominance and wreak destruction on communities of the opposing group. Indeed, one goal of rape in wartime has been to dilute the ethnic group of the enemy by forcing their women to give birth to the babies of the rapists. Another, less obvious, goal is to strengthen the bonds among combatants (Marino, 2011). Hundreds of thousands of women have experienced this war-associated trauma, along with the consequent depression, fear, high suicide rates, risk of unwanted pregnancy, and sexually transmitted disease (Donohoe, 2005). Men too are raped during wartime, although their stories are even less likely to be heard than those of female victims (Sivakumaran, 2007). Some 76 percent of male political prisoners surveyed in El Salvador in the 1980s reported sexual torture, and more than 80 percent of male concentration camp inmates in Sarajevo reported that they had been raped (Storr, 2011). A survey of households in the war-ravaged eastern Democratic Republic of Congo found that almost 40 percent of women and just under 24 percent of men had experienced sexual violence (Johnson *et al.*, 2010). Female combatants may participate in wartime rape: holding the victim down, using objects such as a bottle to perpetrate the rape (Cohen, cited in Marino, 2011). The finding that men as well as women are vulnerable to rape and other forms of sexual assault during armed conflicts, and that female as well as male combatants participate in rape, underlines the notion that sexual violence is more about power and dominance than about sexual passion. Rape is humiliating, frightening, dangerous, and debilitating for women; for men it is also all of these things, with the added dimension of being seen and experienced as emasculating.

Wartime rape victims face some special traumas: while dealing with the aftermath of rape, they are also dealing with the deaths and injuries of friends and families, displacement, and many other losses. Normal support systems may have been destroyed; and victims are often stigmatized and rejected by others. They may even be at risk of further violence by relatives who view them as dishonored (Nolen, 2005). Victims frequently show symptoms of major depression and posttraumatic stress disorder (Johnson *et al.*, 2010). International courts now prosecute wartime rape as a crime against humanity or as a crime of genocide (Henry, 2010).

VIOLENCE AS A PUBLIC PERFORMANCE OF GENDER HIERARCHY AND NORMS

Sometimes violence becomes a public performance of gender hierarchy and male status: an overt enactment of men's claim to ownership of, and right to authority over, "their" women. A tragic example is honor killing: the murder of a woman whose behavior is deemed to have brought dishonor to her husband, father, and/or other family members. Women murdered in defense of family honor have been judged guilty of transgressing cultural boundaries of propriety by dressing in unapproved ways, going without chaperones to public places, appearing in the company of unrelated men, having intimate relationships outside of marriage, being raped, or marrying without family approval. Honor killings, often perpetrated by a male relative such as a brother or through a collaborative effort by several family members (Chesler, 2010), may claim the lives of more than 5000 women every year worldwide, although reliable estimates are virtually impossible. They have been documented in countries as diverse as Turkey, Jordan, Egypt, Pakistan, India, Israel, and Brazil, and are often not prosecuted, or treated leniently by the courts.

The practice of honor killing is rooted in cultural norms that not only legitimize higher status for men than for women, but also link a man's honor and standing in the community to his authority over his wife and daughters. In certain communities where patriarchal norms are strong, a man may feel that his honor is his main possession of value. An indiscreet, independent, or disobedient woman is seen as bringing shame on her family and as destroying that one important possession—a possession that is ranked higher in importance than the woman herself. The cultural assignment of higher value to men's honor and community standing than to women's lives is a sobering dimension of a hierarchical gender system.

For a man in a traditional community, one aspect of protecting his honor is protecting the women in his family from rape and other forms of violation. Ironically, that very man may use rape as a tool of public punishment against women for violating rules of sexual propriety, or for intruding into spaces or situations where they "do not belong." Because of its implications for men's honor, rape may also be used by men as a weapon against other men: one man can lash out at another by raping his wife, daughter, sister, or mother. In one famous case, a young Pakistani woman, Mukhtaran Bibi, was gang-raped by several men on the orders of the rural village tribal council, and then forced to walk home naked in front of villagers who taunted and insulted her. She was being punished because her brother had been seen with a woman from that village (Kristof, 2005).

Public enforcement of the "rules" of gender also takes the form of violent hate crimes against sexual minorities. Perpetrators attack a gay, lesbian, bisexual, or transgender individual because they view that individual as transgressing norms, expectations, or values associated with heterosexual masculinity and/or femininity. Hate crimes, by definition, are terrorizing to whole categories of people, each of whom may legitimately worry that they could be the next target. In the United States in 2015, more than 1100 hate crimes motivated by bias against a particular sexual orientation or sexual identity were documented (Federal Bureau of Investigation, 2016). Police in England and Wales recorded 4267 hate crimes based on sexual orientation in 2012 to 2013 (Office for National Statistics, 2013).

THE BUSINESS OF GENDERED VIOLENCE

There is money in gendered and/or sexualized violence: the profits made by those who sell people (most often women and children) into sexual slavery, or who distribute images of people being raped or sexually humiliated, are significant. Pornography, the depiction of sexually explicit images (of which a significant proportion, though not all, are violent) for the purpose of entertainment and sexual arousal, is big business with a global reach. Globally, it is estimated that pornography is a $97 billion business (NBC News, 2015).

PORNOGRAPHY

There are three reasons for considering pornography under the topic of gendered violence. First, a significant amount of pornography depicts sexual violence, such as the rape and/or humiliation of women or men. Second, there is the possibility that the use of pornography may contribute to sexually violent attitudes and behaviors. Third, there is the question of whether the persons depicted in pornography—the performers—are victims of coercion and violence.

On the first question, portrayals of violence and domination are a significant theme in pornography. A content analysis of top-selling and top-renting popular pornographic videos revealed high levels of both physical and verbal aggression, featuring mostly male perpetrators (70.3%) and female victims (94.4%) (Bridges, Wosnitzer, Scharrer, Sun, and Liberman, 2010). More than 88 percent of the scenes portrayed physical aggression such as spanking, hair-pulling, gagging, slapping, and choking; almost half contained verbal aggression such as insulting or name-calling. Women were far more likely than men in these videos to be insulted or referred to in derogatory ways. Moreover, most targets of aggression were portrayed as responding neutrally or with pleasure to the aggression—leading to the concern that viewers of pornography are learning that aggression during a sexual encounter enhances pleasure.

The fastest-growing medium for the distribution of pornography is the Internet. One analysis of 31 free Internet sites depicting sexual violence found that images strongly emphasized the portrayal of women as victims, usually with no image of the perpetrator. Pain experienced by the victim appeared to be the main emphasis of such sites; there was little or no attempt to portray rape as seduction (Gossett and Byrne, 2002).

Producers of pornography are apparently well aware that violence sells. A content analysis of pornographers' own public descriptions of their products reveals a strong awareness that violence increases the marketability of the films and other media they purvey (Tyler, 2010).

Whether and how exposure to pornography—particularly violent pornography—may contribute to sexual violence has been extensively debated and studied. Do consumers of pornography become more likely to engage in sexually violent behaviors, to adopt more violence-supportive attitudes, to lose empathy for victims of sexual violence? Does the amount of violent content of the pornographic material make a difference? The answers to these questions are still evolving. Some studies show that individuals' use of pornography may be linked to harsher evaluations of other-gender individuals with whom they interact (Jansma, Linz, Mulac, and Imrich, 1997), weakened commitment to their real-life partners (Lambert, Negash, Stillman, Olmstead, and Fincham, 2012), and loss of compassion for female rape victims (Zillmann and Weaver, 1989). Men's consumption of material that objectifies women has been linked to attitudes supportive of violence against women (Wright and Tokunaga, 2016), and convergent evidence from a number of studies indicates that, for men, pornography consumption is associated with an increased risk of sexually aggressive attitudes and behaviors. However, the relationship between pornography and violent outcomes is complicated and does not apply equally to all men and all forms of pornography. For men who are already at high risk for committing sexual aggression because they are hostile and distrustful toward women, gain gratification from controlling women, and take a promiscuous, non-committal approach to sexual relations, the heavy use of pornography, particularly violent pornography, is significantly associated with attitudes supporting violence against women (Malamuth, Hald, and Koss, 2012). These men may be both more likely to seek out violent pornography, and more likely to be influenced by it, than other men. With respect to sexually violent behavior, too, consuming pornography is most likely to affect men who are more predisposed to sexual aggression and who use pornography frequently (Vega and Malamuth, 2007).

Exposure to violent pornography may also have deleterious effects on women. In one study, women who read an eroticized depiction of rape after ingesting a moderate alcohol dose were less likely than sober women to label the incident as rape and were more callous toward the victim (Davis, Norris, George, Martell, and Heiman, 2006). In addition, viewing media portrayals of sexual or non-sexual violence against women can make women feel disempowered (Reid and Finchilescu, 1995).

There is disagreement as to whether the adult performers in pornographic media are always exploited, or whether this work is sometimes a free and rational choice by the individuals who engage in it. Arguably, the practices expected of female performers are dangerous to their health (Bridges *et al.*, 2010). Accounts by experienced women performers often present stories of conflicted emotions, abuse by producers and photographers, and relentless coercive breaking down of their stated boundaries (Boyle, 2011). Performers speak of being discouraged from using condoms, the physical pain of certain acts such as multiple penetrations, vaginal and rectal tears, and exhaustion. However, they often seem to construct these harmful consequences of their work as normal outcomes of a life they have freely chosen, and do not critique the ways in which they have apparently been bullied or threatened into engaging in acts they would rather avoid. Their narratives sometimes emphasize their own lack of sexual inhibitions and suggest that the worst outcomes happen, not to themselves, but to other, more naïve, young women. One study compared pornography actresses to a sample of other women matched on age, ethnicity, and marital status. Results indicated that the actresses were more concerned about contracting a sexually transmitted disease and were more likely to have used drugs, but that they also reported higher levels of self-esteem, positive feelings, social support, sexual satisfaction, and spirituality than did the comparison women (Griffith, Mitchell, Hart, Adams, and Gu, 2013).

Participation in the pornography industry can have some profoundly harmful impacts upon the women who perform before the cameras—indeed, the industry itself acknowledges, even advertises, the use of deception, coercion, and harm of performers (Boyle, 2011; Tyler, 2010). This admission raises troubling questions about the extent to which performers in pornography, even if they are adults, are being paid, and are choosing to show up for work each day, are victims of sexual violence. With respect to performers who are underage, there is no doubt that they are being victimized and exploited.

SEX TRAFFICKING

Trafficking is another violent business that is gendered and global. Its victims are overwhelmingly women and children (Hodge and Lietz, 2007; Miller-Perrin and Wurtele, 2017), but the proportion of men being trafficked is increasing (United Nations Office on Drugs and Crime, 2016). Victims are often deceived by false promises of good jobs or taken against their will from their own countries. They are deprived of legal documents, often kept imprisoned, and forced to work in prostitution, sweatshop labor, or some other form of forced servitude. Although numbers are difficult to substantiate, the International Labour Office (2014) estimated that in 2012 some 20.9 million people were trafficked for labor and/or sexual exploitation or held in slavery-like conditions. The victims most often come from poor countries or those with high unemployment, and are sent to more affluent countries; a disproportionate number of victims come from Asian countries (Crawford, 2010). According to one study, 95 percent of victims experience physical or sexual violence while being trafficked (Zimmerman *et al.*, 2006). Trafficking is an organized and very profitable form of gendered violence: global profits may reach US$150 billion per year (International Labour Organization, 2014).

ECONOMIC AND HEALTH IMPACTS OF GENDERED VIOLENCE

Survivors of physical or sexual violence show physical and mental symptoms of ill-health. In the WHO multi-country study, women reported injuries from bruises and punctures to broken bones, and damage to their ears or eyes (Garcia-Moreno *et al.*, 2005). Women victims of physical or sexual partner violence were significantly more likely than non-victimized women to report that they were in poor health, had difficulties with walking, and experienced symptoms such as memory loss, dizziness, emotional distress, fatigue, and thoughts of suicide. Partner violence frequently occurred during pregnancy, and the rate of miscarriages and induced abortions was higher among women who had experienced partner violence than among other women. A national survey in the United States revealed that both female and male victims of rape, stalking, or intimate partner violence were more likely than their counterparts to report frequent headaches, chronic pain, difficulty sleeping, limitations on their activities, and poor physical and mental health (Black *et al.*, 2011).

The energy-draining physical and psychological impacts of violence have profound implications for victims. In cultural contexts where women hold less power and status than men, even the potential for violence affects women's opportunities to achieve success, or improve their status. Women who live in situations where violence against women is common learn to be alert, careful, and avoidant. Caution limits their mobility and interferes with their economic and social opportunities. In this sense, an atmosphere of potential violence, whether in individual women's homes or in their public streets and communities, serves as an effective way of controlling women's behavior, movements, and aspirations.

The debilitating consequences go beyond the individual women and men who experience the violence. A 2004 World Health Organization report (Waters *et al.*, 2004) concluded that intimate partner violence cost the economy of the United States $12.6 billion annually—an amount equal to 0.1 percent of the gross domestic product. The same report showed that intimate partner violence had costs equal to 1.6 percent of the gross domestic product for Nicaragua, and 2 percent of the gross national product for Chile. One reason for the high economic costs is that victims of intimate partner and sexual violence impact the healthcare system: they are more likely than other people to need and seek out healthcare and to have more and longer hospital stays (Black, 2011). Healthcare costs are significantly higher for victims of intimate partner violence than for non-victims, because there are usually multiple violent episodes and because victims require services, such as psychiatric care, that are less frequently required by non-victims (Kruse, Sørensen, Brønnum-Hansen, and Helweg-Larsen, 2011).

Medical costs are not the only expenses incurred by societies as a consequence of interpersonal violence. Costs of legal services, safe accommodation, and policing are also significant. Furthermore, because they are more likely to be injured or ill, victims are more likely to miss work, so there are costs to individuals and their employers associated with lost earnings, lost time, and lost opportunities for productivity. Such costs are difficult to measure, but one Australian study put the costs of refuge accommodation (including legal services, policing, estimated lost earnings, and opportunity costs) for victims of domestic violence at $14.2 million per year (Australian Institute of Criminology, 2001). A study by the U.S. Department of Justice (1994) estimated that the annual combined cost of direct medical services to victims, lost earnings, and lost opportunities associated with rape was $33 million.

Because violence costs societies so much, programs or interventions to stop interpersonal violence can be very cost-effective. For example, one report estimates that the Violence Against Women Act (VAWA), passed in the United States in 1994 and providing for severe criminal penalties against perpetrators of intimate partner violence and stalking, saved $12.6 billion in averted costs related to victimization over its first five years (Clark, Biddle, and Martin, 2002).

In the light of these diverse consequences, gendered violence is now understood by policy analysts not as a private, interpersonal matter, but as both a public health problem and a human rights issue.

FOR FURTHER EXPLORATION

Aghtaie, Nadia and Gangoli, Geetanjali (eds) (2015). *Understanding gender-based violence: National and international contexts* (New York: Routledge). This book, which takes a feminist, intersectional approach to the problem of gender-based violence, contains articles exploring the history, theory, and methodology of research into this complex topic. Included are research articles in contexts that include the UK, Iran, India, Rwanda, and China.

Branche, R. and Virgili, F. (eds) (2012). *Rape in wartime* (Basing-stoke: Palgrave Macmillan UK). This edited book contains chapters on rape as a weapon of war in a number of different conflicts and historical periods, including World War II, the Bangladesh War of 1971, the Greek civil war, the Spanish civil war, Chechnya, and several African conflicts. Through careful historical scholarship, the book examines the contexts that trigger sexual violence and the functions such violence serves.

Crawford, Mary (2010). *Sex trafficking in South Asia: Telling Maya's story* (Abingdon, Oxon: Routledge). The author, a social psychologist, provides a critical feminist analysis of sex trafficking, focusing on the case of Nepal. She explores how a discourse that characterizes victims as "backward" may lead to strategies for protecting girls and women that may, paradoxically, restrict their human rights.

Frieze, Irene H. (2005). *Hurting the one you love: Violence in intimate relationships* (Belmont, CA: Wadworth/Thompson Learning). The author carefully examines the research on violence in relationships, including violence against and by both women and men.

Gavey, Nicola (2005). *Just sex? The cultural scaffolding of rape* (Hove, UK: Routledge). The author, a New Zealand psychologist, examines the social science literature on rape from a feminist and social constructionist perspective. She argues that we must pay critical attention to the use of dynamics of heterosexual relations as a justification for rape.

UN Women. *Global database on violence against women* (accessible at http://evaw-global-database.unwomen.org/en). This database contains separate listings for every country that has provided data about the measures it has undertaken to address violence against women.

REFERENCES

Archer, J. (2000). Sex differences in aggression between heterosexual partners: A meta-analytic review. *Psychological Bulletin, 126*, 651–680.

Archer, J. (2004). Sex difference in aggression in real-world settings: A meta-analytic review. *Review of General Psychology, 8*, 291–322. doi: 10.1037/1089 2680.8.4.291.

Arias, I. and Pape, K.T. (2015). Psychological abuse: Implications for adjustment and commitment to leave violent partners. In R.D. Maiuro (ed.), *Perspectives on verbal and psychological abuse* (pp. 197–209). New York: Springer Publishing.

Australian Institute of Criminology (2001). *Australian crime – Facts and figures 2002.* www.aic.gov.au/publications/facts/2001/.

Balsam, K.F. and Szymanski, D.M. (2005). Relationship quality and domestic violence in women's same-sex relationships: The role of minority stress. *Psychology of Women Quarterly, 29*, 258–269. doi: 10.1111/j.1471-6402.2005. 00220.x.

Barnes, J.E. and Nissenbaum, D. (2013). Combat ban for women to end. *The Wall Street Journal*, January 24. http://online.wsj.com/article/SB1000142 4127887323539804578260123802564276.html.

Bernard, M. (2013). With women in combat, will military finally address epidemic of sexual assault? *The Washington Post*, January 24. Blog post. www. washingtonpost.com/blogs/she-the-people/wp/2013/01/24/with-woman-in-combat-will-military-finally-address-epidemic-ofsexual-assault/.

Black, M.C., Basile, K.C., Breiding, M.J., Smith, S.G., Walters, M.L., Merrick, M.T., Chen, J., and Stevens, M.R. (2011). *The National Intimate Partner and Sexual Violence Survey (NISVS): 2010 Summary Report*. Atlanta, GA: National Center for Injury Prevention and Control, Centers for Disease Control and Prevention. www.cdc.gov/ViolencePrevention/pdf/ NISVS_Executive_Summary-a.pdf.

Bosson, J.K., Vandello, J.A., Burnaford, R.M., Weaver, J.R., and Wasti, S.A. (2009). Precarious manhood and displays of physical aggression. *Personality and Social Psychology Bulletin, 35*, 623–634. doi: 10.1177/0146167208331161.

Bostwick, T.D. and DeLucia, J.L. (1992). Effects of gender and specific dating behaviors on perceptions of sex willingness and date rape. *Journal of Social and Clinical Psychology, 11*, 14–25.

Boyle, K. (2011). Producing abuse: Selling the harms of pornography. *Women's Studies International Forum, 34*, 593–602. doi: 10.1016/j.wsif.2011.09.002.

Boyle, M., Georgiades, K., Cullen, J. and Racine, Y. (2009). Community influences on intimate partner violence in India: Women's education, attitudes towards mistreatment and standards of living. *Social Science and Medicine, 69*, 691–697. doi: 10.1016/j.socscimed.2009.06.039.

Bridges, A.J., Wosnitzer, R., Scharrer, E., Sun, C., and Liberman, R. (2010). Aggression and sexual behavior in best-selling pornography videos: A content analysis update. *Violence Against Women, 16*, 1065–1085. doi: 10.1177/1077801210382866.

Brownridge, D.A. (2006). Violence against women post-separation. *Aggression and Violent Behavior, 11*, 514–530. doi.org/10.1016/j.avb.2006.01.009.

Card, N.A., Stucky, B.D., Sawalani, G.M., and Little, T.D. (2008). Direct and indirect aggression during childhood and adolescence: A meta-analytic review of gender differences, intercorrelations, and relations to maladjustment. *Child Development, 79*, 1185–1229. doi: 10.1111/j.1467-8624.2008.01184.x.

Chesler, P. (2010). Worldwide trends in honor killings. *The Middle East Quarterly, 17*(2), 3–11. https://phyllis-chesler.com/articles/worldwide-trends-in-honor-killings.

Clark, K.A., Biddle, A.K., and Martin, S.L. (2002). A cost-benefit analysis of the violence against women act of 1994. *Violence Against Women, 8*, 417–428. doi: 10.1177/10778010222183143.

Crawford, M. (2010). *Sex trafficking in South Asia: Telling Maya's Story.* Abingdon, Oxon: Routledge.

Davis, K., Norris, J., George, W.H., Martell, J., and Heiman, J.R. (2006). Rape-myth congruent beliefs in women resulting from exposure to violent pornography: Effects of alcohol and sexual arousal. *Journal of Interpersonal Violence, 21*, 1208–1223. doi: 10.1177/0886260506290428.

Donohoe, M.T. (2005). War, rape and genocide: From ancient times to the Sudan. Abstract #108859. Presentation at the annual meeting of the American Public Health Association, Philadelphia, PA, USA, December 13. https://apha. confex.com/apha/133am/techprogram/paper_108859.htm.

Eagly, A.H. and Steffen, V.J. (1986). Gender and aggressive behavior: A meta-analytic review of the social psychological literature. *Psychological Bulletin, 100*, 309–330. doi: 10.1037/0033-2909.100.3.309.

Emmers-Sommer, T.M. and Allen, M. (1999). Variables related to sexual coercion: A path model. *Journal of Social and Personal Relationships, 16*, 659–678.

Federal Bureau of Investigation (2015). *Crime in the United States 2015.* Expanded offense data. https://ucr.fbi.gov/crime-in-the-u.s/2015/crime-in-the-u.s.-2015/offenses-known-to-law-enforcement/expanded-offense.

Federal Bureau of Investigation (2016). *Hate crime statistics 2015*. https://ucr. fbi.gov/hate-crime/2015.

Frieze, I.H. (2005). *Hurting the one you love: Violence in intimate relationships*. Belmont, CA: Wadworth/Thompson Learning.

Frieze, I.H. (2008). Social policy, feminism, and research on violence in close relationships. *Journal of Social Issues, 64*, 665–684.

Garcia-Moreno, C., Jansen, H.A.F.M., Ellsberg, M., Heise, L., and Watts, C. (2005). *WHO multi-country study on women's health and domestic violence against women: Initial results on prevalence, health outcomes and women's responses*. Geneva: World Health Organization. www.who.int/gender/ violence/who_multicountry_study/Introduction-Chapter1-Chapter2.pdf.

Gavey, N. (2005). *Just sex? The cultural scaffolding of rape*. Hove, Sussex: Routledge.

Giancola, P.R., Helton, E.L., Osborne, A.B., Terry, M.K., Fuss, A.M., and Westerfield, J.A. (2002). The effects of alcohol and provocation on aggressive behavior in men and women. *Journal of Studies on Alcohol, 63*, 64–73.

Gossett, J.L. and Byrne, S. (2002). "CLICK HERE": A content analysis of Internet rape sites. *Gender and Society, 16*, 689–709. doi: 10.1177/089124 302236992.

Griffith, J.D., Mitchell, S., Hart, C.L., Adams, L.T., and Gu, L.L. (2013). Pornography actresses: An assessment of the damaged goods hypothesis. *Journal of Sex Research, 50*, 621–632. doi: 10.1080/00224499.2012.719168.

Henry, N. (2010). The impossibility of bearing witness: Wartime rape and the promise of justice. *Violence Against Women, 16*, 1098–1119. doi: 10.1177/1077801210382860.

Hodge, D.R. and Lietz, C.A. (2007). The international sexual trafficking of women and children: A review of the literature. *Journal of Women and Social Work, 22*, 163–174. doi: 10.1177/0886109907299055.

Hyde, J.S. (1984). How large are gender differences in aggression? A developmental meta-analysis. *Developmental Psychology, 20*, 722–736.

International Labour Office (2014). *Profits and poverty: The economics of forced labour*. Geneva: Author. www.ilo.org/wcmsp5/groups/public/-ed_ norm/-declaration/documents/publication/wcms_243391.pdf.

Jansma, L.L., Linz, D.G., Mulac, A., and Imrich, D.J. (1997). Men's interactions with women after viewing sexually explicit films: Does degradation make a difference? *Communication Monographs, 64*, 1–24. doi: 10.1080/03637759709376402.

Jewkes, R. (2012). *Rape perpetration: A review*. Pretoria, SA: Sexual Violence Research Initiative. www.svri.org/RapePerpetration.pdf.

Johnson, K., Scott, J., Rughita, B., Kisielewski, M., Asher, J., Ong, R., and Lawry, L. (2010). Association of sexual violence and human rights violations with physical and mental health in territories of the Eastern Democratic Republic of Congo. *JAMA, 304*, 553–562. doi: 10.10 01/jama.2010.1086.

Johnson, M.P. and Ferraro, K.J. (2000). Research on domestic violence in the 1990s: Making distinctions. *Journal of Marriage and the Family, 62*, 948–963.

Kahn, A.S., Jackson, J., Kully, C., Badger, K., and Halvorsen, J. (2003). Calling it rape: Differences in experiences of women who do or do not label their sexual assault as rape. *Psychology of Women Quarterly, 27*, 233–242. doi: 10.1111/1471-6402.00103.

Kaukinen, C. (2004). Status compatibility, physical violence, and emotional abuse in intimate relationships. *Journal of Marriage and the Family, 66*, 452–471.

Koss, M.P. (1988). Hidden rape: Incidence, prevalence, and descriptive characteristic of sexual aggression and victimization in a national sample of college students. In A.W. Burgess (ed.), *Sexual Assault*, Vol. 2 (pp. 3–25). New York: Garland Press.

Kristof, N. (2005). Raped, kidnapped and silenced. *The New York Times*, June 14. www.nytimes.com/2005/06/14/opinion/14kristof.html.

Kristof, N. (2017). 11 years old, a mom, *and pushed to marry her rapist in Florida. The New York Times*, May 26. www.nytimes.com/2017/05/26/opinion/sunday/it-was-forced-on-me-child-marriage-in-the-us.html?mwrsm=Email&_r=0.

Kruse, M., Sørensen, J., Brønnum-Hansen, H., and Helweg-Larsen, K. (2011). The health care costs of violence against women. *Journal of Interpersonal Violence, 26*, 3494–3508. doi: 10.1177/0886260511403754.

Kudo, T. (2013). I killed people in Afghanistan. Was I right or wrong? *The Washington Post*, January 25. http://articles.washingtonpost.com/2013-01-25/opinions/36539894_1_bomb-strikes-afghanistan-enemyfire.

Lambert, N.M., Negash, S., Stillman, T.F., Olmstead, S.B., and Fincham, F.D. (2012). A love that doesn't last: Pornography consumption and weakened commitment to one's romantic partner. *Journal of Social and Clinical Psychology, 31*, 410–438. doi: 10.1521/jscp.2012.31.4.410.

Lamothe, D. (2017). Sexual assault on both men and women in the military is declining, Pentagon survey finds. *The Washington Post*, May 1. www.washingtonpost.com/news/checkpoint/wp/2017/05/01/sexual-assault-on-both-men-and-women-in-the-military-is-declining-pentagon-survey-finds/?utm_term=.9e7acbabc0dd.

Lansford, J.E., Skinner, A.T., Sorbring, E., Giunta, L.D., Deater-Deckard, K., Dodge, K.A., Malone, P.S., Oburu, P., Pastorelli, C., Tapanya, S., Tirado, L.M.U., Zelli, A., Al-Hassan, S.M., Alampay, L.P., Bacchini, D., Bombi, A.S., Bornstein, M.H., and Chang, L. (2012). Boys' and girls' relational and physical aggression in nine countries. *Aggressive Behavior, 38*, 298–308. doi: 10.1002/ab.21433.

Legon, J. (2003). Mom, soldier and Hopi Indian: "She fought and died valiantly." CNN.com. http://edition.cnn.com/SPECIALS/2003/iraq/heroes/piestewa.html.

Lenton, R.L. (1995). Power versus feminist theories of wife abuse. *Canadian Journal of Criminology, 37*, 305–330.

Linos, N., Khawaja, M., and Kaplan, R.L. (2012). Women's acceptance of spousal abuse in Iraq: Prevalence rates and the role of female empowerment characteristics. *Journal of Family Violence, 27*, 625–633. doi: 10.1007/s10896-012-9462-0.

Lisak, D.M. and Miller, P.M. (2002). Repeat rape and multiple offending among undetected rapists. *Violence and Victims, 17*, 73–84. doi: 10.1891/vivi.17.1.73.33638.

Loflin, D.C. and Barry, C.T. (2016). "You can't sit with us:" Gender and the differential roles of social intelligence and peer status in adolescent relational aggression. *Personality and Individual Differences, 91*, 22–26. doi: 10.1016/j.paid.2015.11.048.

Lyndon, A.E., Sinclair, H.C., MacArthur, J., Fay, B., Ratajack, E., and Collier, K.E. (2012). An introduction to issues of gender in stalking research. *Sex Roles, 66*, 299–310. doi: 10.1007/s11199-011-0106-2.

Malamuth, N.M., Hald, G.M., and Koss, M. (2012). Pornography, individual differences in risk and men's acceptance of violence against women in a representative sample. *Sex Roles, 66*, 427–439. doi: 10.1007/s11199-011-0082-6.

Marino, K. (2011). Rethinking the causes of wartime rape. The Clayman Institute for Gender Research, Stanford University, October 3. http://gender.stanford.edu/news/2011/rethinking-causes-wartime-rape.

McHugh, M.C., Livingston, N.A., and Ford, A. (2005). A postmodern approach to women's use of violence: Developing multiple and complex conceptualizations. *Psychology of Women Quarterly, 29*, 323–336. doi: 10.1111/j.1471-6402.2005.00226.x.

McNamara, C.L. and Marsil, D.F. (2012). The prevalence of stalking among college students: The disparity between researcher- and self-identified victimization. *Journal of American College Health, 60*, 168–174. doi: 10.1080/07448481.2011.584335.

Miller, S.L. and Meloy, M.L. (2006). Women's use of force: Voices of women arrested for domestic violence. *Violence Against Women, 12*, 89–115. doi: 10.1177/1077801205277356.

Miller-Perrin, C. and Wurtele, S.K. (2017). Sex trafficking and the commercial sexual exploitation of children. *Women & Therapy, 40*, 123–151. doi: 10.1080/02703149.2016.1210963.

NBC News (2015). Things are looking up for America's porn industry. *NBC News*, January 20. www.nbcnews.com/business/business-news/things-are-looking-americas-porn-industry-n289431.

Nelson, D. (2012). Gang rape of Indian woman sparks mass protests. *The Telegraph*, December 19. www.telegraph.co.uk/news/worldnews/asia/india/9755913/Gang-rape-of-Indian-woman-sparks-massprotests.html.

Nolen, S. (2005). "Not women anymore. [...]" The Congo's rape survivors face pain, shame and AIDS. *Ms. Magazine*, spring. www.msmagazine.com/spring2005/congo.asp

Nowinski, S.N. and Bowen, E. (2012). Partner violence against heterosexual and gay men: Prevalence and correlates. *Aggression and Violent Behavior, 17*, 36–52. doi: 10.1016/j.avb.2011.09.005.

Office for National Statistics (2013). *An overview of hate crime in England and Wales*, December. www.gov.uk/government/uploads/system/uploads/attachment_data/file/266358/hate-crime-2013.pdf.

Office for National Statistics (2016a). *Statistical Bulletin: Domestic abuse in England and Wales: Year ending March 2016*. www.ons.gov.uk/people populationandcommunity/crimeandjustice/bulletins/domesticabusein englandandwales/yearendingmarch2016#toc.

Office for National Statistics (2016b). Focus on violent crime and sexual offences, year ending March 2015. Chapter 6. www.ons.gov.uk/people-populationandcommunity/crimeandjustice/compendium/focusonviolent-crimeandsexualoffences/yearendingmarch2015/chapter4intimatepersonal violenceandpartnerabuse#prevalence-of-intimate-violence-extent.

Office for Victims of Crime (2014). *Responding to transgender victims of sexual assault*. Washington, DC: U.S Department of Justice. www.ovc.gov/pubs/forge/sexual_numbers.html.

Reid, P. and Finchilescu, G. (1995). The disempowering effects of media violence against women on college women. *Psychology of Women Quarterly, 19*, 397–411. doi: 10.1111/j.1471-6402.1995.tb00082.x.

Reuter, T.R., Newcomb, M.E., Whitton, S.W., and Mustanski, B. (2017). Intimate partner violence victimization in LGBT young adults: Demographic differences and associations with health behaviors. *Psychology of Violence, 7*, 101–109. doi:10.1037/vio0000031.

Reyns, B.W., Henson, B., and Fisher, B.S. (2012). Stalking in the twilight zone: Extent of cyberstalking victimization and offending among college students. *Deviant Behavior, 33*, 1–25. doi: 10.1080/01639625.2010.538364.

Richardson, D.S. (2005). The myth of female passivity: Thirty years of revelations about female aggression. *Psychology of Women Quarterly, 29*, 238–247.

Rothman, E.F., Exner, D., and Baughman, A.L. (2011). The prevalence of sexual assault against people who identify as gay, lesbian, or bisexual in the United States: A systematic review. *Trauma, Violence, and Abuse, 12*, 55–66. doi: 10.1177/1524838010390707.

Safi, M. (2017). Sex with underage wife is rape, Indian supreme court rules. *The Guardian*, October 11. www.theguardian.com/world/2017/oct/11/sex-with-underage-wife-is-indian-supreme-court-rules.

Santaya, P.O.T. and Walters, A.S. (2011). Intimate partner violence within gay male couples: Dimensionalizing partner violence among Cuban gay men. *Sexuality and Culture: an Interdisciplinary Quarterly, 15*, 153–178. doi: 10.1007/s12119-011-9087-0.

Sheridan, L. and Lyndon, A.E. (2012). The influence of prior relationship, gender, and fear on the consequences of stalking victimization. *Sex Roles, 66*, 340–350. doi: 10.1007/s11199-010-9889-9.

Shotland, R.L. and Goodstein, L. (1992). Sexual precedence reduces the perceived legitimacy of sexual refusal: An examination of attributions concerning date rape and consensual sex. *Personality and Social Psychology Bulletin, 18*, 756–764.

Sivakumaran, S. (2007). Sexual violence against men in armed conflict. *European Journal of International Law, 18*, 253–276. doi: 10.1093/ejil/chm013.

Smith, S.G., Chen, J., Basile, K.C., Gilbert, L.K., Merrick, M.T., Patel, N., Walling, M., and Jain, A. (2017). *The National Intimate Partner and Sexual Violence Survey (NISVS): 2010–2012 State Report*. Atlanta, GA: National Center for Injury Prevention and Control, Centers for Disease Control and Prevention. www.cdc.gov/violenceprevention/pdf/NISVS-StateReportBook.pdf.

Storr, W. (2011). The rape of men. *Observer*, July 16. www.guardian.co.uk/society/2011/jul/17/the-rape-of-men.

Tyler, M. (2010). "Now that's pornography!" Violence and domination in Adult Video News. In K. Boyle (ed.), *Everyday pornography* (pp. 50–62). London and New York: Routledge.

United Nations (1993). Resolution adopted by the General Assembly. *48/104. Declaration on the Elimination of Violence Against Women*, December 20. UN Documents. www.un-documents.net/a48r104.htm.

United Nations (2015). *The world's women: Trends and statistics*. New York: United Nations Statistics Division. https://unstats.un.org/unsd/gender/worldswomen.html.

United Nations Office on Drugs and Crime (2016). *Global report on trafficking in persons 2016*. Vienna, Austria: Author. www.unodc.org/documents/data-and-analysis/glotip/2016_Global_Report_on_Trafficking_in_Persons.pdf.

U.S. Department of Justice (1994). *The costs of crime to victims: Crime data brief*. Bureau of Justice Statistics. www.ojp.usdoj.gov.bjs/pub/.

Vega, V. and Malamuth, N.M. (2007). Predicting sexual aggression: The role of pornography in the context of general and specific risk factors. *Aggressive Behavior, 33*, 104–107. doi: 10.1002/ab.20172.

Walters, M.L. (2011). Straighten up and act like a lady: A qualitative study of lesbian survivors of intimate partner violence. *Journal of Gay and Lesbian Social Services: The Quarterly Journal of Community and Clinical Practice, 23*, 250–270. doi: 10.1080/10538720.2011.559148.

Walters, M.L., Chen, J., and Breiding, M.J. (2013). *The National Intimate Partner and Sexual Violence Survey (NISVS): 2010 findings on victimization by sexual orientation*. Atlanta, GA: National Center for Injury Prevention and Control, Centers for Disease Control and Prevention.

Waters, H., Hyder, A., Rajkotia, Y., Basu, S., Rehwinkel, J.A., and Butchart, A. (2004). *The economic dimensions of interpersonal violence*. Geneva: Department of Injuries and Violence Prevention, World Health Organization. http://whqlibdoc.who.int/publications/2004/9241591609.pdf.

White, J.W. and Kowalski, R.M. (1994). Deconstructing the myth of the nonaggressive woman: A feminist analysis. *Psychology of Women Quarterly, 18*, 487–508. doi: 10.1111/j.1471-6402.1994.tb01045.x.

Williams, S.L. and Frieze, I.H. (2005). Patterns of violent relationships, psychological distress, and marital satisfaction in a national sample of men and women. *Sex Roles, 52*, 771–784. doi: 10.1007/s11199-005-4198-4.

World Health Organization (2012). *Understanding and addressing violence against women. Intimate partner violence.* http://apps.who.int/iris/bitstream/10665/77432/1/WHO_RHR_12.36_eng.pdf.

World Health Organization (2013). *Global and regional estimates of violence against women: Prevalence and health effects of intimate partner violence and non-partner sexual violence.* Geneva: World Health Organization. http://apps.who.int/iris/bitstream/10665/85239/1/9789241564625_eng.pdf?ua=1.

Wright, P.J. and Tokunaga, R.S. (2016). Men's objectifying media consumption, objectification of women, and attitudes supportive of violence against women. *Archives of Sexual Behavior, 45*, 955–964. doi: 10.1007/s10508-015-0644-8.

Yerke, A.F. and DeFeo, J. (2016). Redefining intimate partner violence beyond the binary to include transgender people. *Journal of Family Violence, 31*, 975–979. doi: 10.1007/s10896-016-9887-y.

Zillmann, D. and Weaver, J.B. (1989). Pornography and men's sexual callousness toward women. In D. Zillmann and J. Bryant (eds), *Pornography: Research advances and policy considerations. Communication* (pp. 95–125). Hillsdale, NJ: Lawrence Erlbaum Associates.

Zimmerman, C., Hossain, M., Yun, K., Roche, B., Morison, L., and Watts, C. (2006). *Stolen smiles: A summary report on the physical and psychological health consequences of women and adolescents trafficked in Europe.* London: The London School of Hygiene and Tropical Medicine. http://genderviolence.lshtm.ac.uk/files/Stolen-Smiles-Summary.pdf.

8

GLOBAL PATTERNS OF GENDER AND HEALTH

The World Health Organization (2010a) has reported that 57 percent of the world's blind people are female, and that the proportion of women in the blind population rises at older ages. We do not usually think of blindness as a gender-linked problem, but the report notes that gender inequalities explain much of the disproportionate impact of this problem upon women. Globally, women with cataracts are less likely than men to have the surgery that would prevent blindness—because they have less access than men to financial resources that would pay for medical care or transportation to a healthcare facility, less access to education and health information, and less autonomy to make decisions with respect to healthcare.

It might be expected that women and men would be vulnerable to different health problems. After all, women and men differ in their hormones, their reproductive systems, their secondary sex characteristics, their size, and their muscle strength. However, as the opening example illustrates, there are other differences between women and men that could lead to gender differences in health: different kinds of work and stress, different behavioral norms and expectations, different life priorities, and different access to resources.

GENDERED PATTERNS OF DISEASE

According to the World Health Organization (2017a), in 2015 average global life expectancy at birth was 73.7 years for women and 69.1 years for men. Despite great variations among regions, income groups, and individual countries, women consistently live longer than men. This advantage may be said to be undercut by the fact that women report more ill-health and suffer more illness, chronic health problems, and disabilities than men (Luy and Minagawa, 2014).

These broad statistics obscure a host of differences in the pattern of illnesses that afflict, and kill, women and men. For example, men experience more life-threatening diseases, such as coronary heart disease and cancer, at a younger age; women, on the other hand, suffer higher rates of certain chronic disorders such as autoimmune diseases, and short-term infectious diseases (Rieker and Bird, 2005).

It is impossible to make broad generalizations about the gendered patterns of specific diseases without paying attention to the impact of socio-economic development. In poorer countries, people are more vulnerable to illnesses that are rare in developed countries—simply because preventive care is not available. For example, women's deaths from cervical and breast cancers is far more common in low-income regions, where screening and treatment are less available, than in high-income countries, where such tests and treatment are routine. More than 50 percent of deaths from breast cancer and 88 percent of deaths from cervical cancer occur in less developed regions of the world (Ginsburg, 2013). In poorer countries, diseases of older age may be less prevalent than in richer countries—because people are more likely to die of something else before they have a chance to become old. Alzheimer's disease and other dementias are the third leading cause of death for women in high-income countries, but are not even in the top ten causes of death for women in low- and middle-income countries (World Health Organization, 2016).

Figure 8.1 shows the leading causes of death for women and men in the United States. In developed countries, a small number of major non-communicable diseases—heart disease, cancer, and stroke—are leading causes of death for both women and men

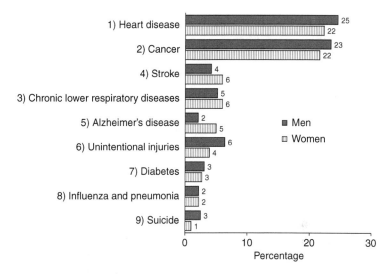

Figure 8.1 Leading causes of death in women and men in the United States, 2014. There are both strong similarities and notable differences in the leading causes of death for women and for men. Whereas heart disease and cancer are by far the top killers of both sexes in the United States, men are more likely than women to die of unintentional injuries or of suicide, and women are more likely than men to die of Alzheimer's disease.

Source: Based on data from Centers for Disease Control and Prevention (2014a, 2014b), and National Center for Health Statistics (2017).

(World Health Organization, 2016). Cardiovascular disease is the leading cause of death for both women and men globally, but it occurs at later ages for women than for men. Until menopause, women's estrogen levels may protect against the build-up of the artery-blocking plaque that can produce heart attacks. Women are more likely than men to suffer from two specific types of heart disease: coronary microvascular disease and broken heart syndrome (National Heart, Lung, and Blood Institute, 2014). For women, cardiovascular disease is the leading cause of death in high-income regions, but in low-income countries women are more likely to die of lower respiratory tract infections, HIV/AIDS, or diarrheal diseases than of heart disease (World Health Organization, 2016).

Cancer rates in high-income countries are more than double those in low-income countries. Breast cancer is the most common cancer among women worldwide and the leading cause of cancer deaths for them, followed by lung, colorectal, cervical, and stomach cancers (World Health Organization, 2016). In high-income countries, most women who develop breast or cervical cancer survive; in low-income countries, such cancers are more likely to result in death (Ginsburg *et al.*, 2017). Globally, the most cancer deaths for men occur from lung, liver, stomach, colorectal, and prostate cancers. Prostate cancer, which affects only men, accounts for about 7 percent of men's cancer deaths worldwide (World Health Organization, 2016).

Autoimmune diseases, characterized by problems in the immune system that cause the body to attack its own organs, tissues, and cells, are far more likely to affect women than men. Most common among these diseases are multiple sclerosis, lupus, and rheumatoid arthritis. In the United States, nearly 80 percent of those suffering from autoimmune diseases are women; these diseases comprise a leading cause of death for young and middle-aged women (National Institute of Allergy and Infectious Diseases, 2016). Reasons for women's greater susceptibility to autoimmune diseases are not clear. Some researchers point to a possible protective effect conferred by androgens (hormones that are at higher levels in males than in females) (Voskul, 2011). Some suggest that an important contributing factor may be male–female differences in intestinal bacteria—differences which somehow affect hormone levels (Markle *et al.*, 2013). Among the consequences of women's greater susceptibility to autoimmune diseases is that women are more likely to suffer from chronic pain. Ironically, women's complaints of pain are more likely than men's to be dismissed as emotional in origin and to be untreated, and clinical trials of pain medication have often omitted women (Edwards, 2013).

Gender is also a factor in patterns of infectious diseases, such as malaria and tuberculosis. In some cultures, girls are less likely than boys to be vaccinated against common diseases; in others, gender role constraints upon mothers make it extraordinarily difficult for them to access vaccinations for their children (Merten *et al.*, 2015). One comparison across 90 less developed countries revealed that women were more protected from malaria in nations where their legal and economic status was higher (Austin, Noble, and Meja, 2014). In Africa, adolescent girls and pregnant women are particularly vulnerable to malaria; pregnant adolescents, who often face stigma and negative attitudes when they seek prenatal medical care, are especially vulnerable (World Health Organization, 2007). Gender differences in sleeping arrangements and gendered division of labor may determine exposure to the mosquitoes that carry malaria. If women work outside before dawn, or if men do most of their work in the forest, their work may place them at high risk of mosquito bites. Gender norms may also affect access to malaria treatment. A woman may need her husband's permission to visit a clinic, or a man may feel he cannot give priority to traveling to a clinic when he has economically important work to do close to home. Women often carry the heaviest burden of malaria and other tropical diseases because they bear the main responsibility of caring for ill family members; however, they are often not the decision-makers with respect to treatment.

The reported incidence of tuberculosis is almost twice as high for men than for women. The reasons for this difference are poorly understood, but some analysts have suggested that, in those countries most heavily affected, the stigma of tuberculosis is seen as greater for women, discouraging them from seeking treatment (and thus from being diagnosed and counted). Gender differences in certain behaviors may affect the progression of this disease. Smoking and alcohol abuse are linked to reduced immunity—and men are far more likely than women to smoke and abuse alcohol in the countries where tuberculosis is prevalent. Men are also less likely than women to complete treatment. Independent of these factors, some research indicates that men may be biologically more susceptible to tuberculosis—perhaps because of hormones (Neyrolles and Quintana-Murci, 2009). Biology and gender-related norms, values, and expectations can shape gendered patterns of illness in a multitude of complex ways, as explored in the following sections.

NUTRITION

Around the world, women are more likely than men to suffer from malnutrition. Reasons include the practice in some societies of giving priority to men and boys when food is available, and women's reduced access to the financial resources necessary to ensure food security. A large study in India showed that girls were less likely than boys to receive supplemental food and were more likely than boys to be malnourished. However, when mothers had higher individual status or lived in communities where women's status was higher, this status apparently reduced the nutrition gap between boys and girls (Bose, 2011). Cross-national research shows that women's empowerment, as indicated by education level, control over reproduction, political representation and life expectancy, predicts lower levels of child malnutrition (Burroway, 2016).

Women in older age groups also face a nutritional disadvantage. One US study of homebound elders showed that, after controlling for health and demographic factors, women reported significantly lower nutrient intake than did men (Sharkey and Branch, 2004). Elderly women are more likely than men to suffer from malnutrition in rural Lebanon (Boulos, Salameh, and Barbeger-Gateau, 2013) and rural India (Das and Das, 2012).

Where food is plentiful, women are still sometimes more likely than men to be malnourished, perhaps because of their acceptance of the cultural notion that they must be thin. Women are more likely than men to be weight conscious and to restrict their food intake in order to lose weight (Aruguete, DeBord, Yates, and Edman, 2005; Yeung, 2010).

STRESS

When external events or conditions feel threatening or debilitating, they become stressors: sources of upset, worry, discomfort, and general distress. Too much stress leads to negative health consequences; increased stress often precedes the onset of illness. Are there differences between women and men in the amount and type of stress they encounter?

Stressful life events are unique occurrences, such as the death of a family member, loss of one's job, destruction of one's home, or being the victim of a physical attack. Stressful life conditions, on the other hand, are chronic situations that persist day after day, such as food insecurity, fear of violence, overwork, or hostility from co-workers. Daily minor irritations, such as traffic, annoying tele-marketing calls, or unexpected messes at home are a third cause of stress. Women report higher levels of both chronic stress and minor daily stressors than do men; however, men and women report similar numbers of stressful life events (Matud, 2004). Whereas women and men do not differ in the number of stressful life events, they may differ in the kinds of events they experience, in the magnitude and type of reaction to these events, and in their coping styles. Matud (2004) found, in a large sample of adults in Spain, that women were more likely to list family and health-related stressful events, and men were more likely to list relationship, financial, and work-related events. Women rated their stressful life events as more negative and less controllable, and they scored higher than men on psychosomatic symptoms and psychological distress. Thus, women seemed more affected than men by the stressors they experienced. Women were also more likely than men to use emotion-focused coping (trying to regulate their emotional responses to the situation) rather than problem-focused coping (trying to change the situation) to deal with stress.

Women are more likely than men to experience one category of stressor: sexist prejudice or discrimination. In one US sample, 99 percent of women said they had experienced a sexist event at least once in their lives; women of color reported more such incidents than did Whites (Klonoff and Landrine, 1995). Most common events were exposure to sexist or sexually degrading jokes, sexual harassment, sexist insults, and disrespectful treatment associated with being female. More than half of the sample reported that being female had led to their being picked on, hit, shoved, or threatened; 40 percent said they had been denied a raise or promotion because they were women; and more than 19 percent said they had taken serious action such as filing a lawsuit or grievance because of sexist discrimination. Women's greater exposure to sexist treatment may partially explain why they report higher rates of depressive, anxious, and somatic symptoms than do men. One survey of US students showed that women who reported experiencing frequent sexist treatment displayed significantly more of these symptoms than did men, but women who reported little sexism did not differ from men on any of the symptoms measured (Klonoff and Landrine,

2000). The impact of gender discrimination intersects with racial or other forms of discrimination. One study of African American women revealed that experiencing both racial and gender discrimination increased these women's risk for poor health and also made them more vulnerable to the impact of individual stressors such as personal injury, victimization, and relationship losses (Perry, Harp, and Oser, 2013).

HEALTH-RELATED BEHAVIORS ARE INFLUENCED BY GENDER STEREOTYPES

Women and men tend to differ in behaviors and attitudes linked to health outcomes. Men engage in more health risk behaviors (Pengpid and Peltzer, 2015). Women are more likely than men to engage in "preventive nutrition" by eating healthy foods and avoiding foods believed to be dangerous (Schüz, Sniehotta, Scholz, and Mallach, 2005). Female medical students display more positive attitudes than men toward using nutrition as a therapeutic tool (Schulman and Karney, 2003). When possible, women are more likely than men to eat the recommended five servings per day of fruit and vegetables, and to be aware of the recommendations (Baker and Wardle, 2003; El Ansari *et al.*, 2011). How might these kinds of male–female differences in health behaviors be linked to gender socialization and expectations? Here are some possibilities. Part of the masculine role entails taking risks rather than being cautious. Part of the feminine role involves an orientation toward nurturing and caretaking, which could encompass being knowledgeable about health issues. In many contexts it is more acceptable for women than for men to admit weakness, seek help, or take advice, and women are socialized more than men to be concerned about their bodies.

SMOKING

All over the world, men are far more likely to use tobacco, with men's average prevalence 4.4 times that of women (World Health Organization, 2011). Historically, in most countries men have been first to adopt the practice of smoking—a pattern that has been reinforced by gender roles that have traditionally deemed smoking unfeminine or unladylike. For example, the World Health Organization (2003) cites a study in Vietnam in which the most common reason given by women for avoiding tobacco was that "women shouldn't smoke." On the other hand, smoking often represents masculinity and may form an important aspect of social relationships among males. Smoking advertisements tend to bolster this notion, with portrayals of men smoking while in rough terrain, undertaking adventurous or strenuous activities, and wearing rugged clothing.

Tobacco companies have targeted girls and women, particularly in developing countries, with the message that smoking is sophisticated, sexy, and associated with breaking constraints for women. Cultural emphasis on thinness for women adds to the pressure to use tobacco; many young women report that they start or continue to smoke in order to avoid weight gain. Perhaps for these reasons, tobacco use appears to be increasing among girls in some countries, particularly in Asia and the Pacific region (World Health Organization, 2011).

For women more than for men, smoking appears to be associated with avoiding depression and other negative emotions (Richardson, He, Curry, and Merikangas, 2012); for men, smoking is more strongly linked to positive sensations and habit. It appears harder for women than for men to quit smoking—perhaps because they rely on it to cope with stress (Legleye, Khlat, Beck, and Peretti-Watel, 2011; World Health Organization, 2011).

Smoking is responsible for most cases of lung cancer, and is implicated in many cases of heart disease and other illnesses. As smoking rates have increased among women over the decades, the rates of lung cancer have followed, with about a 30-year lag (Weiss, 1997). In the United States, the prevalence of cigarette smoking peaked for men in 1940, remained steady until 1955, and then began to decline; consequently, the lung cancer rate for men peaked in 1990 and then began to drop. For women, whose smoking increased steadily from no higher than 2 percent in 1930 to 38 percent in 1960 and then dropped more slowly than men's, lung cancer mortality began to rise in about 1965. Women's mortality rate from lung cancer has increased sixfold since 1950; lung cancer overtook breast cancer as the leading cause of death for women in the United States in the 1980s and remains a more frequent cause of death for US women (National Center for Health Statistics, 2016). Figure 8.2 shows the changes in lung cancer mortality rates for women and men over the past several decades. Compared to men, women may develop lung cancer with lower

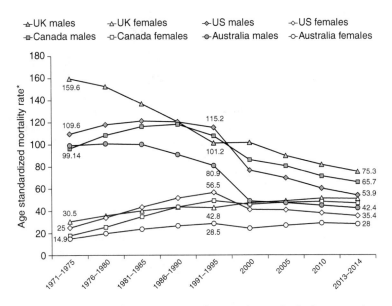

Figure 8.2 Patterns in lung cancer mortality rates by gender in four countries. Changes in lung cancer mortality rates (deaths per 100,000 people) among women and men are an example of how changes in gendered patterns of behavior can affect health. In all four countries shown here, there was a trend for lung cancer mortality rates to begin dropping among men as the delayed impact of a drop in the percentage of men who smoke took effect. For women, on the other hand, lung cancer mortality rates continued to increase steadily, reflecting a rise in women's smoking that peaked years later than the peak for men.

Note: *Rates for Australia since the year 2000 are crude rather than standardized.

Source: Based on data from Liaw, Huang, and Lien (2005), National Cancer Institute (2014), Cancer Research UK (2016), Canadian Cancer Society (2017), and Australian Institute of Health and Welfare (2017).

levels of smoking and are more likely to contract aggressive small cell lung cancer. Tobacco use is also especially problematic for women because their bodies metabolize nicotine more quickly if they are pregnant or using oral contraceptives (World Health Organization, 2011).

ALCOHOL AND OTHER DRUGS

Multinational studies show a consistent tendency for men to use alcohol and drink more heavily than women, and for more women than men to abstain from alcohol or give up drinking (Wilsnack, Wilsnack, Kristjanson, Vogeltanz-Holm, and Gmel, 2009). Illicit drug use and dependence is also higher among males (National Center for Health Statistics, 2016). Cultural norms are more tolerant of male than female intoxication, and may emphasize restraint as a sign of appropriate femininity. In addition, men often have greater access to money for alcohol and drugs and to freedom to go out and indulge. The importance of such cultural factors is illustrated by the large variation among countries in drinking behavior. For example, one 35-country study reported rates of current drinking that ranged from 97 percent of men and 94 percent of women in Denmark to 37 percent of men and 3 percent of women in the Indian state of Karnataka (Wilsnack *et al.*, 2009).

Although women drink less alcohol, they typically achieve higher blood alcohol concentrations than do men, even when consuming the same amount (Mumenthaler, Taylor, O'Hara, and Yesavage, 1999). Thus, women are likely to experience alcohol-related problems at lower levels of drinking than men. Studies have shown that college women reported blackouts at the same rate as men, even though they drank less (White, Jamieson-Drake, and Swartzwelder, 2002), and that they experienced alcohol-related physical illnesses with lower levels of drinking than did men (Nolen-Hoeksema, 2004).

Women and men may be at risk of different consequences of drinking owing to differences in the ways their bodies respond to alcohol and differences in gender norms and expectations (Nolen-Hoeksema and Hilt, 2006). One study examined gender differences in the consequences of drinking, after controlling for the reported amount of alcohol consumed per week and the estimated average blood alcohol level of participants. Even after accounting for these variables, women who drank alcohol had a higher risk than men of developing tolerance for higher levels of alcohol, blacking out, passing out, drinking after promising not to, and getting injured. Men, on the other hand, had a higher risk of damaging property and going to school drunk (Sugarman, DeMartini, and Carey, 2009). For women, a dangerous consequence of binge drinking is an increased vulnerability to rape (McCauley, Calhoun, and Gidycz, 2010). Another consequence unique to women is danger to a developing fetus of maternal alcohol use (Tsai, Floyd, Green, and Boyle, 2007).

The misuse and abuse of prescription drugs is a topic of serious concern. Indeed, in the United States and some other countries, there is agreement that there is an "opioid epidemic" involving addiction to prescription painkillers. The role of gender in this situation is complex. Overdose deaths from prescription painkillers are increasing faster among women than among men (Office on Women's Health, 2016). Men are somewhat more likely than women to report misusing prescription drugs; however, women are more likely than men to be prescribed both painkillers and antidepressants (National Center for Health Statistics, 2016). Women are more often prescribed painkillers because they are more likely than men to experience severe pain, and that experience appears to increase with age (Grol-Prokopczyk, 2017). Women who use opioids may also progress more quickly to dependence than do men, and experience more cravings (Office on Women's Health, 2016).

RISK-TAKING

Men tend to engage in more physically risky behaviors than do women (Pengpid and Peltzer, 2015)—perhaps because taking risks is part of stereotypic masculinity. Men may use risk-taking to signal their masculinity to potential mates; one study showed that young men were more likely to take risks when sexually aroused and in the presence of a romantically available woman (Baker and Maner, 2009). Men may build up masculine "capital" by engaging in traditionally masculine activities. Such "masculinity points" bolster a man's perceived masculinity and compensate for non-masculine behaviors (de Visser and McDonnell, 2013). For example, a man may be able to compensate for being a non-drinker if he takes other kinds of risks, is a good athlete, or is known to be heterosexually active.

The orientation toward risk can make men, especially certain groups of men, particularly vulnerable to accidental injury and death. For example, some young working-class men in Australia enact a risk-heavy masculine automobile culture, which emphasizes male power and excludes women (Walker, Butland, and Connell, 2000). Attempts to fit in with this culture may encourage young men to speed, avoid seat belt use, drive while intoxicated, and engage in other risky behaviors that can lead to disastrous results. Indeed, in 2015 more than three times as many boys and men as girls and women died from road traffic accidents around the world (World Health Organization, 2016).

For women, health-related risky behaviors often entail body change strategies, such as extreme dieting or cosmetic surgery. Such behaviors are not often discussed in the framework of "risk-taking," and are less public and/or social than risks associated with masculinity. Thus, they may be overlooked when researchers make gender comparisons in risky behaviors.

RISKY SEXUAL BEHAVIORS

Having many sexual partners exposes an individual to increased risk of sexually transmitted disease. Globally, men are more than twice as likely as women to die from sexually transmitted diseases other than HIV/AIDS and almost 1.4 times as likely to die from HIV/AIDS (World Health Organization, 2016). Having many sexual partners may also increase the likelihood of sexual victimization, particularly for women, by raising the probability of encountering an assaultive partner. Men are more likely than women to engage in unprotected sex with multiple partners (Nkansah-Amankra, Diedhiou, Agbanu, Harrod, and Dhawan, 2011); having plenty of sex with multiple women is sometimes seen as an important aspect of masculinity (Bowleg et al., 2011).

For both women and men, one predictor of sexual risk-taking and other forms of health risk behaviors is a history of sexual assault. Women who have been sexually assaulted report higher levels of depression and anxiety, more dangerous drinking, and risky sexual behavior than do other women (McCauley, Ruggiero, Resnick, Conoscenti, and Kilpatrick, 2009). In one diverse sample of US college women, women in all ethnic groups used risky sexual behavior as a way of coping with the depression and anxiety caused by sexual assault (Littleton, Grills-Taquechel, Buck, Rosman, and Dodd, 2013). Among US male college students, sexual victimization is also linked to higher levels of sexual risk-taking behaviors and problem drinking (Turchik, 2012).

EXERCISE AND FITNESS

Men are more likely than women to engage in recommended levels of regular physical activity—although the majority of men and women do not meet minimum guidelines in developed countries (Centers for Disease Control and Prevention, 2014; Zach et al., 2013). Men's higher frequency of exercise may stem partly from gender stereotypes and norms that emphasize strength and activity for men more than for women. Linked to these stereotypes are differences in encouragement and opportunities for women and men in the realm of sports and fitness. For example, for many years, the running of marathons was considered impossible or dangerous for women. It was 1972 before women were allowed to compete in the famous Boston Marathon (although Roberta Gibb sneaked onto the field and completed the race in 1966, and Kathrine Switzer made a famous "unofficial" run in 1967 by registering for the race as K.V. Switzer and nonchalantly lining up with the men). There was no marathon race for women included in the Summer Olympics until 1984.

In countries where there are strong sanctions against the display of women's bodies, restrictions on women's opportunities for exercise and sports participation have been especially stringent. In some Muslim majority countries, female athletes abide by very modest dress codes and do not join in mixed-gender fitness classes. Female athletes in these countries have adjusted by wearing a variety of very modest fitness clothing, adopting forms of exercise that allow for comfortable clothing (or solitude), and flocking to single-sex gyms and women-only beaches (Moaveni, 2009). With accommodations for dress codes, Muslim women have made their mark in international competitive sports. For example, an Iranian skier, Marjan Kalhor, participated in the 2010 Winter Olympics wearing a uniform that covered her body completely, and female boxers from Afghanistan have worn the hijab in competitions sponsored by the International Boxing Association (WISE, 2010).

HIV/AIDS AND OTHER SEXUALLY TRANSMITTED DISEASES

Women make up about half of the approximately 37 million people around the world who are living with human immunodeficiency virus (HIV); HIV/AIDS is the leading cause of death worldwide among women of reproductive age (World Health Organization, 2016). Globally, among persons aged 15 to 24, women's rates of HIV infection are significantly higher than men's (UNAIDS, 2015). Both biology and gender-related norms and power relations contribute to the high prevalence of this disease among women. During heterosexual intercourse, women are at higher risk than men for transmission of HIV and some other sexually transmitted infections, partly because the mucous membranes of the female reproductive tract receive substantial and protracted exposure to any virus present in seminal fluid. Women's biological vulnerability is magnified, moreover, by cultural factors: their exposure to rape, pressure by partners to have sex without the protection of condoms, and their lack of control over high-risk behaviors of their partners—who may have unprotected sex or use intravenous drugs with shared needles (Higgins, Hoffman, and Dworkin 2010). For similar reasons, women are also more vulnerable than men to a variety of other sexually transmitted diseases such as human papilloma virus (HPV), trichomoniasis, genital herpes, and chlamydia.

Men's vulnerability to HIV/AIDS is increased under conditions such as homelessness and incarceration. In the United States, where the overwhelming majority of prisoners are Black men, the rate of AIDS is five times higher in the prison population than in the general population (Centers for Disease Control and Prevention, 2017a). However, in some contexts men's wealth and income are positively related to HIV risk—perhaps because wealth is linked to the ability to have more leisure time, spend more on alcohol and drugs, and acquire more sexual partners. In some sub-Saharan African countries, adults in the wealthiest segments of the population have the highest prevalence of HIV (Mishra *et al.*, 2007).

The impact of HIV/AIDS differs by gender. Pregnant women who are HIV positive can transmit the virus to their newborns during pregnancy, childbirth, or breastfeeding—something that occurs between 15 and 45 percent of the time in the absence of effective interventions. Interventions such as antiretroviral treatment can reduce this rate to 5 percent (World Health Organization, 2017b). Women may face barriers to HIV prevention and treatment due to lack of resources, childcare responsibilities, and restrictions on their mobility and decision-making power. Men may avoid seeking HIV prevention or treatment services for fear of stigma, worry about losing their jobs, or concern that they may be perceived as weak or unmanly.

REPRODUCTIVE HEALTH AND MATERNAL MORTALITY

In the realm of reproductive health, differences in health-related issues between women and men are most stark, since women deal with pregnancy, childbirth, and the complications associated with these processes, and are also concerned with preventing or terminating pregnancies. Maternal mortality is a major health issue in the developing world, complicated in some cases by female genital cutting procedures that leave women vulnerable to terrible injuries when giving birth. In developed countries, too, reproductive health issues impact women and men quite differently, particularly in terms of access to contraception and abortion.

CONTRACEPTION AND ABORTION

The availability of reliable ways to prevent pregnancy has a significant impact upon individual heterosexual relationships and upon the broader picture of male–female relations. In 2010, the fiftieth anniversary of the birth control pill, analysts opined that it was the pill that changed women's lives (e.g. Rubin, 2010). The large impact came because women taking the pill could control their reproduction, even without the knowledge and/or consent of their partners—a significant shift in the balance of power within relationships. Even if women were in relationships where they had little choice about whether to have sex, they at least did not have to face a series of unwanted pregnancies. This was a dramatic change from earlier decades, when women often bore more children than they wanted, could afford, or had the health and strength to nurture. And the development of better pills and contraceptive methods over the intervening years—now including morning-after pills—has increased women's options in this regard.

Around the world, however, in 2010, about 12.3 percent of women aged 15 to 49, who were married or in sexual relationships and who wanted to avoid a pregnancy, either did not have access to, or were not using, any effective method of contraception. In Africa, the unmet need for contraception was highest, at more than 25 percent (Alkema, Kantorova, Menozzi, and Biddlecome, 2013). Even where contraception is theoretically available (though perhaps not very affordable or accessible), it is not always used. In the United States, about one in every ten women who are at risk from an unintended pregnancy do not use any form of contraception (Daniels, Daugherty, and Jones, 2014).

Contraceptive methods for men have emphasized the condom and sterilization through vasectomy. The approaches have not advanced significantly for years, perhaps because women are the ones who get pregnant. One possible reversible method of male contraception (thus far tested only on mice) uses a molecular approach to reduce sperm numbers and motility without affecting hormone levels (Matzuk *et al.*, 2012). If such a method were successfully developed, it might increase the proportion of men who take on the major responsibility for contraception.

When contraception is unavailable or fails, women faced with unintended pregnancies may turn to abortion. In the United States where abortion is legal, there were 12.5 abortions reported per 1000 women of reproductive age in 2013, with highest rates for women aged 20 to 29 (Jatlaoui *et al.*, 2016). It is rare for these abortions to end in death or serious injury for the women involved; in developing countries, however, grim statistics reveal that abortion is unsafe for women, and is often carried out under illegal or unsanitary conditions. Worldwide, approximately 13 percent of maternal deaths (about 47,000 per year) are linked to abortion-related complications—and almost all of these deaths occur in developing countries (World Health Organization, Human Reproduction Program, 2017).

PREGNANCY, CHILDBIRTH, AND MATERNAL HEALTH

The vast majority of women experience pregnancy at some point in their lives. Pregnancy and its outcomes and complications provide the single most obvious set of reasons why women may require healthcare. Life-threatening complications include severe bleeding during or after childbirth, infections, and problems linked to hypertension, heart disease, diabetes, and botched abortions.

For women in the developed world, pregnancy and childbirth are relatively safe. For example, in 2015, globally, a woman's lifetime risk of death associated with complications of pregnancy or childbirth was one in 180. However, women's risk of death was only one in 23,700 in Greece, one in 8800 in Canada, one in 5800 in the United Kingdom, and one in 3800 in the United States (Alkema *et al.*, 2015). In the United States, maternal mortality increased by more than 26 percent from 2000 to 2014—to 23.8 maternal deaths per 100,000 live births. This makes the United States the only developed country in which maternal mortality is rising. Among the 31 OECD countries, the USA ranks worse than every country apart from Mexico in maternal mortality (MacDorman, Declercq, Cabral, and Morton, 2016). The situation is worse in less developed countries. In 2015, a woman's lifetime risk of dying from pregnancy or childbirth complications was one in 17 in Sierra Leone, one in 22 in Somalia, and one in 52 in Afghanistan. Although the number of maternal deaths decreased worldwide from 385 deaths per 100,000 live births in 1990 to 216 in 2015, women continue to die at high rates, mainly in low-income countries. Poverty is a key factor: research across developing countries shows a consistent link between increasing poverty and an increasing proportion of women dying from pregnancy-related causes (Paruzzolo, Mehra, Kes, and Ashbaugh, 2010). Within developed countries, too, maternal deaths are more common among women who lack economic resources and access to good medical care. In the United States, for example, pregnancy-related deaths are more than three times as high for African American women than for white women (Centers for Disease Control and Prevention, 2017b) and are highest in regions of the country with high poverty rates and high immigrant populations.

Pregnancy and childbirth are riskier for teenaged women, who are about one-third more likely than women in their twenties to die from maternal causes (Restrepo-Méndez and Victora, 2014). This consideration, along with concerns about the ability of very young mothers to provide and care for their children, has driven efforts to reduce teen birth rates. In the United States, a 67 percent decline in teen birth rates from 1991 to 2016, to a historic low of 20.3 births per 1000 women aged 15 to 19, was hailed with pride by health officials (Hamilton, Martin, Osterman, Driscoll, and Rossen, 2017). However, in some low-income countries, women are expected to marry and begin childbearing at very young ages, often without having any power to refuse such arrangements; about 11 percent of births around the world are to mothers aged 15 to 19 (World Health Organization, 2014). Among teenaged mothers globally, complications of pregnancy and childbirth are the second leading cause of death—and babies born to teen mothers also have a lower risk of survival (World Health Organization, 2014). Where gender norms prescribe that women be kept subservient to men, denied opportunities for education and income, and refused the choice to delay marriage and motherhood, this pattern is likely to persist.

FEMALE GENITAL MUTILATION

A traditional practice in some cultures involves a rite of passage in which a girl's genital area is cut. Sometimes called female circumcision, female genital mutilation (FGM) is a cultural practice rooted in the notion that women's sexuality is dangerous and must be controlled. In some cases, the clitoris and labia are excised completely and the genital area is sewn up; in others, the clitoris and labia are partially removed. Millions of girls are affected; for example, in Indonesia in 2010, between 86 and 100 percent of households surveyed said their daughters were subjected to genital cutting (Haworth, 2012). In Africa, the Middle East, and Asia, more than 200 million girls and women alive today have undergone FGM (World Health Organization, 2017c).

This procedure, which is justified as a way of ensuring that a girl grows into a sexually virtuous woman, is dangerous and painful, and later interferes with the woman's sexual pleasure. Furthermore, this genital cutting and sewing often creates a smaller vaginal opening, leading to obstructed labor when the woman gives birth. Obstructed labor can produce a dangerous condition called obstetric fistula: a hole torn in the birth canal. Without repair, the fistula leads to unrelenting urinary incontinence and the possibility of infection—and the sufferer is often shamed and segregated in her community.

Male circumcision, which involves surgical removal of the foreskin of the penis when the boy is a few days old, also affects millions. This procedure also has its roots in cultural and religious traditions (both Jewish and Muslim). Male circumcision (unlike the procedures described above for females) appears to confer more potential health benefits than risks: prevention of urinary tract infections, prostate cancer, and some sexually transmitted infections and reduced risk of cervical cancer, herpes, chlamydia, and syphilis in female partners (Morris, Bailis, and Wiswell, 2014; Morris and Hankins, 2017). International clinical trials in Africa demonstrated that men who had been randomly assigned to be circumcised had significantly lower incidence of HIV infection than control groups of men circumcised at the end of the study (Byakika-Tusiime, 2008). Unlike FGM, male circumcision does not typically have deleterious effects on sexual pleasure or expose boys to the risk of serious health problems or death.

DEPRESSION AND SUICIDE

Women and men have similar overall levels of mental health, but differ in the frequency with which they experience specific conditions: women are more likely to experience depression and anxiety disorders; men are likely to show substance abuse, antisocial behavior, and to commit suicide (Rieker and Bird, 2005). Although there is little doubt that women are more likely than men to be depressed, part of the difference in diagnosis rates may be due to gender-related stereotypes and expectations. When women and men score similarly on measures of depressive symptoms, women are more likely than men to be diagnosed as depressed by their primary care physician (Bertakis *et al.* 2001).

Beginning by age 12 and peaking during adolescence, there is a significant gender difference in depression: women are about twice as likely as men to be diagnosed as depressed—a ratio that seems to hold all over the world (Salk, Hyde, and Abramson, 2017). Some explanations for this gender difference focus on the amount and kinds of distress experienced by women and men, and some focus on how distress is handled. Women may experience different kinds of stressors than men, or may, owing to biological and socialization differences, be more likely than men to react to stress in ways that lead to depression (Nolen-Hoeksema, 2006). One major research emphasis has been on rumination: focusing on and thinking about problems. Women and girls are more likely than men and boys to ruminate when they are distressed—and people who tend to ruminate when they are distressed experience more depressive symptoms and are more likely to develop major depression (McLaughlin and Nolen-Hoeksema, 2011).

Social support from peers and friends seems to buffer the effects of stress and reduce the likelihood of depression. However, even though adolescent girls report more supportive peer relationships than do boys, they also have higher rates of depression. Upon investigation, researchers discovered that adolescent girls were more likely than boys to spend time co-ruminating with their close friends—focusing their conversations mainly on problems and negative emotions (Stone, Hankin, Gibb, and Abela, 2011). Higher levels of co-rumination were associated with more, longer, and more severe episodes of depression among the sample of adolescents they studied. The causes of gender differences in rumination and co-rumination may lie in the different ways girls and boys are socialized. For example, girls apparently expect that disclosing problems to friends will make them feel cared for and understood, whereas boys expect to feel that they are wasting time (Rose *et al.*, 2012)—a difference that may be rooted in early parent–child interactions that emphasize conversation for girls more than for boys.

Although women are more likely than men to be depressed and to think about and attempt suicide (McKinnon, Gariépy, Sentenac, and Elgar, 2016), men are more likely than women to actually commit suicide (World Health Organization, 2017d). The ratio of male to female suicides varies widely among countries, with, for example, the number of male suicides for every female suicide being about 3.4 in the United States, 2.7 in Australia, 5.7 in the Russian Federation, and 2.3 in Japan (World Health Organization, 2017c). Among the Inuit people in Canada, whose suicide rate is among the highest in the world, 22 percent of 15- to 24-year-old men and 39 percent of young women report having attempted suicide (Fraser, Geoffroy, Chachamovich, and Kirmayer, 2015). For both males and females, having been a victim of sexual assault predicts increased likelihood of suicide attempts (Tomasula, Anderson, Littleton, and Riley-Tillman, 2012), as does being a victim of school bullying (Sampasa-Kanyinga, Dupuis, and Ray, 2017). Among transgender and other gender nonconforming adults, family rejection related to gender identity is linked to increased risk of suicidal behavior (Klein and Golub, 2016).

Different factors may push women and men toward suicide. One South African study found, for example, that men tended to take their own lives as a means of escape when their ideals of masculinity, dominance, and success were thwarted, whereas women committed suicide to protest against miserable conditions in their lives—often caused by the dominance of the men around them (Niehaus, 2012). Perpetrators of a particular type of suicide—murder-suicide—in the United States are overwhelmingly male, most often use guns, and most often target family members, although a smaller group targets strangers in "rampage killings" before committing suicide (Violence Policy Center, 2012). These statistics fit with the idea of suicide growing out of rage and frustration at being unable to succeed in controlling a situation—as a man is supposed to be able to do—and/or the desire to escape failure by going out in a blaze of "masculine" glory. However, little actual research confirms or disputes this interpretation.

Gender differences in completed suicides do not parallel gender differences in depression, and researchers have struggled to comprehend the underlying factors. Some have suggested that men are more likely than women to have access to very lethal tools for suicide: firearms. Others have noted that certain personality traits congruent with the masculine role—stoicism and sensation-seeking—are linked to capability of suicide (Witte, Gordon, Smith, and Van Orden, 2012). However, many unanswered questions remain.

HEALTH DISPARITIES AMONG WOMEN AND AMONG MEN

Although there is considerable data that may be used to compare health issues and outcomes *between* women and men, disparities exist *within* both genders—affected by the intersection of gender with such factors as race/ethnicity, economic status, sexual orientation, and culture. For example, in the United States, African American women are significantly more likely than women of other groups to die from breast cancer and from cervical cancer, and White women are more likely than other women to die from ovarian cancer. Among US men, African Americans are much more likely than men of other groups to die from prostate cancer (Centers for Disease Control and Prevention, 2017c). Within the USA, women living in economically deprived counties are more than three times as likely as women in other counties to have late-stage breast cancer (Anderson *et al.*, 2013). Such disparities may be fueled by a combination of factors, such as access to care, stress, environmental pollution, and lifestyle.

Sexual orientation and gender identity are also associated with health disparities. For example, young people who identify as lesbian, gay, bisexual, or transgender are two to three times more likely than their gender-conforming counterparts to attempt suicide; lesbian women are less likely than other women to receive preventive services for cancer; and transgender persons have an especially high rate of victimization and mental health issues (Office of Disease Prevention and Health Promotion, 2017). Many of these health issues are linked to discrimination and to difficulties in finding medical providers who are knowledgeable about and accepting of LGBT patients.

Globally, one issue affecting the health of millions of women and men is migration—both planned and unplanned, chosen, or forced. Worldwide, 65.6 million people were forcibly displaced from their homes in 2016. The total number seeking refuge across international borders was greater than 22.5 million —the highest number since the United Nations began keeping records (UNHCR, 2017). Gender intersects with the sources of stress and distress experienced by refugees, and also with the sources of resilience and strength. Among refugees, women often face the risk of rape and other gender-based violence while they are fleeing, and they often have to deal with pregnancy, childbirth, and caring for small children. Both women and men have long-term health consequences of grief, loss, and trauma, which may affect their health for years to come. The impact of shattered expectations about gender roles may also be important. For example, one study of Afghan refugees who resettled in the United States found that family ties and English ability were linked with lower levels of distress among women, but had little association with distress among men. With respect to gender ideology, traditionally oriented women and egalitarian men showed lower distress, and men were particularly distressed by dissonance between their home culture and their new one. These patterns were attributed by researchers to the difficulty of adaptation to very different gender roles in their new country (Stempel *et al.*, 2017).

ACCESS TO MEDICAL CARE

When access to medical care is readily available, women are more likely than men to consult with physicians for physical and mental health issues (Centers for Disease Control and Prevention, 2017d). One explanation for the differences appears to be the constraints of the masculine gender role. In the USA, both men and women consider it "not masculine" to see a doctor for minor health concerns or to consult a psychologist or psychiatrist for emotional issues (de Visser and McDonnell, 2013). US researchers have also found that men with traditional beliefs about masculinity (that men should be tough, strong, and self-reliant) were more likely to put off dealing with medical problems and more likely to choose male physicians, in the belief that male doctors were more competent. However, when seeing male doctors, these men were not open with them about their symptoms, perhaps because they did not want to appear weak or dependent. Interestingly, the men were more likely to be honest about symptoms with female doctors (Himmelstein and Sanchez, 2016).

Access to medical care is not always readily available, however. Among older Americans, women have greater healthcare needs but fewer economic resources than men; in this population, women may have fewer physician visits and hospital stays than men with similar health profiles (Cameron, Song, Manheim, and Dunlop, 2010). There are gender disparities in access to care, screening, treatment decisions, and follow-up care. In the United States in 2015, 10.7 percent of women, as compared to 8.9 percent of men, reported delaying or forgoing medical care, 8.4 percent of women and 5.4 percent of men did not receive prescription drugs, and 13.6 percent of women and 10 percent of men did not receive dental care due to cost (National Center for Health Statistics, 2016). Even in Canada, a country with universally accessible, publicly funded healthcare, gender has been a reliable predictor of having an unmet healthcare need (Bryant, Leaver, and Dunn, 2009). Specifics of care may be shaped by patient gender; for example, female patients with atrial fibrillation are less likely than males to receive anticoagulation medication (Bhave, Lu, Girotra, Kamel, and Vaughan Sarrazin, 2015), and women with heart attack symptoms are less likely than men to receive angioplasty treatment (Donnelly, 2015). Gender stereotypes may account for some gender disparities in treatment decisions. For example, physicians whose prototypical heart attack patient is a middle-aged man may be slow to diagnose a heart attack in a middle-aged woman, even though women who have a heart attack are actually more likely to die than men (Travis, Meltzer, and Howerton, 2010).

In the developing world as well, gender inequities in access to healthcare are linked to gendered norms, stereotypes, and resource allocation. Women often lack economic support for seeking treatment for themselves or for their children, and may have to defy the opinions of male family members in order to do so. In some settings, women may be reluctant to deal with male healthcare workers (World Health Organization, 2007). Men may use healthcare services less than women do when significant commitments of time and energy, such as walking long distances to a clinic, are involved. Perhaps masculinity ideology makes it embarrassing to appear to place so much emphasis on obtaining help.

Attempts to understand gendered patterns of health must go beyond biological differences between women and men. Gendered cultural norms, expectations, and restrictions play a significant role in shaping threats to, and supports for, individuals' well-being. The lifelong impact of these cultural forces culminates in the way older age is experienced by men and women, as seen in Chapter 9.

FOR FURTHER EXPLORATION

Bird, Chloe E. and Rieker, P.P. (2008). *Gender and health: The effect of constrained choices and social policies* (New York: Cambridge University Press). These sociologist authors examine ways in which gender differences in health may be constructed by social arrangements and societal norms and laws with respect to gender. They include discussions of the impact of gendered work and family patterns, community supports, and gender-differentiated pressures toward particular individual health choices.

Chrisler, J.C. (ed.) (2012). *Reproductive justice: A global concern* (Santa Barbara, CA: Praeger). Contributions from social scientists in many different countries examine a variety of issues related to reproductive health. Included are chapters on partner selection, power in partner relationships, genital cutting, sexual assault, trafficking and sexual exploitation, contraception and abortion, pregnancy, birthing, and public policy for reproductive justice.

Jack, Dana C. and Ali, Alisha A. (eds) (2010). *Silencing the self across cultures: Depression and gender in the social world* (Oxford: Oxford University Press). The editors have gathered the perspectives of 21 contributors from 13 countries to examine the social and psychological aspects of gender differences in depression. The contributions include consideration of such factors as relationships, drugs, self-censorship, immigration, violence, and illness in the development of gendered patterns of depression in different cultural contexts.

McHugh, Maureen C. and Chrisler, Joan C. (eds) (2015). *The wrong prescription for women: How medicine and the media create a "need" for treatments, drugs, and surgery* (Santa Barbara, CA: Praeger). The editors have collected articles that critique the medicalized approach to a variety of health issues for women, including reproductive issues, sexuality, body image, and depression. Each article critiques the medicalization of a particular issue, and then follows with recommendations for a different approach.

REFERENCES

Alkema, L., Kantorova, V., Menozzi, C., and Biddlecome, A. (2013). National, regional, and global rates and trends in contraceptive prevalence and unmet need for family planning between 1990 and 2015: A systematic and comprehensive analysis. *The Lancet, 381*, 1642–1652. doi: 10.1016/S0140-6736(12)62204-1.

Alkema, L., Chou, D., Hogan, D., Zhang, S., Moller, A., Fat, D.M., *et al.* (2015, November 12). Global, regional, and national levels and trends in maternal mortality between 1990 and 2015, with scenario-based projections to 2030: a systematic analysis by the UN Maternal Mortality Estimation Inter-Agency Group. *The Lancet*, November 12. Published online http://dx.doi.org/10.1016/S0140-6736(15)00838-7 and Appendix, www.thelancet.com/pb/assets/raw/Lancet/pdfs/S0140673615008387_appendix.pdf.

Anderson, R.T., Yang, T., Matthews, S.A., Camacho, F., Kern, T., Mackley, H.B., Kimmick, G., Louis, C., Lengerich, E., and Yao, N. (2013). Breast cancer screening, area deprivation, and later stage breast cancer in Appalachia: Does geography matter? *Health Services Research, 49*, 546–567. doi: 10.1111/1475-6773.12108.

Aruguete, M.S., DeBord, K.A., Yates, A., and Edman, J. (2005). Ethnic and gender differences in eating attitudes among black and white college students. *Eating Behaviors, 6*, 328–336. doi: 10.1016/j.eatbeh.2004.01.014.

Austin, K.F., Noble, M.D., and Meja, M.T (2014). Gendered vulnerabilities to a neglected disease: A comparative investigation of the effect of women's legal economic rights and social status on malaria rates. *International Journal of Comparative Sociology, 55*, 204–228.

Australian Institute of Health and Welfare (2017). Australian cancer incidence and mortality (ACIM) books. Lung cancer. www.aihw.gov.au/reports/cancer/acim-books/contents/acim-books.

Baker, A.H. and Wardle, J. (2003). Sex differences in fruit and vegetable intake in older adults. *Appetite, 40*, 269–275. doi: 10.1016/S0195-6663(03)00014-X.

Baker Jr., M.D. and Maner, J.K. (2009). Male risk-taking as a context-sensitive signaling device. *Journal of Experimental Social Psychology, 45*, 1136–1139. doi: 10.1016/j.jesp. 2009.06.006.

Bertakis, K.D., Helms, L.J., Callahan, E.J., Azari, R., Leigh, P., and Robbins, J.A. (2001). Patient gender differences in the diagnosis of depression in primary care. *Journal of Women's Health and Gender Based Medicine, 10*, 689–698.

Bhave, P.D., Lu, X., Girotra, S., Kamel, H., and Vaughan Sarrazin, M.S. (2015). Race- and sex-related differences in care for patients newly diagnosed with atrial fibrillation. *Heart Rhythm, 12*, 1406–1412.

Bose, S. (2011). The effect of women's status and community on the gender differential in children's nutrition in India. *Journal of Biosocial Science, 43*, 513–533. doi: 10.1017/S002193201100006X.

Boulos, C., Salameh, P., and Barberger-Gateau, P. (2013). The AMEL study, a cross sectional population-based survey on aging and malnutrition in 1200 elder Lebanese living in rural settings: Protocol and sample characteristics. *BMC Public Health*, June 12, *13*, 573. doi: 10.1186/1471-2458-13-573.

Bowleg, L., Teti, M., Massie, J.S., Patel, A., Malebranche, D.J., and Tschann, J.M. (2011). 'What does it take to be a man? What is a real man?': Ideologies of masculinity and HIV sexual risk among black heterosexual men. *Culture, Health and Sexuality, 13*, 545–559. doi: 10.1080/13691058.2011.556201.

Bryant, T., Leaver, C., and Dunn, J. (2009). Unmet healthcare need, gender, and health inequalities in Canada. *Health Policy, 91*, 24–32. doi: 10.1016/j.healthpol.2008.11.002.

Burroway, R. (2016). Empowering women, strengthening children: A multi-level analysis of gender inequality and child malnutrition in developing countries. *Advances in Gender Research, 22*, 117–142. doi: 10.1108/S1529-212620160000022016.

Byakika-Tusiime, J. (2008). Circumcision and HIV infection: Assessment of causality. *AIDS and Behavior, 12*, 835–841.

Cameron, K.A., Song, J., Manheim, L.M., and Dunlop, D.D. (2010). Gender disparities in health and healthcare use among older adults. *Journal of Women's Health, 19*, 1643–1650. doi: 10.1089/jwh.2009.1701.

Canadian Cancer Society (2017). Canadian cancer statistics 2017. www.cancer.ca/~/media/cancer.ca/CW/publications/Canadian%20Cancer%20Statistics/Canadian-Cancer-Statistics-2017-EN.pdf.

Cancer Research UK (2016). Lung cancer mortality statistics. www.cancer researchuk.org/health-professional/cancer-statistics/statistics-by-cancer-type/lung-cancer/mortality#heading-Two.

Centers for Disease Control and Prevention (2014a). Leading causes of death in females, 2014. www.cdc.gov/women/lcod/2014/race-ethnicity/index.htm.

Centers for Disease Control and Prevention (2014b). Leading causes of death in males, 2014. www.cdc.gov/healthequity/lcod/men/2014/race-ethnicity/index.htm.

Centers for Disease Control and Prevention (2014c). *Physical activity. Data and statistics.* www.cdc.gov/physicalactivity/data/facts.html.

Centers for Disease Control and Prevention (2017a). *HIV among incarcerated populations.* www.cdc.gov/hiv/group/correctional.html.

Centers for Disease Control and Prevention (2017b). *Pregnancy mortality surveillance system.* www.cdc.gov/reproductivehealth/maternalinfanthealth/pmss.html.

Centers for Disease Control and Prevention (2017c). *Cancer rates by race/ethnicity and sex.* www.cdc.gov/cancer/dcpc/data/race.htm.

Center for Disease Control and Prevention (2017d). FastStats. *Ambulatory care use and physician office visits.* www.cdc.gov/nchs/fastats/physician-visits.htm.

Daniels, K., Daugherty, J., and Jones, J. (2014). Current contraceptive status among women aged 15–44: United States, 2011–2013, *National Health Statistics Reports*, No. 173. www.cdc.gov/nchs/data/databriefs/db173.pdf.

Das, S. and Das, D. (2012). Women's health status and healthcare in rural India—A case study of Barak Valley in Assam. *Journal of Social and Economic Policy, 9*, 53–66.

de Visser, R.O. and McDonnell, E.J. (2013). "Man points": Masculine capital and young men's health. *Health Psychology, 32*, 5–14. doi: 10.1037/a0029045.

Donnelly, l. (2015). Women more likely to die following heart attack than men. *The Telegraph*, August 30. www.telegraph.co.uk/news/health/news/11833480/Women-more-likely-to-die-following-heart-attack-than-men.html.

Edwards, L. (2013). The gender gap in pain. *The New York Times*, March 16. www.nytimes.com/2013/03/17/opinion/sunday/women-and-the-treatment-of-pain.html?ref=painand_r=1and.

El Ansari, W., Stock, C., John, J., Deeny, P., Phillips, C., Snelgrove, S. *et al.* (2011). Health promoting behaviours and lifestyle characteristics of students at seven universities in the UK. *Central European Journal of Public Health, 19*(4), 197–204.

Fraser, S.L., Geoffroy, D., Chachamovich, E., and Kirmayer, L. (2015). Changing rates of suicide ideation and attempts among Inuit youth: A gender-based analysis of risk and protective factors. *Suicide & Life-threatening Behavior*, *45*, 141–156.

Ginsburg, O.M. (2013). Breast and cervical cancer control in low and middle-income countries: Human rights meet sound health policy. *Journal of Cancer Policy*, *1*, e35–e41. doi: 10.1016/j.jcpo.2013.07.002.

Ginsburg, O.M., Bray, F., Coleman, M.P. *et al.* (2017). Health, equity, and women's cancers 1. The global burden of women's cancers: A grand challenge in global health. *The Lancet*, *389*, 847–860. http://dx.doi.org/10.1016/S0140-6736(16)31392-7.

Grol-Prokopczyk, H. (2017). Sociodemographic disparities in chronic pain, based on 12-year longitudinal data. *Pain*, *158*, 313–322. http://dx.doi.org/10.1097/j.pain.0000000000000762.

Hamilton, B.E., Martin, J.A., Osterman, M.J.K., Driscoll, A.K., and Rossen, L.M. (2017). Births: Provisional data for 2016. *NVSS Vital Statistics Rapid Release*, Report No. 002, June. www.cdc.gov/nchs/data/vsrr/report002.pdf.

Haworth, A. (2012). The day I saw 248 girls suffering genital mutilation. *Observer*, November 17. www.guardian.co.uk/society/2012/nov/18/female-genital-mutilation-circumcision-indonesia.

Higgins, J.A., Hoffman, S., and Dworkin, S.L. (2010). Rethinking gender, heterosexual men, and women's vulnerability to HIV/AIDS. *American Journal of Public Health*, *100*, 435–445. doi: 10.2105/AJPH.2009.159723.

Himmelstein, M.S. and Sanchez, D.T. (2016). Masculinity in the doctor's office: Masculinity, gendered doctor preference and doctor–patient communication. *Preventive Medicine*, *84*, 34–40. doi: 10.1016/j.ypmed.2015.12.008.

Jatlaoui, T.C., Ewing, A., Mandel, M.G. *et al.* (2016). Abortion Surveillance—United States, 2013. *MMWR Surveillance*, *65* (summer), 1–44. doi: http://dx.doi.org/10.15585/mmwr.ss6512a1.

Klein, A. and Golub, S.A. (2016). Family rejection as a predictor of suicide attempts and substance misuse among transgender and gender nonconforming adults. *LGBT Health*, *3*(3), 193–199.

Klonoff, E.A. and Landrine, H. (1995). The Schedule of Sexist Events: A measure of lifetime and recent sexist discrimination in women's lives. *Psychology of Women Quarterly*, *19*, 439–472. doi: 10.1111/j.1471-6402.1995.tb00086.x.

Klonoff, E.A. and Landrine, H. (2000). Sexist discrimination may account for well-known gender differences in psychiatric symptoms. *Psychology of Women Quarterly*, *24*, 93–99. doi: 10.1111/j.1471-6402.2000.tb01025.x.

Legleye, S., Khlat, M., Beck, F., and Peretti-Watel, P. (2011). Widening inequalities in smoking initiation and cessation patterns: A cohort and gender analysis in France. *Drug and Alcohol Dependence, 117,* 233–241. doi: 10.1016/j. drugalcdep. 2011.02.004.

Liaw, Y., Huang, Y., and Lien, G. (2005). Patterns of lung cancer mortality in 23 countries: Application of the age-period-cohort model. *BMC Public Health, 5*(22). http://europepmc.org/articles/PMC555565.

Littleton, H.L., Grills-Taquechel, A.E., Buck, K.S., Rosman, L. and Dodd, J.C. (2013). Health risk behavior and sexual assault among ethnically diverse women. *Psychology of Women Quarterly* **37**, 7–21. doi: 10.1177/03616843124 51842.

Luy, M., and Minagawa, Y. (2014). Gender gaps – Life expectancy and proportion of life in poor health. *Health Reports, 25* (12), 12–19. (Statistics Canada Catalogue no. 82-003-X).

MacDorman, M.F., Declercq, E., Cabral, H., and Morton, C. (2016). Recent increases in the U.S. maternal mortality rate: Disentangling trends from measurement issues. *Obstetrics & Gynecology, 128,* 44–455. doi: 10.1097/AOG.0000000000001556.

Markle, J.G.M., Frank, D.N., Mortin-Toth, S., Robertson, C.E., Feazel, L.M., Rolle-Kampczyk, U., von Bergen, M., McCoy, K.D., Macpherson, A.J., and Danska, J.S. (2013). Sex differences in the gut microbiome drive hormone-dependent regulation of autoimmunity. *Science*, published online January 17. doi: 10.1126/science.1233521. www.sciencemag.org/content/early/2013/01/16/science.1233521.

Matud, M.P. (2004). Gender differences in stress and coping styles. *Personality and Individual Differences, 37,* 1401–1415. doi: 10.1016/j.paid.2004.01.010.

Matzuk, M.M., McKeown, M.R., Filippakopoulos, P., Li, Q., Ma, L., Agno, J.E., Lemieux, M.E., Picaud, S., Yu, R.N., Qi, J., Knapp, S., and Bradner, J.E. (2012). Small-molecule inhibition of BRDT for male contraception. *Cell, 150,* 673–684. doi: 10.1016/j.cell.2012.06.045.

McCauley, J.L., Calhoun, K.S., and Gidycz, C.A. (2010). Binge drinking and rape: A prospective examination of college women with a history of previous sexual victimization. *Journal of Interpersonal Violence, 25,* 1655–1668. doi: 10.1177/0886260509354580.

McCauley, J., Ruggiero, K.J., Resnick, H.S., Conoscenti, L.M., and Kilpatrick, D.G. (2009). Forcible, drug–facilitated, and incapacitated rape in relation to substance use problems: Results from a national sample of college women. *Addictive Behaviors, 34,* 458–462. doi: 10.1016/j.addbeh.2008.12.004.

McKinnon, B., Gariépy, Sentenac, M., and Elgar, F.J. (2016). Adolescent suicidal behaviours in 32 low- and middle-income countries. *Bulletin of the World Health Organization, 94,* 340–350F. doi: http://dx.doi.org/10.2471/BLT.15.163295.

McLaughlin, K. and Nolen-Hoeksema, S. (2011). The role of rumination in promoting and preventing depression in adolescent girls. In T.J. Strauman, P.R. Costanzo, and J. Garber (eds), *Depression in adolescent girls: Science and prevention*. Duke Series in Child Development and Public Policy (pp. 112–129). New York: Guilford Press.

Merten, S., Martin Hilber, A., Biaggi, C., Secula, F., Bosch-Capblanch, X., Namgyal, P, and Hombach, J. (2015). Gender determinants of vaccination status in children: Evidence from a meta-ethnographic systematic review. *PLoS ONE, 10*(8): e0135222. doi: 10.1371/journal.pone.0135222.

Mishra, V., Assche, S.B., Greener, R., Vaessen, M., Hong, R., Ghys, P.D., Boerma, J.Y., Van Assche, A., Khan, S., and Rutstein, S. (2007). HIV infection does not disproportionately affect the poorer in sub-Saharan Africa. *AIDS, 21*(Suppl 7), S17–S28.

Moaveni, A. (2009). How to work out while Muslim—and female. *Time.com*, August 16. www.time.com/time/magazine/article/0,9171,1924488,00.html.

Morris, B.J. and Hankins, C.A. (2017). Effect of male circumcision on risk of sexually transmitted infections and cervical cancer in women. *The Lancet, Global Health, 5*, e1054-e1055. doi: http://dx.doi.org/10.1016/S2214-109X(17)30386-8.

Morris, B.J., Bailis, S.A., and Wiswell, T.E. (2014). Circumcision rates in the United States: Rising or falling? What effect might the new affirmative pediatric policy statement have? *Mayo Clinic Proceedings, 89*, 677–686. doi: http://dx.doi.org/10.1016/j.mayocp. 2014.01.001.

Mumenthaler, M.S., Taylor, J.L., O'Hara, R., and Yesavage, J.A. (1999). Gender differences in moderate drinking effects. *Alcohol Research and Health, 23*, 55–64.

National Cancer Institute (2014). Cancer of the lung and Bronchus. Annual death rates. Table 15.9. https://seer.cancer.gov/archive/csr/1975_2013/results_merged/sect_15_lung_bronchus.pdf.

National Center for Health Statistics (2016). *Health, United States, 2016*. www.cdc.gov/nchs/hus/contents2016.htm.

National Center for Health Statistics (2017). *Health, United States 2016*. Table 17. www.cdc.gov/nchs/data/hus/hus16.pdf#listfigures.

National Heart, Lung, and Blood Institute, US Department of Health and Human Services (2014). *How does heart disease affect women?* www.nhlbi.nih.gov/health/health-topics/topics/hdw/.

National Institute of Allergy and Infectious Diseases (2016). *Gender-specific health challenges facing women*. www.niaid.nih.gov/research/gender-specific-health-challenges.

Neyrolles, O. and Quintana-Murci, L. (2009), Sexual inequality in tuberculosis. *PLoS Medicine, 6*, 12. http://dx.doi.org/10.1371/journal.pmed.1000199.

Niehaus, I. (2012). Gendered endings: Narratives of male and female suicides in the South African lowveld. *Culture, Medicine and Psychiatry, 36*, 327–347. doi: 10.1007/s11013-012-9258-y.

Nkansah-Amankra, S., Diedhiou, A., Agbanu, H.L.K., Harrod, C., and Dhawan, A. (2011). Correlates of sexual risk behaviors among high school students in Colorado: Analysis and implications for school-based HIV/ AIDS programs. *Maternal and Child Health Journal, 15*, 730–741. doi: 10.1007/s10995-010-0634-3.

Nolen-Hoeksema, S. (2004). Gender differences in risk factors and consequences for alcohol use and problems. *Clinical Psychology Review, 24*, 981–1010.

Nolen-Hoeksema, S. (2006). The etiology of gender differences in depression. In C.M. Mazure and G.P. Keita (eds), *Understanding depression in women: Applying empirical research to practice and policy* (pp. 9–43). Washington, DC: American Psychological Association. doi: 10.1037/11434-001.

Nolen-Hoeksema, S. and Hilt, L. (2006). Possible contributors to the gender differences in alcohol use and problems. *Journal of General Psychology, 133*, 357–374. http://dx.doi.org/10.3200/GENP.133.4.357-374.

Office of Disease Prevention and Health Promotion (2017). *Lesbian, gay, bisexual, and transgender health.* www.healthypeople.gov/2020/topics-objectives/topic/lesbian-gay-bisexual-and-transgender-health.

Office on Women's Heath (2016). *White paper: Opioid use, misuse, and overdoes in women.* www.womenshealth.gov/files/documents/white-paper-opioid-508.pdf.

Paruzzolo, S., Mehra, R., Kes, A., and Ashbaugh, C. (2010). *Targeting poverty and gender inequality to improve maternal health.* New York: Women Deliver. www.womendeliver.org/assets/Targeting_poverty.pdf.

Pengpid, S. and Peltzer, K. (2015). Gender differences in health risk behavior among university students: An international study. *Gender & Behaviour, 13*, 6576–6583.

Perry, B.L., Harp, I.L., and Oser, A.B. (2013). Racial and gender discrimination in the stress process: Implications for African American women's health and well-being. *Sociological Perspectives, 56*, 25–48. doi: 10.1525/sop.2012.56.1.25.

Restrepo-Méndez, M.C. and Victora, C.G. (2014). Maternal mortality by age: Who is most at risk? *The Lancet, Global Health, 2*(3), e120-e121. doi: http://dx.doi.org/10.1016/S2214-109X(14)70007-5.

Richardson, A., He, J-P., Curry, L., and Merikangas, K. (2012). Cigarette smoking and mood disorders in US adolescents: Sex-specific associations with symptoms, diagnoses, impairment and health services use. *Journal of Psychosomatic Research, 72*, 269–275. doi: 10.1016/j.jpsychores.2012.01.013.

Rieker, P.P. and Bird, C.E. (2005). Rethinking gender differences in health: Why we need to integrate social and biological perspectives. *Journal of Gerontology*, Series B, *60B*, 40–47.

Rose, A.J., Schwartz-Mette, R.A., Smith, R.L., Asher, S.R., Swenson, L.P., Carlson, W., and Waller, E.M. (2012). How girls and boys expect disclosure about problems will make them feel: Implications for friendships. *Child Development, 83*, 844–863.

Rubin, R. (2010). The pill: 50 years of birth control changed women's lives. *USA Today*, May 8. http://usatoday30.usatoday.com/news/health/2010-05-07-1Apill07_CV_N.htm.

Salk, R.H., Hyde, J.S., and Abramson, L.Y. (2017). Gender differences in depression in representative national samples: Meta-analyses of diagnoses and symptoms. *Psychological Bulletin, 143*, 783–822. http://dx.doi.org/10.1037/bul0000102.

Sampasa-Kanyinga, H., Dupuis, L.C., and Ray, R. (2017). Prevalence and correlates of suicidal ideation and attempts among children and adolescents. *International Journal of Adolescent Medicine and Health*, April 1, *29*(2). https://doi.org/10.1515/ijamh-2015-0053.

Schulman, J.A. and Karney, B.R. (2003). Gender and attitudes toward nutrition in prospective physicians. *American Journal of Health Behavior, 27*, 623–632. doi: 10.5993/AJHB.27.6.5.

Schüz, B., Sniehotta, F.F., Scholz, U., and Mallach, N. (2005). Gender differences in preventive nutrition: An exploratory study addressing meat consumption after livestock epidemics. *The Irish Journal of Psychology, 26*, 101–113.

Sharkey, J.R. and Branch, L.G. (2004). Gender differences in physical performance, body composition, and dietary intake in homebound elders. *Journal of Women and Aging, 16*, 71–89. doi: 10.1300/J074v16n03_06.

Stempel, C., Sami, N., Koga, P.M., Alemi, Q., Smith, V., and Shiraze, A. (2017). Gendered sources of distress and resilience among Afghan refugees in northern California: A cross-sectional study. *International Journal of Environmental Research and Public Health, 14*(1), 25–47. doi: 10.3390/ijerph14010025.

Stone, L.B., Hankin, B.L., Gibb, B.E., and Abela, J.R.Z. (2011). Co-rumination predicts the onset of depressive disorders during adolescence. *Journal of Abnormal Psychology, 120*, 752–757. doi: 10.1037/a0023384.

Sugarman, D.E., DeMartini, K.S., and Carey, K.B. (2009). Are women at greater risk? An examination of alcohol-related consequences and gender. *The American Journal on Addictions, 18*, 194–197. doi: 10.1080/10550490902786991.

Tomasula, J.L., Anderson, L.M., Littleton, H.L., and Riley-Tillman, T.C. (2012). The association between sexual assault and suicidal activity in a national sample. *School Psychology Quarterly, 27*, 109–119. doi: 10.1037/a0029162.

Travis, C.B., Meltzer, A.I., and Howerton, D.M. (2010). Gender issues in health care utilization. In J. Chrisler and D.R. McCreary (eds), *Handbook of gender research in psychology* (Vol. 2, pp. 517–540). New York: Springer.

Tsai, J., Floyd, R.L., Green, P.P., and Boyle, C.A. (2007). Patterns and average volume of alcohol use among women of childbearing age. *Maternal and Child Health Journal, 11*, 437–445. doi: 10.1007/s10995-007-0185-4.

Turchik, J.A. (2012). Sexual victimization among male college students: Assault severity, sexual functioning, and health risk behaviors. *Psychology of Men and Masculinity, 13*, 243–255. doi: 10.1037/a0024605. Special Section: Recent Research on Sexual Harassment and Victimization of Men.

UNAIDS (2015). *Global factsheets 2015.* http://aidsinfo.unaids.org/.

UNHCR (2017). *Forced displacement worldwide at its highest in decades.* www.unhcr.org/uk/news/stories/2017/6/5941561f4/forced-displacement-worldwide-its-highest-decades.html.

Violence Policy Center (2012). *American roulette: Murder-suicide in the United States* (4th edn). Washington, DC: Author. www.vpc.org/studies/amroul2012.pdf.

Voskul, R. (2011). Sex differences in autoimmune diseases. *Biology of Sex Differences, 2.* www.bsd-journal.com/content/2/1/1.

Walker, L., Butland, D., and Connell, R.W. (2000). Boys on the road: Masculinities, car culture, and road safety education. *The Journal of Men's Studies, 8*, 153–169. doi: 10.3149/jms.0802.153.

Weiss, W. (1997). Cigarette smoking and lung cancer trends. A light at the end of the tunnel? *Chest, 111*, 1414–1416.

White, A.M., Jamieson-Drake, D.W., and Swartzwelder, H.S. (2002). Prevalence and correlates of alcohol-induced blackouts among college students: Results of an e-mail survey. *Journal of American College Health, 51*, 117–131.

Wilsnack, R.W., Wilsnack, S.C., Kristjanson, A.F., Vogeltanz-Holm, N.D., and Gmel, G. (2009). Gender and alcohol consumption: Patterns from the multinational GENACIS project. *Addiction, 104*, 1487–1500. doi: 10.1111/j.1360-0443.2009.02696.x.

WISE (2010). Women's Islamic initiative in spirituality and equality. Current issues: Sports. www.wisemuslimwomen.org/currentissues/sports/.

Witte, T.K., Gordon, K.H., Smith, P.N., and Van Orden, K.A. (2012). Stoicism and sensation seeking: Male vulnerabilities for the acquired capability for suicide. *Journal of Research in Personality, 46*, 384–392. doi: 10.1016/j.jrp.2012.03.004.

World Health Organization (2003). Gender, health and tobacco. www.who. int/gender/documents/Gender_Tobacco_2.pdf.

World Health Organization (2007). Gender, health, and malaria. www.who. int/gender/documents/gender_health_malaria.pdf.

World Health Organization (2010). *Gender and blindness—Eye surgery in Egypt*. www.who.int/gender/egypt_20101108_en.pdf.

World Health Organization (2011). Gender, health, tobacco, and equity. www.who.int/tobacco/publications/gender/gender_tobacco_2010. pdf?ua=1.

World Health Organization (2013). *Fact sheet: Women's health*, September. www.who.int/mediacentre/factsheets/fs334/en/.

World Health Organization (2014). *Adolescent pregnancy. Fact sheet*. www.who. int/mediacentre/factsheets/fs364/en/.

World Health Organization (2016). *Global health estimates 2015: Deaths by cause, age, sex, by country and by region, 2000–2015*. www.who.int/health-info/global_burden_disease/estimates/en/index1.html.

World Health Organization (2017a). *World Health Statistics 2017*. http://apps. who.int/iris/bitstream/10665/255336/1/9789241565486-eng.pdf?ua=1.

World Health Organization (2017b). HIV/AIDS. *Mother-to-child transmission of HIV*. http://who.int/hiv/topics/mtct/en/.

World Health Organization (2017c). *Female genital mutilation. Fact sheet*. www. who.int/mediacentre/factsheets/fs241/en/.

World Health Organization (2017d). Global health Observatory data repository. *Suicide rates, age-standardized, data by county*. http://apps.who.int/ gho/data/node.main.MHSUICIDEASDR?lang=en.

World Health Organization, Human Reproduction Program (2017). *Preventing unsafe abortion*. www.who.int/reproductivehealth/topics/unsafe_abortion/ magnitude/en/.

Yeung, W.T.L. (2010). Gender perspectives on adolescent eating behaviors: A study on the eating attitudes and behaviors of junior secondary students in Hong Kong. *Journal of Nutrition Education and Behavior, 42*, 250–258. doi: 10.1016/j.jneb.2009.05.008.

Zach, S., Zeev, A., Dunsky, A., Goldbourt, U., Shimony, T., Goldsmith, R., and Netz, Y. (2013). Adolescents' physical activity habits—Results from a national health survey. *Child: Care, Health and Development, 39*, 103–108. doi: 10.1111/j.1365-2214.2012.01392.x.

9

THE SHAPE OF OUR FUTURE

GENDER AND THE AGING POPULATION

Aging represents the future—not only for each of us as individuals but for many facets of our collective experience within culture. As it happens, each of us is getting older, but also we are currently in a situation in which the world's population is shifting toward an older average age. Like so many other things, the experience of aging is shaped by gender roles and expectations. Some analysts have written about a "double standard of aging," by which older women in North America are judged as unattractive, less feminine, and frail, whereas older men are judged as distinguished, still masculine, and wise (Deutsch, Zalenski, and Clark, 1986). Some researchers have identified a mellowing of gender stereotypes with older age, so that women become more comfortable with agency, power, and authority as they age (e.g., Stewart, Ostrove, and Helson, 2001), whereas men become more nurturing and less concerned with dominance and competition (Sinnott and Shifren, 2001; Villereal and Cavazos, 2005). All this is of particular interest to gender scholars because women live longer than men—so there is an increasing majority of women as we consider older age groups.

CHANGING DEMOGRAPHICS: AN AGING POPULATION MEANS MORE WOMEN

In all regions of the world, the proportion of people aged 60 and older is increasing. By 2050 it is expected that in 65 countries more than 30 percent of their population will be over the age of 60 (United Nations Population Fund, 2012).

As was noted in Chapter 8 and detailed in Figure 9.1, women's life expectancy is longer than men's around the world, although the gender difference is smaller in poorer countries, where overall life expectancy is lower. Thus women make up the majority of persons in older age brackets, and that majority increases in size at increasing

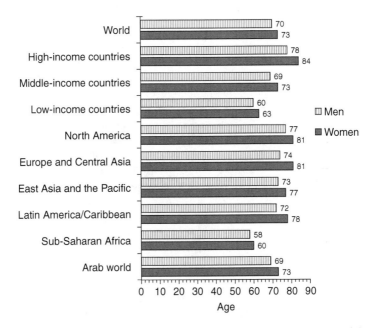

Figure 9.1 Life expectancy at birth for women and men. In all regions of the world, women's life expectancy at birth is longer than that of men. However, the difference is smaller in poorer countries.

Source: Based on data from The World Bank (2017). World Development Expectancy Indicators: https://data.worldbank.org/indicator/SP.DYN.LE00.FE.IN.

age, as shown in Figure 9.2. Worldwide, men comprise 95 percent of 60-year-olds, 72.8 percent of 80-year-olds, 48.4 percent of 90-year-olds, and only 23.1 percent of persons aged 100 or older (U.S. Census Bureau, 2017a). These ratios vary somewhat by region; for example, men make up 76.2 percent of 80-year-olds in North America, but only 43.1 percent of 80-year-olds in Eastern Europe (U.S. Census Bureau, 2017b). By the time they reach older age, women and men have absorbed the cumulative impact of years of differential treatment and access to resources and opportunities. Thus it is not surprising if their experiences of old age are different on many dimensions, including work, health, and relationships.

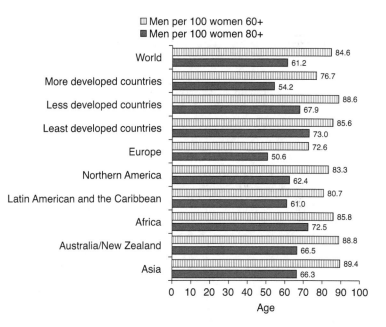

Figure 9.2 Ratio of men to women among people aged 60 years and over and 80 years and over. Because, on average, women live longer than men do, there are more women than men in older segments of the population. Women outnumber men among seniors aged 60 years and over, and the proportion of women to men increases with age.

Source: Based on data from the U.S. Census Bureau (2017a, 2017b).

WORK AND THE GENDERED ECONOMICS OF AGING: WHO CAN AFFORD A RESTFUL RETIREMENT?

The proportions of older women and men in the labor force differ from country to country. In the United States in 2016, almost 37 percent of men and 28 percent of women aged 65 to 69 were in the civilian labor force; among those aged 70 to 74, 23.8 percent of men and 15.2 percent of women were in the labor force (U.S. Bureau of Labor Statistics, 2017a). In Canada, the labor force participation rate of those aged 65 and over was 10.1 percent for women and 17.9 percent for men in 2016; in Korea, the rate was 23.7 percent for women and 42.2 percent for men; in France, the rate was 2.2 percent for women and 3.9 percent for men (Organization for Economic Cooperation and Development, 2017).

In recent years, the proportion of women working past traditional retirement age has increased more than the proportion of men doing the same, and older women are increasingly likely to be in the labor market. By 2024, the projection is for the labor force participation rate of women aged 65 and older to be 18.4 percent—an increase of 3.3 percent over the previous decade—while similar-aged men's participation is projected to increase 2.7 percent (U.S. Bureau of Labor Statistics, 2015). In most of the world, the participation of women aged 55 and over has risen over the past two decades, while that of men in the same age group has remained the same or dipped slightly (United Nations, 2015).

Why might the proportion of older women in the workforce be increasing more rapidly than the proportion of men? One possibility is that, because of their disproportionate share of family responsibilities, many women joined the workforce later or had more gaps in their workforce participation than did men, leaving them not ready to retire "on schedule" because they were still building their careers. Another possibility is that, having put in fewer years of work and been paid lower salaries, women are less likely than men to have the economic resources to retire.

A gender wage gap persists among older workers. In the United States in 1979 older women's median weekly earnings were 77.6 percent of men's; 28 years later, in 2007, the women's earnings were still only 77.8 percent of men's. By 2016, women aged 65 and over earned only 75.5 percent of what similar-aged men earned (U.S. Bureau of Labor Statistics, 2017b). The wage gap increases with age among US women. In 2016, women in the 16 to 24 age range earned just under 95 percent of similar-aged men's earnings. That percentage dropped to 88.8 for women in the 25 to 34 age range, 83.3 for women in the 35 to 44 age range, and 77.8 and 73.7 respectively, for women aged 45 to 54 and 55 to 64.

The cumulative impact of the gender wage gap over many years of work means that women are more likely than men to have insufficient resources when they approach retirement. The situation is exacerbated by the fact that women are less likely than men to have adequate pensions (International Labour Office, 2016). Traditionally, state-funded pensions were not designed to be directly available to persons who had not made contributions while employed—meaning that women who spent much of their lives in homemaking roles could access pension income only through their spouses. Women are also less likely to be in jobs that provide private pensions, and to have had fewer years in the workforce to accumulate pension contributions and retirement savings.

The problems with inadequate pensions and retirement income for women are global. Worldwide, the percentage of men above retirement age receiving a pension is 68.4 percent, whereas only 57.8 percent of women above retirement age receive a pension (International Labour Office, 2016). The gender gap in pension beneficiaries in northern Africa, the Arab states, and eastern Asia is particularly large; in these regions, more than 20 percent fewer women than men above retirement age receive a pension. The size of pension benefits also shows a significant gender gap—reflecting women's lower wages, career breaks, higher incidence of part-time work, and other factors. For instance, women's pensions are 60.1 percent the size of men's in the United Kingdom, 80.5 percent of men's in Iceland, and 88. 8 percent of men's in the Russian Federation (International Labour Office, 2016). In the United States, retired women are significantly more likely than men to depend on Social Security payments as their only or main source of income— and such payments are, on average, lower for women than for men (Joint Economic Committee United States Congress, 2016). In

Britain, single female pensioners have significantly lower gross income, and lower occupational and personal pension income than single male pensioners (Department for Work and Pensions, 2016). Furthermore, women's longer life expectancy means that they must stretch their already smaller retirement savings over a longer period than must men. All this adds up to considerable worry for women. The European Social Survey (2010) showed that in almost all countries surveyed, women were more concerned than men that their retirement income would be inadequate to support them through their old age.

Whether or not they can afford a "restful retirement," many elders spend their early old age making important contributions to their families and communities through unpaid work. The Australian government once calculated that, among persons aged 65 to 74, women contributed $16 billion per year in unpaid caregiving and voluntary work, while men contributed $10 billion (de Vaus, Gray, and Stanton, 2003). In Canada, older adults devote an average of 223 hours per year in volunteer work (Mei, Eales, and Fast, 2013). Unpaid work by older Americans, including formal volunteering, informally helping community members, and care for family members, has been valued at more than $161 billion per year (Johnson and Schaner, 2005).

AGING AND THE FEMINIZATION OF POVERTY

Women who are old and single are especially vulnerable to poverty. Because women live longer than men, they are more likely than men to lose their life partners, less likely to remarry, and to spend more time at the ends of their lives living in poverty. We have already seen that women tend to have fewer retirement savings and are less likely than men to have adequate pensions. Widowhood decreases women's income (except in the rare cases where the husband leaves a large inheritance), and often pushes women over the line into poverty. In the United States, where 34 percent of older women were widows in 2016 (Administration on Aging, 2016), widowhood has been found to decrease a woman's household income by 37 percent, but decreases a man's by only 22 percent (U.S. Government Accountability Office, 2012). In China,

Ghana, India, the Russian Federation, and South Africa, widowhood for women is linked to being in the poorest wealth quintile (Lloyd-Sherlock, Corso, and Minicuci, 2015).

In the United States in 2015, the poverty rate for older women was significantly higher (10.3%) than for men (7.0%) (Proctor, Semega, and Kollar, 2016). Women, minorities, and older persons living alone are more likely to be poor. There are staggeringly high poverty rates for Hispanic women living alone (40.7%) (Administration on Aging, 2016). Older women are at higher risk of poverty than older men in all countries where data are available (Organization for Economic Cooperation and Development, 2015a). The largest gender gaps are in Estonia, Slovenia, and the United States, where older women's poverty rates are between 8 and 12 percentage points higher than older men's—but large gaps also exist in Germany, Hungary, Poland, and Switzerland. Sexual orientation also interacts with age with respect to poverty: among couples aged 65 or over in the United States, women in same-sex couples have the highest poverty rate (Badgett, Durso, and Schneebaum, 2013).

GENDERED ASPECTS OF AGING AND HEALTH

Gender stereotypes and age stereotypes interact, often resulting in *ageism* (bias against individuals on the basis of their age) that is colored by sexism, and vice versa. Women, already stereotyped as weaker than men, are viewed as increasingly frail as they age. Stereotypes of post-menopausal women include frailty, poverty, disengagement, dependency, and incompetence (Chrisler, Barney, and Palatino, 2016; Velkoff and Kinsella, 1998). Young people view "old age" as starting earlier for women than for men (Barrett and von Rohr, 2008), and there are greater pressures on women than on men to hide signs that they are aging (Dingman, Otte, and Foster, 2012).

For men, masculine stereotypes of dominance and sexual agency interact with age stereotypes to shape anti-aging messages. Advertisements targeted to older men urge them to forestall aging via supplemental testosterone, to continue to view women in terms of their sexual availability, and to continue to prove masculinity through competence and competition (Calasanti and King, 2007).

Clearly, gender stereotypes play a role in individuals' experience of aging and health.

MEDIA MESSAGES TO OLDER MEN AND WOMEN

Both popular and scientific media produce competing narratives of aging and contradictory messages aimed at older women and men (Lips and Hastings, 2012). Ads in the popular media careen between portrayals of silver-haired, carefree, heterosexual couples enjoying a leisurely retirement of golf and Caribbean cruises, and depictions of older individuals wincing in pain as they try to move. The medical literature sounds dire warnings about decline in the form of arthritis, osteoporosis, and erectile dysfunction, but also preaches healthy diet, exercise, and fitness to hold back the ravages of aging.

The increasing proportion of older people in the population has produced a rise in targeting of seniors by advertisers. Whereas older women were once ignored in the media or treated as anything but sexy, they are now bombarded by the message that they should do or buy whatever is necessary to maintain their sex appeal. At the same time, powerful and accomplished mature women in the public eye, such as Hillary Clinton, Theresa May, and Angela Merkel, are sometimes deliberately portrayed as unattractive and unlikable—with stereotypic attributions such as "ice queen," unflattering photographs emphasizing wrinkles and sags, and abrasive-sounding quotes (Vandiver, 2011).

Media messages also target older men, exhorting them to look and act younger than their age. A torrent of advertisements advises men on ways to prevent or reverse hair loss or graying. Yet the media also provide many favorable images of men in their seventies and eighties—in which craggy faces and gray hair are portrayed as handsome and distinguished. We may think of Clint Eastwood, Harrison Ford, Sean Connery, Morgan Freeman, and many older men who are depicted as attractive and interesting; it is more difficult to come up with similar-aged women who are portrayed equally favorably.

WOMEN, MEN, BODIES, AND FITNESS AT OLDER AGES

Aging correlates with changes in our physical bodies: changes in appearance, and in the ease with which we see, hear, think, and move. Indeed, the body is the crucial locus for the social construction of aging. By looking at how people internalize age stereotypes and then physically express them through their bodies, theories of embodiment analyze the impact of aging upon individuals.

Not surprisingly, physical appearance is a central aspect of women's experience of aging (Maguire, 2008). Women are judged heavily on their appearance, and a youthful appearance is prized as a *sine qua non* of women's attractiveness. Many women express concerns about how they can hold back the tide of changes in appearance (wrinkles, grey hair, sagging breasts, weight gain) that accompany advancing age. However, older women's vulnerability to anxiety or dissatisfaction based on appearance may vary among ethnic and cultural groups. For example, older African American women show more body satisfaction than do older European American women (Sabik and Cole, 2017).

Appearance concerns frequently translate into spending money on anti-aging treatments, ranging from expensive skins creams to cosmetic surgery. One market research firm projects annual spending on anti-aging products globally will reach $260 billion by 2022 (Global Industry Analysts, 2016). In the United States in 2016, there were 387,000 cosmetic surgeries and a total of 4.1 million cosmetic procedures performed on persons aged 55 and over—and 92 percent of all cosmetic procedures in 2016 were performed on women (American Society of Plastic Surgeons, 2016).

Although we may decry the association of age with unattractiveness in women and exhort women to think of aging as beautiful, there are real and serious cultural reasons for women's concerns about "looking old." For not only are negative stereotypes of the aged pervasive, but these stereotypes are often internalized. Through a lifelong process of first observing and then experiencing the prejudiced evaluations directed at old persons, older persons begin to accept the stereotypes and apply them to themselves. Furthermore, the more strongly these stereotypes are internalized, the more they become self-fulfilling prophecies: older persons who accept that they are frail, incapable, and vulnerable become less healthy and less capable on a variety of dimensions.

Levy's (2009) *stereotype embodiment theory* outlines how individuals assimilate stereotypes of aging from the surrounding culture, leading to self-definitions that influence their own functioning and health. Aging, she argues, is at least in part a social construct; thus, while we should try to change negative stereotypes of aging, we should also acknowledge the real impact of the current stereotypes upon older persons. When individuals resist the appearance changes associated with aging through such strategies as coloring their hair, trying to lose weight, or seeking cosmetic surgery, they are responding to a genuine threat from their social environment. Dismissive or disparaging reactions of others to older persons can literally drag those older persons down and confirm the stereotypes.

Women are judged more negatively than men for the effects of aging (Tiggemann, 2004), but men are also subjected to media pressures to maintain a youthful appearance. Research is mixed as to how serious this concern is for men. Some research suggests that older men respond neutrally or positively to the ways in which their appearance changes with age (Halliwell and Dittmar, 2003), and that older men may experience less body dissatisfaction than may younger men (Peat, Peyerl, Ferraro, and Butler, 2011). Other researchers have found men to be very concerned about aging (Shirani, 2013) and more distressed than women by age-related changes in appearance (Kaminski and Hayslip, 2006). Older men have been found to have less dissatisfaction than younger men with height and muscularity; however, older men who adhere most rigidly to traditional masculine roles appear particularly prone to dissatisfaction with their bodies (Murray and Lewis, 2014). For some aging gay men, loss of sexual attractiveness is a concern that intersects with age-related stigma (Lyons, Croy, Barrett, and Whyte, 2015).

Stereotypes about aging bodies are not all about appearance; they are also about physical strength and weakness—and both women and men are targeted by competing messages in this domain. Older individuals are warned of the many health dangers and possibilities of decline with age, but they are offered strategies for staving off these dangers through drugs and lifestyle changes. However, the messages targeted at women and men are somewhat different, shaped by stereotypes of femininity and masculinity.

When stereotypes of femininity and aging combine, their emphases on weakness, delicacy, and frailty are mutually reinforcing; they are unlikely to convey strength and power. Even media portrayals of older women intended to depict positive aging, such as television advertisements for bone-strengthening drugs, tend to focus on fluidity and flexibility rather than on power and strength. Such images are countered to some extent by media attention to outstanding older female athletes: Sister Madonna Bruder, the 87-year-old American "iron nun" running triathlons, or Ernestine Shepherd, at 78 the world's oldest female bodybuilder. However, the latter images appear notable simply because they are unusual; they may be more easily discounted than the constant drumbeat of emphasis on decline. As is the case with appearance, exposure to images related to physical strength can affect the ways in which aging is embodied—and thus experienced and lived—by women. If Levy's (2009) stereotype embodiment theory is correct, we might expect that an older woman who watches television and/or reads magazines in a Western culture is likely to have internalized the expectation that, as she ages, her bones will become increasingly fragile, her joints painful, her muscles weak, and her stamina increasingly limited. The internalized expectancies turn into self-fulfilling prophecies, causing individuals to circumscribe their own activities—perhaps resulting in the very loss of physical capacity contained in the expectations. Interestingly, older African American women appear to be somewhat buffered from such "old and weak" media portrayals: these women express more satisfaction than do their European American counterparts with physical functioning (Sabik and Cole, 2017). This may be because older African American women are less often portrayed in the media, and/or because African American culture promotes a more accepting and multifaceted definition of attractiveness and of aging.

In terms of attitudes toward their aging bodies, women and men's concerns and sources of dissatisfaction appear to differ in emphasis, with women focusing more strongly on their appearance and men on the functionality of their bodies (Halliwell and Dittmar, 2003). For men, strength and a muscular physique are an aspect of masculinity, and men generally express more desire than women do for a lean, muscular body (Tiggemann, Martins, and Kirkbride, 2007). However, even as they become less muscular, older men may take comfort from satisfaction in other dimensions of masculinity: achievement, success, self-confidence, and independence—all things that may be higher in older men than in younger men.

Individuals in older age ranges continue a gender-differentiated pattern of physical activity. In the United States, women (33.2 percent) are more likely than men (29.9 percent) to report that they never exercise (American Heart Association, 2013). Among Americans aged 65 to 74, 12.2 percent of women, as opposed to 18.8 percent of men, engage in the recommended physical activity guidelines for both aerobic and muscle-strengthening activities (Centers for Disease Control and Prevention, 2017).

For those who engage in it, physical activity has important benefits: both older women and older men who are athletically active can evade some age stereotypes, and can focus their self-views on capability age rather than on numerical age (Eman, 2012). Even in the oldest age groups, men who maintain higher levels of physical activity suffer less cognitive decline than men whose activity levels drop (van Gelder et al., 2004). Among older women too, physical activity correlates with a reduced risk of cognitive decline: among one large sample of women aged 65 and older, women with higher levels of physical activity were between 26 percent and 34 percent less likely to experience a reduction in their cognitive abilities over 6 to 8 years (Yaffe, Barnes, Nevitt, Lui, and Covinsky, 2001). Research on elite senior athletes participating in the Senior Olympics showed that, between the ages of 50 and 75, performance declined very slowly (about 3.4 percent per year) for both men and women who continued to compete. Among these active seniors, subjective physical and mental health was significantly higher than in the US population as a whole (Wright and Perricelli, 2008).

DISABILITY AND DISEASE

Some important issues with respect to disability and disease in older age groups cannot be ignored. One in particular is the rise in

Alzheimer's disease and other forms of dementia among elders in developed nations, where an increasing number of individuals may expect to live to older ages. A longitudinal population-based study estimated that in 2010 there were 4.7 million people aged 65 and older suffering from Alzheimer's disease in the United States—and that this number will nearly triple to 13.8 million by 2050 (Hebert, Weuve, Scherr, and Evans, 2013). Globally, the total number of people with dementia is estimated at 47 million and is projected to reach a total of 132 million in 2050 (World Health Organization, 2017).

Older women are somewhat more likely than their male counterparts to develop one form (non-amnestic) of mild cognitive impairment (MCI), which can be a precursor to Alzheimer's disease (Au, Dale-McGrath, and Tierney, 2017). Since women, on average, live longer than men, they are also more likely to be diagnosed with Alzheimer's disease. In addition to their longer life expectancy, women are at increased risk, relative to men, of Alzheimer's disease and of more rapid cognitive decline once it develops—although the reasons for this increased risk are not clear (Snyder et al., 2016). Besides their greater likelihood of experiencing Alzheimer's disease, women's longer lifespan makes it more likely that they will be engaged in caring for a spouse or other family member with the disease. Interestingly, women's cognitive performance in later life is correlated with societal attitudes toward gender roles: in countries with more egalitarian attitudes, older women's performance on cognitive tests is better (Bonsang, Skirbekk, and Staudinger, 2017).

For their part, men have a higher risk than women of vascular dementia (a much less common form of dementia), linked to other heart and blood vessel problems that are relatively common in older men (Podcasy and Epperson, 2016).

In addition to dementia, there is an increased prevalence of other disabilities with older age, and disability is more likely among women and among people in low-income countries. Visual impairment, hearing loss, and osteoarthritis, the most common forms of disability, are much more prevalent in developing countries (United Nations Population Fund, 2012). Women live longer than men, and they experience more disabilities related to activities of daily living in old age. One study in Singapore showed that, among people aged 65 and older, women, in comparison to men, could expect a larger proportion of their remaining years to include bone and joint problems, hypertension, vision impairments, and walking difficulties (Yong, Saito, and Chan, 2011). A US study found that, after controlling for resource differences, women of all racial/ethnic groups experienced more disability-related limitations than did White men or men of the same race/ethnicity (Warner and Brown, 2011). Among the oldest old, women experience more illnesses, describe themselves as less healthy, have lower scores on such functional capacity measures as gait and balance, experience more depression, and report lower levels of subjective well-being and quality of life than do men (Borglin, Jakobssen, Edberg, and Hallberg, 2005; Smith and Baltes, 1998). Women's greater experience of disability is linked both to their tendency to recover more slowly from illness or injury and the lower likelihood that they will die from these events (Hardy, Allore, Guo, and Gill, 2008).

One significant source of injury, illness, and unhappiness in old age is elder abuse and neglect. In one large community-based survey in the United States, 1 in 10 respondents aged 60 years or older reported emotional, physical, or sexual mistreatment or neglect during the previous year—with the most significant risk factor being a lack of social support (Acierno *et al.* 2010). Although elder abuse is often discussed in gender-neutral terms, gender is an important factor: women are more likely than men to be victims of elder abuse (e.g., Hightower, 2010; Kissal and Beşer, 2011). One Canadian study of family medical practice clients estimated that the prevalence of elder abuse ranged from 13.6 to 15.2 percent among women and from 9.1 to 9.7 percent among men (Yaffe, Weiss, Wolfson, and Lithwick, 2007). A comprehensive study, using data from the National Incident-Based Reporting System in the United States between 2000 and 2005, found that victims were more likely to be female (about 53%), and that more than 70 percent of perpetrators were male (Krienert, Walsh, and Turner, 2009). As in other forms of violence, men were more likely than women to be abused by a stranger or acquaintance; women were more likely than men to be abused by a son or daughter, spouse, or other family member. Women were also more likely than men to be abused in their homes. Men were more likely than women to be victims of aggravated assaults and to report major injuries; women were more likely to experience simple assaults and intimidation, and to report either no injury or minor injury. The latter finding suggests that some of the elder abuse experienced by women may be hidden and difficult to identify.

Globally, the prevalence of several types of elder abuse has been investigated (Pillemer, Burnes, Riffin, and Lachs, 2016). The one-year prevalence of physical abuse against elderly community residents ranges from 0.5 percent (Canada) and 1.4 percent (United States) to 4.9 percent (China) and 14.6 percent (Nigeria). Sexual abuse is less common, ranging from 0.04 to 0.8 percent across countries. Financial abuse presents a serious problem for many seniors, with an average of 4.7 percent of elders victimized globally. The one-year prevalence of serious emotional/psychological abuse—usually defined as 10 or more events over the past year—is reported to range from 1.4 percent (Canada) to 10.8 percent (India). Taking all types together, abuse prevalence ranges from a low of 4.0 percent (Canada) to a high of 14.0 percent (India). Across countries, women are more likely than men to be victims of elder abuse, especially emotional and financial abuse.

Economic and cultural factors affect the risk of elder abuse. In cultures where women's social and economic status relative to men is especially low, elderly women are likely to be at higher risk than men for neglect as well as abuse, especially if they are widowed (World Health Organization, 2011). Abuse is also linked to compassion fatigue and frustration—suggesting that more adequate societal supports for caregivers might reduce the incidence of abuse (Krienert, Walsh, and Turner, 2009).

The relationship between gender and vulnerability to elder abuse is complicated by the availability of social support, financial dependence, and gender stereotypes. Social support is a protective factor against elder maltreatment (Melchiorre *et al.*, 2013), and women are likely to have higher levels of social support than men during the early part of old age. However, since women live longer than men, they may spend more years in relative isolation, having outlived much of their social network. Women are also more likely than men to be poor in old age, and thus may find themselves financially dependent on family caretakers—leaving them more vulnerable to abuse by those caretakers. For men, vulnerability to abuse in old age may be increased by masculinity stereotypes that do not encompass the possibility of men as victims—making it difficult for men to report such abuse and for observers such as health professionals to see it (Kosberg, 2007).

One study using mock criminal cases found that women were more likely than men to believe the testimony of alleged victims of elder abuse and to render a guilty verdict—and this difference was largest when the alleged perpetrator was the elder's daughter (Golding, Yozwiak, Kinstle, and Marsil, 2005). Women's greater readiness to believe that abuse occurred in such situations may be linked to their capacity to identify with both the caregiver and the recipient of care—both roles they know they are likely to inhabit at some point.

THE GENDERING OF CAREGIVING

Women are more likely than men both to need and provide caregiving services in their old age. In the European Union, women are about twice as likely as men are to receive formal care of some type during their senior years (Bettio and Verashchagina, 2012). In the United States, sometime after turning 65, 46.7 percent of men and 57.5 percent of women will have a need for long-term care; men will need care for an average of 1.5 years and women will need care for an average of 2.5 years (Favreault and Dey, 2016). Among adults aged 85 and older, 23 percent of women and 14 percent of men will need help with personal care (Administration on Aging, 2016). Women's greater need for formal care in older age is linked in part to their longer lifespan and the related tendency to outlive a spouse. In the United States in 2015, 70 percent of men but only 45 percent of women aged 65 and older lived with a spouse. Among women aged 75 and older, 46.3 percent lived alone (Administration on Aging, 2016). In Great Britain, 1.5 million women and only 577,000 men aged 75 and older lived alone in 2016 (Statista, 2016). Thus, most older women encounter the illnesses and disabilities of old age without a spouse, whereas most men encounter them *with* a spouse and can often expect to be cared for by that spouse.

Due to illness or disability, a significant number of older persons spend time in nursing homes or assisted living situations. Far from ideal for many seniors, residential care may be experienced as especially inadequate by members of the LGBT community. The working assumptions and social organization in these residences may be heteronormative or even homophobic—leading to invisibility, anxiety, discomfort, and loneliness (Westwood, 2016)

Providing healthcare for family members burdens women disproportionately. In 2013, among 17 OECD countries, women comprised 61 percent of persons over the age of 50 who were providing unpaid informal care (Organization for Economic Cooperation and Development, 2015b). In the United States, where arrangements for pre- and after-school care for children of employed parents tend to be a patchwork, grandparents often fill in the gaps. One group of researchers calculated that women and men over the age of 65 spend an average of 1.9 hours and 1.6 hours per day on unpaid childcare (Bianchi, Folbre, and Wolf, 2012). In Britain, 19 percent of grandmothers and 8 percent of grandfathers surveyed said they had reduced working hours, given up a job, or taken leave time to care for a grandchild (Save the Children, 2014). In France, 22.8 percent of grandmothers and 16.5 percent of grandfathers report providing regular childcare for their grandchildren; in Italy, 32.5 percent of grandmothers and 26.1 percent of grandfathers report doing so (Zanella, 2016).

One factor driving the necessity for elders to provide caregiving to children is the prevalence of children orphaned by AIDS, natural disasters, or wars. The impact of HIV/AIDS, in particular, has been the subject of much attention in the international community. Grandparents, particularly grandmothers, often end up as the primary caretakers of AIDS orphans (Karimli, Ssewamala, and Ismayilova, 2012). In certain communities studied in rural Kenya, one out of every three children had lost one parent, and one out of every nine children had lost both parents (Nyambedha, Wandibba, and Aagaard-Hansen, 2003). Their grandparent caretakers encountered significant hardships in providing education, food, and medical care for these children. Furthermore, because their own children had died, these elderly caretakers lost the higher status, respect, and entitlement to care that had traditionally been accorded older persons in the community.

Even grandparents with few resources tend, in such situations, to become providers rather than receivers of care. One South African study showed that AIDS orphans were more likely to be taken in by their grandparents in the poorest economic groups (Ardington *et al.*, 2009). Most of the grandparents taking responsibility for AIDS orphans are women. Gender norms and stereotypes constrain these women, assigning lower value to their needs, health, and lives than to men's, and prescribing that it is their duty to provide care for others, even at the cost of their own well-being (Olowu, 2012).

When they do accept it, the caretaking role may be harder on men than on women. Among AIDS caregivers in two poor districts of Nairobi, male caregivers reported higher levels of disability and severe health problems than men who were not caregivers; no such differences between caregivers and non-caregivers were found for women (Chepngeno-Langat, Madise, Evandrou, and Falkingham, 2011). The authors suggest that men do not expect to have to become active caretakers in this situation and have not developed appropriate coping strategies.

Much of the informal caregiving provided by the elderly, however, focuses on parents and spouses. Worldwide, between 57 and 81 percent of caregivers of the elderly are women (Sharma, Chakrabarti, and Grover, 2016). However, demographic changes such as increases in men's life expectancy have increased the likelihood that men will take on caregiving roles for spouses. Little research focuses specifically on male caregivers. However, there is some evidence that they seek help from others less often than female caregivers, are less aware of available community services, and are concerned about appearing to be incompetent and weak if they signal that they cannot manage the caregiving situation on their own (Baker and Robertson, 2008). All of these responses are congruent with traditional expectations for masculinity. However, these response patterns may not reflect the experience of men in the LGBT community, who report providing more hours of care than female caregivers and more than men in the general population (Family Caregiver Alliance, 2016).

Informal caregiving takes a large physical and emotional toll on caregivers. Caregivers of spouses with dementia experience stress that results in lowered immunity response to vaccines, slower wound healing, and higher inflammation—and some measures of psychological well-being, such as depression and loneliness, do not rebound to normal levels even three years after the death of the cared-for spouse (Glaser, Sheridan, Malarkey, MacCallum, and Kiecolt-Glaser, 2000; Gouin, Hantsoo, and Kiecolt-Glaser, 2008). Caregivers also often neglect their own self-care because they are too busy or too wrapped up in their caregiving tasks to attend to their own well-being; this too contributes to negative health consequences (Vitaliano, Zhang, and Scanlan 2003).

Even when women and men provide equivalent amounts and types of care, women may experience a higher subjective burden of care (e.g., they may be more likely than men to say that they feel trapped or that providing care is an excessive burden) (del Pino-Casado, Frías-Osuna, Palomino-Moral, and MartínezRiera, 2012; Pinquart and Sorensen, 2003). Exposure to the suffering of the person receiving care can, through empathy or mirroring of the care recipient's feelings, provoke strong emotional responses that contribute to the caregiver's psychological and physical distress. Since women are more sensitive than men to others' emotions and more empathetic under many conditions, they may be more distressed than men by the suffering of a care recipient—particularly one with whom they have a close relationship (Monin and Schulz, 2009).

The toll on caregivers can also be financial, since caregiving may involve taking time away from paid work—something that most women, in particular, can ill afford to do. Caregiving is associated with unemployment, temporary and part-time work, reduction in hours of paid work, lower income, early retirement, and an increased risk of poverty (Family Caregiving Alliance, 2015). The increased risk of lower income and poverty is particularly striking for female caregivers.

Of course, not all caregiving is informal; paralleling the growth of the aging population is a large and growing long-term care workforce in developed countries. Most of these workers (90 percent in the United States, 84 percent in England) are female and many are women of color (Hussein, 2011; Rodrigues, Huber, and Lamura, 2012). They fill jobs as nurse aids, nursing assistants, orderlies, personal care attendants, home care workers, and other paraprofessional caregivers to the elderly or disabled in hospitals, nursing homes, daycare settings, and private homes. It is projected that there will be a need for 6 million such direct care workers in the United States by 2050 (Bouchard, 2013).

A growing proportion of these women are immigrants from countries where they cannot find good jobs (Eckenwiler, 2014). In 2016, 28 percent of direct care workers in the United States were immigrants. The availability of these immigrant women workers fills an important need, but it may also fuel the devaluation of eldercare as a profession by keeping wages low. In the United States, wages for direct care workers are significantly lower than the median wage for all US workers; almost a quarter of home care workers and 17 percent of nursing assistants working in nursing homes live below the federal poverty line (Paraprofessional Healthcare Institute, 2017). Another problem is that the countries from which these workers come may find their own supply of both formal eldercare workers and informal family caretakers drained. It is difficult to predict the impact of the latter development upon the gendering of caregiving in these "source" countries.

IDENTITY AND RELATIONSHIPS: WIDOWHOOD, SOCIAL NETWORKS, SOCIAL SUPPORT

Both social isolation (having little social contact, living alone, without a partner or a network of social support) and feeling lonely (being dissatisfied with the frequency and/or closeness of one's social contacts) are connected to poor health outcomes. Among over 2000 elderly people studied in the Netherlands, older persons who reported feeling lonely were at higher risk for dementia, even if they were not, by objective measures, socially isolated (Holwerda et al., 2012). In a nationally representative US sample of individuals aged 50 and over, feelings of loneliness were associated with increased mortality risk over a six-year period (Luo, Hawkley, Waite, and Cacioppo, 2012). Among 6500 British people aged 52 and older, both social isolation and loneliness were linked to increased mortality from all causes, but only the effect of social isolation was independent of other predictors of mortality (Steptoe, Shankar, Demakakos, and Wardle, 2013). Among community-dwelling elderly people in

France, feelings of loneliness and living alone independently predicted mortality 22 years after being measured (Teguo *et al.*, 2016). Both socially isolated and lonely individuals are at higher risk for cardiovascular disease, high blood pressure, and heightened inflammatory response to stress (Steptoe *et al.*, 2013).

These findings suggest major problems for older people, who are much more likely than younger people to be isolated. Furthermore, there is a gender dimension to this issue, as women are especially likely to be isolated in older age. In the United States, 35 percent of women and 20 percent of men aged 65 and over live alone (Administration on Aging, 2016). In Japan, one in every eight men and one in five women aged 65 or older lives alone (Yoshida, 2016). In some European countries, more than 40 percent of women aged 65 and older live alone (United Nations Population Fund, 2012). In the large British sample studied by Steptoe and his colleagues (2013), there was no male–female difference in social isolation, but women were significantly more likely than men to be lonely.

Women's increased risk for isolation and loneliness in old age is linked to their longer lifespan, tendency to outlive their spouses, and greater likelihood of experiencing depression and other illnesses. However, the gender difference is complicated. Yes, women are more likely than men to find themselves widowed in their senior years (Antonucci *et al.*, 2002). For example, in the United States in 2016, there were three times as many widows (8.8 million) as widowers (2.6 million) (Administration on Aging, 2016). However, in developed countries, widowhood appears harder on men than on women (Stroebe, Stroebe, and Schut, 2001), and marital status has a larger effect on loneliness for men than for women (Rokach, Matalon, Rokach, and Safarov, 2007). This may be because, for men, marriage is likely to be both central to their feelings of intimate attachment and emotional well-being, *and* a key aspect in their wider social involvement (perhaps because their wives mediate social arrangements). Thus, when men lose their wives, they lose not only an important close relationship but also a link to a variety of other social relationships. Indeed, among older adults living alone in the United Sates, men are much less likely (48%) than women (71%) to say that they are "very satisfied" with the number of friends they have (Stepler, 2016).

For women, marriage or couplehood offers one source of intimate attachment, but they are also likely to find both emotional and social support in other close ties with friends and family members (Dykstra and de Jong Gierveld, 2004). Women, even in their seventies, have larger social networks than men, and these networks tend to be less impacted than men's by widowhood or divorce (McLaughlin, Vagenas, Pachana, Begum, and Dobson, 2010). The positive quality of older women's social relations can buffer the negative emotional consequences and resource deficits they face in terms of financial security and health (Antonucci *et al.*, 2002). Even under the difficult conditions found in Kenyan slums, elderly women maintain larger, stronger social networks than men, allowing them to be more resourceful and cooperative in dealing with needs for food, information, and healthcare (Mudege and Ezeh, 2009).

In cultures where women derive their identity and status, as well as their livelihood, from their husbands, the impact of widowhood upon women may be more serious than upon men. In some areas of Africa, a widow risks being labeled and persecuted as a witch, losing her property, and/or forfeiting her social standing (Remi, 2009; Rosenblatt and Nkosi, 2007). In parts of rural India, a widow may be considered a non-person. There is even a Hindu tradition (called *Sati*, now illegal, but still practiced on occasion) that a widow should throw herself on the funeral pyre of her husband, since her life is no longer worth living; there is no parallel tradition for widowers (Kayoda and Yin, 2015; Vijayakumar, 2004). Attitudes toward widows continue to evolve in India, and middle-class widows in urban settings can now often anticipate rebuilding their lives as single women (Czerenda, 2010; Kayoda and Yin, 2015). However, among a nationally representative sample of persons aged 60 and over, widowed persons of both genders were more vulnerable than married persons in terms of health status and access to healthcare services, and widows were the most disadvantaged group (Sreerupa and Rajan, 2010).

PURPOSE AND MEANING: RETHINKING WHAT MATTERS

Although aging is associated with a variety of losses and declines in certain areas, older people tend to adapt by readjusting their priorities, goals, and behavior. The process has been described as *selective optimization with compensation* (Baltes and Baltes, 1990), referring to a narrowing of one's set of goals by picking only the most important as targets of one's resources, and using alternative methods or resources to make up for losses or deficiencies. This winnowing of goals may take somewhat different forms for women and for men, especially if they have been engaged in traditional gender roles. For example, men may rethink the importance of career achievement and success, and women may re-evaluate the importance of feminine ideals of pleasing others, looking attractive, and prioritizing others' needs.

For women, moving into older age may sometimes be associated with a new sense of freedom: moving in new directions and stepping out of the constraints of feminine stereotypes and roles (Arnold, 2005). Whereas, for women, aging often used to be framed mainly as the loss of reproductive roles and transition to an "empty nest," midlife and older age now present women with opportunities to enhance self-development, confidence, and self-acceptance (Picard, 2000).

As aging individuals narrow their goals and focus, one interesting result appears to be that they focus more on emotion-related goals than on information-related goals—and they emphasize the positive emotions. Framing this process as *socio-emotional selectivity* (Carstensen, Fung, and Charles 2003), researchers have used it to explain why older age is linked, somewhat unexpectedly, to happiness. The theory posits that, with age, adults realize that remaining life is short, and begin to focus on reducing the amount of time they spend on negative emotions and experiences. They make choices in order to better meet their needs and protect their emotional health. Older adults appear to respond with less anger and to disengage more from offending interpersonal situations than do younger adults (Charles and Carstensen, 2008). They narrow their social networks, with increasing emphasis on close friends and people who elicit more positive and less negative emotions (English and Carstensen, 2014). In laboratory experiments they pay less attention to, and recall, fewer negative stimuli than do younger people—a phenomenon labeled the *positivity effect* (Carstensen and Mikels, 2005).

Women and men may differ in the degree and manner of achieving this focus on the positive. Positivity effects in autobiographical memory appear stronger for older men than for older women: women remember more negative memories than do men (Ros and Latorre, 2010). And women seem more likely than men to focus on positive social exchanges (experiencing care, support, and companionship) to buffer or ameliorate the damaging impact upon their emotions of negative social exchanges (tension, conflict, neglect) (Fiori, Windsor, Pearson, and Crisp, 2013). This may be because, as we have seen, women tend to place more emphasis on social networks and interpersonal relationships than do men.

For both men and women, there may be a shift away from traditional gender expectations with increasing age. Transitions such as job loss or retirement, or the illness or loss of a spouse, may cause men to re-evaluate long-held assumptions and beliefs about aspects of gender roles such as division of labor, or important sources of identity (Emslie, Hunt, and O'Brien, 2004). However, with few cultural norms about how older men should be masculine, many men continue, at older ages, to try to enact traditional masculinities (Thompson and Langendoerfer, 2016). For women, age may sometimes be accompanied by a stronger sense of their own power, competence, and inner strength (Boneham and Sixsmith, 2006; Friedman and Pines, 1992; Hammoudeh *et al.*, 2017; Feldman, 1999). However, older women may still embrace physical attractiveness as a critical dimension of femininity, and thus fret about their aging bodies (Carter, 2016). Most of the vast literature on gender roles, norms, and stereotypes has focused on the young; as we move into a future that includes an increasing proportion of older women and men, many questions remain to be answered about gender and aging.

FOR FURTHER EXPLORATION

Cruikshank, Margaret (2013). *Learning to be old: Gender, culture, and aging* (3rd edn) (Lanham, MD: Rowman & Littlefield). This book, framed by a feminist perspective, takes a good look at cultural myths about aging and the fears people have about an aging population. The book focuses on the American situation, but most of the issues are relevant to many countries. Included are discussions of sickness and social roles, overmedication, ageism, the different experiences of different ethnic and economic groups, and "countercultural gerontology."

Holstein, Martha (2015). *Women in later life: Critical perspectives on gender and age* (Lanham, MD: Rowman & Littlefield). The author, a feminist scholar on aging, brings personal, political, theoretical, and scientific approaches to the examination of the many gender-related issues women confront as they age. She explores body image and beauty, stereotyping, retirement, caregiving, poverty, and death. The book ends with a call for activism to confront ageism.

Lamb, Sarah (2000). *White saris and sweet mangoes: Aging, gender, and body in North India* (Berkeley, CA: University of California Press). The author, an anthropologist, explores the expectations and practices associated with aging and gender in one part of the world—and in doing so sheds light on many broad assumptions about older women and men. Through fascinating stories of individuals in Mangaldihi, India, she entices the reader to examine issues of economics, health, separation, widowhood, death, and love.

Muhlbauer, V. and Chrisler, J.C. (eds) (2007). *Women over 50: Psychological perspectives* (New York: Springer). This collection of ten chapters examines the challenges and opportunities associated with women's entry into the "middle" time of life, commonly thought of as a bridge to old age. The issues are considered from a research perspective, and range from body image, love and sex, relationships, and retirement, to empowerment.

REFERENCES

Acierno, R., Hernandez, M.A., Amstadter, A.B., Resnick, H.S., Stever, K., Muzzy, W., and Kilpatrick, D.G. (2010). Prevalence and correlates of emotional, physical, sexual, and financial abuse and potential neglect in the United States: The National Elder Mistreatment Study. *American Journal of Public Health*, *100*, 292–297. doi: 10.2105/AJPH.2009. 163089.

Administration on Aging, U.S. Department of Health and Human Services (2016). *A portrait of older Americans 2016.* www.giaging.org/documents/A_Profile_of_Older_Americans__2016.pdf.

American Heart Association (2013). *Physical inactivity. Statistical fact sheet.* www.heart.org/idc/groups/heart-public/@wcm/@sop/@smd/documents/downloadable/ucm_319589.pdf.

American Society of Plastic Surgeons (2016). *Plastic surgery statistics report 2016.* ASPS National Clearinghouse of Plastic Surgery Procedural Statistics. www.plasticsurgery.org/documents/News/Statistics/2016/plastic-surgery-statistics-full-report-2016.pdf.

Antonucci, T.C., Lansford, J.E., Akiyama, H., Smith, J., Baltes, M.M., Takahashi, K., Fuhrer, R., and Dartigues, J-F. (2002). Differences between men and women in social relations, resource deficits, and depressive symptomatology during later life in four nations. *Journal of Social Issues, 58,* 767–783. doi: 10.1111/1540-4560.00289.

Ardington, C., Case, A., Islam, M., Lam, D., Leibbrandt, M., Menendez, A., and Olgiati, A. (2009). *The impact of AIDS on intergenerational support in South Africa: Evidence from the Cape Area Panel Study.* Paper prepared for the conference on "The Impact of AIDS on Older Persons in Africa and Asia," February. University of Michigan. www.princeton.edu/~accase/downloads/AIDS_and_intergenerational_support_in_Cape_Town.pdf.

Arnold, E. (2005). A voice of their own: Women moving into their fifties. *Health Care for Women International, 26,* 630–651. doi: 10.1080/07399330500177014.

Au, B., Dale-McGrath, S., and Tierney, M.C. (2017). Sex differences in the prevalence and incidence of mild cognitive impairment: A meta-analysis. *Ageing Research Reviews, 35,* 176–199. doi: http://dx.doi.org/10.1016/j.arr.2016.09.005.

Badgett, M.V.L., Durso, L.E., and Schneebaum, A. (2013). New patterns of poverty in the lesbian, gay, and bisexual community. The Williams Institute, University of California School of Law. http://williamsinstitute.law.ucla.edu/wp-content/uploads/LGB-Poverty-Update-Jun-2013.pdf.

Baker, K.L. and Robertson, N. (2008). Coping with caring for someone with dementia: Reviewing the literature about men. *Aging and Mental Health, 12,* 413–422.

Baltes, P.B. and Baltes, M.M. (1990). Psychological perspectives on successful aging: The model of selective optimization with compensation. In P.B. Baltes and M.M. Baltes (eds), *Successful aging: Perspectives from the behavioral sciences* (pp. 1–34). New York: Cambridge University Press.

Barrett, A.E. and von Rohr, C. (2008). Gendered perceptions of aging: An examination of college students. *International Journal of Ageing and Human Development, 67*, 359–386.

Bettio, F. and Verashchagina, A. (2012). *Long-term care for the elderly. Provisions and providers in 33 European countries.* Technical Report. Luxembourg: Publications Office of the European Union. doi: 10.2838/87307. file:///C:/Users/hlips/AppData/Local/Microsoft/Windows/INetCache/ IE/YUK45KH4/elderly_care_en.pdf.

Bianchi, S., Folbre, N., and Wolf, D. (2012), Unpaid care work. In N. Folbre (ed.), *For love and money: Care provision in the United States* (pp. 40–64). New York: Russell Sage Foundation.

Boneham, M.A. and Sixsmith, J.A. (2006). The voices of older women in a disadvantaged community: Issues of health and social capital. *Social Science & Medicine, 62*, 269–279. http://dx.doi.org/10.1016/j.socscimed.2005. 06.003.

Bonsang, E., Skirbekk, V., and Staudinger, U.M. (2017). As you sow, so shall you reap: Gender-role attitudes and late-life cognition. *Psychological Science.* Published online, July 24. doi: https://doi.org/10.1177/ 0956797617708634.

Borglin, G., Jakobssen, U., Edberg, A., and Hallberg, I.R. (2005). Self-reported health complaints and prediction of overall and health-related quality of life among elderly people. *International Journal of Nursing Studies, 42*, 147–158. http://dx.doi.org/10.1016/j.ijnurstu.2004. 06.003.

Bouchard, S. (2013). Immigration reform may solve long-term care worker shortage. *Health Care Finance News*, March 12. www.healthcarefinancenews.com/news/immigration-reform-may-solve-longterm-care-worker-shortage.

Calasanti, T. and King, N. (2007). "Beware of the estrogen assault": Ideals of old manhood in anti-aging advertisements. *Journal of Aging Studies, 21*, 357–368. doi: 10.1016/j.jaging.2007.05.003.

Carter, C. (2016). Still sucked into the body image thing: The impact of anti-aging and health discourses on women's gendered identities. *Journal of Gender Studies, 25*, 200–214.

Carstensen, L.L. and Mikels, J. (2005). At the intersection of emotion and cognition: Aging and the positivity effect. *Current Directions in Psychological Science, 14*, 117–121.

Carstensen, L.L., Fung, H.H., and Charles, S.T. (2003). Socioemotional selectivity theory and the regulation of emotion in the second half of life. *Motivation and Emotion, 27*, 103–123. http://dx.doi.org/10.1080/095892 36.2014.927354.

Centers for Disease Control and Prevention (2017). *Early release of selected estimates based on data from the National Health Interview Study 2016.* www.cdc. gov/nchs/data/nhis/earlyrelease/Earlyrelease201705_07.pdf.

Charles, S.T. and Carstensen, L.L. (2008). Unpleasant situations elicit different emotional responses in younger and older adults. *Psychology and Aging, 23,* 495–504. doi: 10.1037/a0013284.

Chepngeno-Langat, G., Madise, N., Evandrou, M., and Falkingham, J. (2011). Gender differentials on the health consequences of care-giving to people with AIDS-related illness among older informal carers in two slums in Nairobi, Kenya. *AIDS Care, 23,* 1586–1594. doi: 10.1080/09540121. 2011. 569698.

Chrisler, J.C., Barney, A., and Palatino, B. (2016). Ageism can be hazardous to women's health: Ageism, sexism, and stereotypes of older women in the healthcare system. *Journal of Social Issues, 72, 86–104.* doi: 10.1111/ josi.12157.

Czerenda, A.J. (2010). The meaning of widowhood and health to older middle-class Hindu widows living in a south Indian community. *Journal of Transcultural Nursing, 21,* 351–360. doi: 10.1177/1043659609360715.

de Vaus, D., Gray, M., and Stanton, D. (2003). *Measuring the value of unpaid household, caring and voluntary work of older Australians.* Research Paper No. 34. Melbourne, Australia: Australian Institute of Family Studies. www.pc. gov.au/_data/assets/pdf_file/0011/14033/sub010.pdf.

del Pino-Casado, R., Frías-Osuna, A., Palomino-Moral, P.A., and Martín-ezRiera, J.R. (2012). Gender differences regarding informal caregivers of older people. *Journal of Nursing Scholarship, 44,* 349–357. doi: 10.1111/j.1547-5069. 2012.01477.x.

Department for Work and Pensions (2016, June 28). Pensioners' incomes series: Financial year 2014/15. June 28.www.jec.senate.gov/public/_ cache/files/0779dc2f-4a4e-4386-b847-9ae919735acc/gender-pay-inequality-us-congress-joint-economic-committee.pdf.

Deutsch, F.M., Zalenski, C.M., and Clark, M.E. (1986). Is there a double standard of aging? *Journal of Applied Social Psychology, 16,* 771–785.

Dingman, S., Otte, M.E.M., and Foster, C. (2012). Cosmetic surgery: Feminist perspectives. *Women & Therapy, 35,* 181–192. doi: 10.1080/ 02703149.2012.684536.

Dykstra, P.A. and de Jong Gierveld, J. (2004). Gender and marital-history differences in emotional and social loneliness among Dutch older adults. *Canadian Journal on Aging, 23,* 141–155. doi: 10.1353/cja.2004.0018.

Eckenwiler, L. (2014). Care worker migration, global health equity, and ethical place-making. *Women's Studies International Forum, 47*(Part B), 213–222.

Eman, J. (2012). The role of sports in making sense of the process of growing old. *Journal of Aging Studies, 26*, 467–475. doi: 10.1016/j.jaging. 2012.06.006.

Emslie, C., Hunt, K., and O'Brien, R. (2004). Masculinities in older men: A qualitative study in the west of Scotland. *The Journal of Men's Studies, 12*, 207–226. doi: 10.3149/jms.1203.207.

English, T. and Carstensen, L.L. (2014). Selective narrowing of social networks across adulthood is associated with improved emotional experience in daily life. *International Journal of Behavioral Development, 38*, 195–202. http://dx.doi.org/10.1177/0165025413515404.

European Social Survey (2010). www.europeansocial survey.org/index.

Family Caregiver Alliance (2015). Women and caregiving: Facts and figures. Updated February. www.caregiver.org/women-and-caregiving-facts-and-figures.

Family Caregiver Alliance (2016). Caregiver statistics: Demographics. www. caregiver.org/caregiver-statistics-demographics.

Favreault, M. and Dey, J. (2016). *Long-term services and supports for older Americans: Risks and financing research brief.* U.S. Department of Health & Human Services, Office of the Assistant Secretary for Planning and Evaluation. https://aspe.hhs.gov/basic-report/long-term-services-and-supports-older-Americans-risks-and-financing-research-brief.

Feldman, S. (1999). Please don't call me "dear": Older women's narratives of health care. *Nursing Iquiry, 6*, 269–276. http://dx.doi.org/10.1046/j.1440-1800.1999.00041.x.

Fiori, K.L., Windsor, T.D., Pearson, E.D., and Crisp, D.A. (2013). Can positive social exchanges buffer the detrimental effects of negative social exchanges? Age and gender differences. *Gerontology, 59*, 40–52. doi: 10.1159/000339747.

Friedman, A. and Pines, A.M. (1992). Increase in Arab women's perceived power in the second half of life. *Sex Roles, 26*, 1–9. doi: 10.1007/BF00290121.

Glaser, R., Sheridan, J., Malarkey, W.B., MacCallum, R.C., and Kiecolt-Glaser, J.K. (2000). Chronic stress modulates the immune response to a pneumococcal pneumonia vaccine. *Psychosomatic Medicine, 62*, 804–807.

Global Industry Analysts, Inc. (2016). *Desire to remain youthful among the middle aged & older adults drives the global anti-aging products market.* October. www. strategyr.com/MarketResearch/Anti_Aging_Products_Market_Trends. asp.

Golding, J.M., Yozwiak, J.A., Kinstle, T.L., and Marsil, D.F. (2005). The effect of gender in the perception of elder physical abuse in court. *Law and Human Behavior, 29*, 605–614. doi: 10.1007/s10979-005-6831-8.

Gouin, J.P., Hantsoo, L., and Kiecolt-Glaser, J.K. (2008). Immune dysregulation and chronic stress among older adults: A review. *Neuroimmunomodulation, 15*, 251–259. doi: 000156468[pii]10.1159/000156468.

Halliwell, E. and Dittmar, H. (2003). A qualitative investigation of women's and men's body image concerns and their attitudes toward aging. *Sex Roles, 49*, 675–684.

Hammoudeh, D., Coast, E., Lewis, D., van der Meulen, Y., Leone, T., and Giacaman, R. (2017). Age of despair or age of hope? Palestinian women's perspectives on midlife health. *Social Science & Medicine, 184*, 108–115. https://doi.org/10.1016/j.socscimed.2017.05.028.

Hardy, S.E., Allore, H.G., Guo, Z., and Gill, T.M. (2008). Explaining the effect of gender on functional transitions in older persons. *Gerontology, 54*, 79–86. doi: 10.1159/000115004.

Hebert, L.E., Weuve, J., Scherr, P.A., and Evans, D.A. (2013). Alzheimer disease in the United States (2010–2050) estimated using the 2010 census. *Neurology, 80*, 1778–1783. doi: 10.1212/WNL.0b013e318 28726f5.

Hightower, J. (2010). Abuse in later life: When and how does gender matter? In G. Gutman and C. Spencer (eds), *Aging, ageism and abuse: Moving from awareness to action*. Elsevier Insights (pp. 17–29). San Diego, CA: Elsevier Academic Press.

Holwerda, T.J., Deeg, D.J.H., Beekman, A.T.F., van Tilburg, T.G., Stek, M.L., Jonker, C., and Schoevers, R.A. (2012). Feelings of loneliness, but not social isolation, predict dementia onset: Results from the Amsterdam Study of the Elderly (AMSTEL). *Journal of Neurology, Neurosurgery and Psychiatry*. doi: 10.1136/jnnp-2012-302755.

Hussein, S. (2011, May 11). *Migrants and the state of long term care in England: Opportunities and challenges*. Social Care Workforce Research Unit, King's College, London, UK, May 11.www.academia.edu/2424356/Migrants_and_the_state_of_long_term_care_in_England_opportunities_and_challenges_Filling_the_Gaps_on_the_Impacts_of_Immigration.

International Labour Office (2016). *Women at work. Trends 2016*. Geneva, Switzerland: Author. www.ilo.org/wcmsp5/groups/public/-dgreports/-dcomm/-publ/documents/publication/wcms_457317.pdf.

Johnson, R.W. and Schaner, S.G. (2005). Value of unpaid activities by older Americans tops $160 billion per year. *Perspectives on Productive Aging, 4*. Washington, DC: The Urban Institute. www.urban.org/sites/default/files/publication/42896/311227-Value-of-Unpaid-Activities-by-Older-Americans-Tops-Billion-Per-Year.PDF.

Joint Economic Committee United States Congress (2016). *Gender pay inequality. Consequences for women, families and the economy*. April. www.jec.senate.gov/

public/_cache/files/0779dc2f-4a4e-4386-b847-9ae919735acc/gender-pay-inequality-us-congress-joint-economic-committee.pdf.

Kaminski, P.L. and Hayslip, B. (2006). Gender differences in body esteem among older adults. *Journal of Women and Aging, 18*, 19–35.

Karimli, L., Ssewamala, F.M., and Ismayilova, L. (2012). Extended families and perceived caregiver support to AIDS orphans in Rakai district of Uganda. *Child and Youth Services Review, 34*, 1351–1358. doi: 10.1016/j.childyouth.2012.03.015.

Kayoda, Y. and Yin, T. (2015). Widow discrimination and family caregiving in India: Evidence from microdata collected from six major cities. *Journal of Women & Aging, 27*, 59–67. doi: 10.1080/08952841.2014.9.

Kissal, A. and Beşer, A. (2011). Elder abuse and neglect in a population offering care by a primary health care center in Izmir, Turkey. *Social Work in Health Care, 50*, 158–175. doi: 10.1080/00981389.2010.527570.

Kosberg, J.I. (ed.) (2007). *Abuse of older men.* New York: Routledge.

Krienert, J.L., Walsh, J.A., and Turner, M. (2009). Elderly in America: A descriptive study of elder abuse examining National Incident-Based Reporting System (NIBRS) data, 2000–2005. *Journal of Elder Abuse and Neglect, 21*, 325–345. doi: 10.1080/08946560903005042.

Levy, B. (2009). Stereotype embodiment: A psychosocial approach to aging. *Current Directions in Psychological Science, 18*, 332–336. doi: 10.1111/j.1467-8721.2009.01662.x.

Lips, H.M. and Hastings, S.L. (2012). Competing discourses for older women: Agency/leadership vs. disengagement/retirement. *Women and Therapy, 35*, 1–20.

Lloyd-Sherlock, P., Corso, B., and Minicuci, N. (2015). Widowhood, socio-economic status, health and wellbeing in low and middle-income countries. *Journal of Developmental Studies, 51*, 1374–1388.

Luo, Y., Hawkley, L.C., Waite, L.J., and Cacioppo, J.T. (2012). Loneliness, health, and mortality in old age: A national longitudinal study. *Social Science and Medicine, 74*, 907–914. doi: 10.1016/j.socscimed.2011.11.028.

Lyons, A., Croy, S., Barrett, C., and Whyte, C. (2015). Growing old as a gay man: How life has changed for the gay liberation generation. *Ageing & Society, 35*, 2229–2250. http://dx.doi.org/10.1017/S0144686X14000889.

Maguire, M. (2008). "Fade to grey": Older women, embodied claims and attributions in English university departments of education. *Women's Studies International Forum, 31*, 474–482. doi: 10.1016/j.wsif.2008.09.001.

McLaughlin, D., Vagenas, D., Pachana, N.A., Begum, N., and Dobson, A. (2010). Gender differences in social network size and satisfaction in adults in their 70s. *Journal of Health Psychology, 15*, 671–679. doi: 10.1177/1359105310368177.

Mei, Z., Eales, J., and Fast, J. (2013). Older Canadians are volunteers and charitable donors. Sage Seniors Association. www.mysage.ca/public/download/documents/4058.

Melchiorre, M.G., Chiatti, C., Lamura, G., Torres-Gonzales, F., Stankunas, M., Lindert, J., Ioannidi-Kapolou, E., Barros, H., Macassa, G., and Soares, J.F.J. (2013). Social support, socio-economic status, health and abuse among older people in seven European countries. *PLoS One, 8*, e54856. Published online January 30. doi: 10.1371/journal.pone.0054856.

Monin, J.K. and Schulz, R. (2009). Interpersonal effects of suffering in older adult caregiving relationships. *Psychology and Aging, 24*, 681–695. doi: 10.1037/a0016355.

Mudege, N.N. and Ezeh, A.C. (2009). Gender, aging, poverty and health: Survival strategies of older men and women in Nairobi slums. *Journal of Aging Studies, 23*, 245–257.

Murray, T. and Lewis, V. (2014). Gender-role conflict and men's body satisfaction: The moderating role of age. *Psychology of Men & Masculinity, 15*, 40–48. http://dx.doi.org/10.1037/a0030959.

Nyambedha, E., Wandibba, S., and Aagaard-Hansen, J. (2003). Retirement lost—The new role of the elderly as caretakers for orphans in western Kenya. *Journal of Cross-Cultural Gerontology, 18*, 33–52.

Olowu, D. (2012). Gendered imbalances in AIDS-related burden of care: Lessons from Lesotho. *Gender and Behaviour, 10*, 4344–4357.

Organization for Economic Cooperation and Development (2015a). Old-age income poverty. In *Pensions at a glance 2015: OECD and G20 indicators.* Paris: OECD Publishing. www.keepeek.com/Digital-Asset-Management/oecd/social-issues-migration-health/pensions-at-a-glance-2015/old-age-income-poverty_pension_glance-2015-28-en#page3.

Organization for Economic Cooperation and Development (2015b). Informal carers. In *Health at a glance 2015.* Paris: OECD Publishing. http://dx.doi.org/10.1787/health_glance-2015-76-en.

Organization for Economic Cooperation and Development (2017). *OECD.Stat.* LFS by sex and age.https://stats.oecd.org/Index.aspx?DataSetCode=LFS_SEXAGE_I_R.

Paraprofessional Healthcare Institute (2017, September 6). *PHI releases data on home care workers and nursing assistants.* September 6.https://phinational.org/blogs/phi-releases-data-home-care-workers-and-nursing-assistants.

Peat, C.M., Peyerl, N.L., Ferraro, F.R., and Butler, M. (2011). Age and body image in Caucasian men. *Psychology of Men and Masculinity, 12*, 195–200. doi: 10.1037/a0021478.

Picard, C. (2000). Pattern of expanding consciousness in midlife women: Creative movement and the narrative as modes of expression. *Nursing Science Quarterly, 13*, 150–157.

Pillemer, K., Burnes, D., Riffin, C., and Lachs, M.S. (2016). Elder abuse: Global situation, risk factors, and prevention strategies. *The Gerontologist, 56* (Issue Suppl_2), S194–S205. https://doi.org/10.1093/geront/gnw004.

Pinquart, M. and Sorensen, S. (2003). Differences between caregivers and non-caregivers in psychological health and physical health: A meta-analysis. *Psychology and Aging, 18*, 250–267.

Podcasy, J.L. and Epperson, C.N. (2016). Considering sex and gender in alzheimer disease and other dementias. *Dialogues in Clinical Neuroscience, 18*(4), 437–446.

Proctor, B., Semega, J.L., and Kollar, M.A. (2016). *Income and poverty in the United States: 2015.* U.S. Census Bureau Current Population Reports P60–256 (RV). Washington, DC: U.S. Government Printing Office. www.census.gov/content/dam/Census/library/publications/2016/demo/p60-256.pdf.

Remi, A. (2009). "Yesterday you were divorced. Today I am a widow": An appraisal of widowhood practices and the effects on the psyche of widows in Africa. *Gender & Behaviour, 7*, 2457–2468. http://dx.doi.org/10.4314/gab.v7i2.48699.

Rodrigues, R., Huber, M., and Lamura, G. (eds) (2012). *Facts and figures on healthy ageing and long-term care.* Vienna: European Centre for Social Welfare Policy and Research. www.euro.centre.org/data/LTC_Final.pdf.

Rokach, A., Matalon, R., Rokach, B., and Safarov, A. (2007). The effects of gender and marital status on loneliness of the aged. *Social Behavior and Personality, 35*, 243–254. doi: 10.2224/sbp.2007.35.2.243.

Ros, L. and Latorre, J.M. (2010). Gender and age differences in the recall of affective autobiographical memories using the autobiographical memory test. *Personality and Individual Differences, 49*, 950–954. https://doi.org/10.1016/j.paid.2010.08.002.

Rosenblatt, P.C. and Nkosi, B.C. (2007). South African Zulu widows in a time of poverty and social change. *Death Studies, 31*, 67–85. doi: 10.1080/07481180600995214.

Sabik, N.J. and Cole, E.R. (2017). Growing older and staying positive: Associations between diverse aging women's perceptions of age and body satisfaction. *Journal of Adult Development, 24*, 177–188. http://dx.doi.org/10.1007/s10804-016-9256-3.

Save the Children (2014). 1.9 million cut working hours to look after grandchildren. www.savethechildren.org.uk/2014-07/19-million-cut-working-hours-look-after-grandchildren.

Sharma, N., Chakrabarti, S., and Grover, S. (2016). Gender differences in caregiving among family—Caregivers of people with mental illnesses. *World Journal of Psychiatry*, 6(1), 7–17. http://doi.org/10.5498/wjp.v6. i1.7.

Shirani, F. (2013). The spectre of the wheezy dad: Masculinity, fatherhood and ageing. *Sociology*, 47, 1104–1119. http://dx.doi.org/10.1177/0038038 512469063.

Sinnott, J.D. and Shifren, K. (2001). Gender and aging: Gender differences and gender roles. In J.E. Birren and K.W. Schaie (eds), *Handbook of the psychology of aging* (5th edn) (pp. 454–476). San Diego, CA: Academic Press.

Smith, J. and Baltes, M.M. (1998). The role of gender in very old age: Profiles of functioning and everyday life patterns. *Psychology and Aging*, 13, 676–695. doi: 10.1037/0882-7974.13.4.676.

Snyder, H.M., Asthana, S., Bain, L., Brinton, R., Craft, S., Dubal, D.B. *et al.* (2016). Sex biology contributions to vulnerability to Alzheimer's disease: A think tank convened by the Women's Alzheimer's Research Initiative. *Alzheimer's & Dementia*, 12, 1186–1196. https://doi.org/10.1016/j. jalz.2016.08.004.

Sreerupa and Rajan, S.I. (2010). Gender and widowhood: Disparity in health status and health care utilization among the aged in India. *Journal of Ethnic and Cultural Diversity in Social Work: Innovation in Theory, Research and Practice*, 19, 287–304. doi: 10.1080/15313204.2010.523650.

Statista (2016). Number of people living alone in the United Kingdom (UK) 2016, by age and gender. www.statista.com/statistics/281616/people-living-alone-in-the-united-kingdom-uk-by-age-and-gender/.

Stepler, R. (2016). *Well-being of older adults living alone*. Pew Social Trends. www.pewsocialtrends.org/2016/02/18/3-well-being-of-older-adults-living-alone/.

Steptoe, A., Shankar, A., Demakakos, P., and Wardle, J. (2013). Social isolation, loneliness, and all-cause mortality in older men and women. *Proceedings of the National Academy of Sciences of the United States of America*, March 25. doi: 10.1073/pnas.1219686110.

Stewart, A.J., Ostrove, J.M., and Helson, R. (2001). Middle aging in women: Patterns of personality change from the 30s to the 50s. *Journal of Adult Development*, 8, 23–37. doi: 10.1023/A:1026445704288.

Stroebe, M., Stroebe, W., and Schut, H. (2001). Gender differences in adjustment to bereavement: An empirical and theoretical review. *Review of General Psychology*, 5, 62–83.

Teguo, M.T., Simo-Tabue, N., Stoykova, R., Meillon, C., Cogne, M., Amiéva, H., and Dartigues, J. (2016). Feelings of loneliness and living alone as predictors of mortality in the elderly: The PAQUID study. *Psychosomatic Medicine*, *78*, 904–909. http://dx.doi.org/10.1097/PSY.0000000000000386.

The World Bank (2017). World Development Expectancy Indicators: Life expectancy at birth. https://data.worldbank.org/indicator/SP.DYN.LE00.FE.IN (female data) and https://data.worldbank.org/indicator/SP.DYN.LE00.MA.IN (male data).

Thompson Jr., E.H. and Langendoerfer, K.B. (2016). Older men's blueprint for "being a man." *Men and Masculinities*, *19*, 119–147. http://dx.doi.org/10.1177/1097184X15606949.

Tiggemann, M. (2004). Body image across the adult life span: Stability and change. *Body Image*, *1*, 29–41.

Tiggemann, M., Martins, Y., and Kirkbride, A. (2007). Oh to be lean and muscular: Body image ideals in gay and heterosexual men. *Psychology of Men and Masculinity*, *8*, 15–24.

United Nations (2015). *The world's women 2015: Trends and statistics.* https://unstats.un.org/unsd/gender/worldswomen.html.

United Nations Population Fund (2012). *Ageing in the twenty-first century: A celebration and a challenge.* New York: United Nations Population Fund and HelpAge International. http://unfpa.org/ageingreport/.

U.S. Bureau of Labor Statistics (2015). *Employment projections. Civilian labor force participation rate by age, gender, race, and ethnicity.* www.bls.gov/emp/ep_table_303.htm.

U.S. Bureau of Labor Statistics (2017a). *Labor force statistics from the current population survey. Household data annual averages.* Table 3: Employment status of the civilian noninstitutional populations by age, sex, and race. www.bls.gov/cps/cpsaat03.pdf.

U.S. Bureau of Labor Statistics (2017b). Highlights of women's earnings in 2016. www.bls.gov/opub/reports/womens-earnings/2016/pdf/home.pdf.

U.S. Census Bureau (2017a). *International data base. World population by age and sex.* www.census.gov/population/international/data/idb/worldpop.php.

U.S. Census Bureau (2017b). International Data Base. www.census.gov/population/international/data/idb/informationGateway.php.

U.S. Government Accountability Office (2012). *Retirement security: Women still face challenges.* July 19. www.gao.gov/products/GAO-12-699.

Vandiver, L. (2011). Portrayal of women in the media. Politics. Media Representation Group. http://mediarepresentation. wordpress.com/women mediapolitics/.

van Gelder, B.M., Tijhuis, M.A.R., Kalmijn, S., Giampaoli, S., Nissinen, A., and Kromhout, D. (2004). Physical activity in relation to cognitive decline in elderly men: The FINE Study. *Neurology*, *63*, 2316–2321.

Velkoff, V.A. and Kinsella, K. (1998). Gender stereotypes: Data needs for ageing research. *Ageing International, spring*, 18–38.

Vijayakumar, L. (2004). Altruistic suicide in India. *Archives of Suicide Research, 8*, 73–80. doi: 10.1080/13811110490243804.

Villereal, G.L. and Cavazos Jr., A. (2005). Shifting Identity: Process and change in identity of aging Mexican-American males. *Journal of Sociology and Social Welfare, 32*, 33–41.

Vitaliano, P.P., Zhang, J., and Scanlan, J.M. (2003). Is caregiving hazardous to one's physical health? A meta-analysis. *Psychological Bulletin, 129*, 946–972. doi: 10.1037/0033-2909.129.6.946.

Warner, D.F. and Brown, T.H. (2011). Understanding how race/ethnicity and gender define age-trajectories of disability: An intersectionality approach. *Social Science and Medicine, 72*, 1236–1248. doi: 10.1016/j.socscimed.2011.02.034.

World Health Organization (2011). *Elder maltreatment.* August. www.who.int/mediacentre/factsheets/fs357/en/index.html.

World Health Organization (2017). 10 facts on dementia. http://origin.who.int/features/factfiles/dementia/en/.

Westwood, S. (2016). "We see it as being heterosexualised, being put into a care home": Gender, sexuality and housing/care preferences among older LGB individuals in the UK. *Health & Social Care in the Community, 24*, e155–e163. http://dx.doi.org/10.1111/hsc.12265.

Wright, V.J. and Perricelli, B.C. (2008). Age-related rates of decline in performance among elite senior athletes. *American Journal of Sports Medicine, 36*, 443–450.

Yaffe, M.J., Weiss, D., Wolfson, C., and Lithwick, M. (2007). Detection and prevalence of abuse of older males: Perspectives from family practice. *Journal of Elder Abuse and Neglect, 19*, 47–60. doi: 10.1300/J084v19n01_04.

Yaffe, K., Barnes, D., Nevitt, M., Lui, L-Y., and Covinsky, K. (2001). A prospective study of physical activity and cognitive decline in elderly women. *Archives of Internal Medicine, 161*, 1703–1708.

Yong, V., Saito, Y., and Chan, A. (2011). Gender differences in health and health expectancies of older adults in Singapore: An examination of diseases, impairments, and functional disabilities. *Journal of Cross-Cultural Gerontology, 26*, 189–203. doi: 10.1007/s10823-011-9143-0.

Yoshida, R. (2016). Japan census report shows surge in elderly population, many living alone. *The Japan Times*, June 29. www.japantimes.co.jp/news/2016/06/29/national/japan-census-report-shows-surge-elderly-population-many-living-alone/#.WbbB0-T2Y5s.

Zanella, G. (2016). *How does grandparent childcare affect labor supply?* IZA World of Labor. https://wol.iza.org/articles/how-does-grandparent-childcare-affect-labor-supply/long.

EPILOGUE

THE FUTURE OF GENDER

In her incisive book *The dialectic of sex*, Shulamith Firestone (1970) offered a radical feminist analysis of the oppression of women—along with even more radical solutions. Firestone argued that inequality between women and men was rooted in the biological assignment to women the task of childbearing. She envisioned a feminist future in which reproduction would be separated from both sexuality and gender: conception would happen through artificial insemination and gestation would take place, not in women's bodies, but in artificial wombs in carefully controlled environments. By divorcing the act of sex from procreation and the female body from pregnancy and childbirth, Firestone posited that the biological, genital distinction between women and men would cease to matter. Male privilege would be undercut, and the stage would be set for cultural equality between women and men.

As a vision of the future, Firestone's scenario was startling and controversial. More than 45 years later, despite advances in reproductive technology that have significantly weakened the link between sex and pregnancy, there appears to be little appetite for her imagined world of laboratory-dominated reproduction. However, many may still agree that, by focusing on childbearing, she had pinpointed a key issue among barriers to gender equality.

Women's health is often held hostage to their roles as mothers. Maternal mortality and maternity-related illnesses take an enormous toll on women in regions of the world where availability of good healthcare is scant, childbearing is emphasized as the key task for women, and access to control over reproduction is elusive at best. That toll is exacerbated in cultures that place a lower value on women's lives than on men's.

In developed countries, maternal mortality is less common (although, as noted in Chapter 8, maternal mortality has actually been rising in the United States), but the motherhood penalty is a major economic issue. We have seen that motherhood is associated with lower pay and fewer advancement opportunities for employed women; that the logistics of balancing childcare with paid work remain daunting for many women; that mothers, much more often than fathers, must make impossible choices between attending to family responsibilities and focusing on their jobs. Women, not men, are still deemed the primary caretakers of children and families; this assumption colors government and corporate policies about employment, and can disadvantage women at every stage of their working life. Furthermore, the association of women with motherhood strengthens gender stereotypes that emphasize caring and "softness" as opposed to the competence and decisiveness expected of public leaders and high-achieving workers. (Even though anyone who has been a mother is well aware that competence and decisiveness are critical aspects of this role.)

It is difficult to imagine a scenario in which the health, economic, and social stereotype-related disadvantages linked to motherhood would vanish completely—without doing away with the biological necessity for women to bear the children. Perhaps that is why Firestone focused her revolutionary vision on separating reproduction from sex and pregnancy, and why science fiction writer Ursula LeGuin (1969) fantasized a world where there were not two sexes but one—and anyone could become pregnant. Neither of these solutions is realistic, but they do help us to clarify how female–male relations are shaped by childbearing—and perhaps to envision a world in which more gender equality is possible.

Predicting the future of gender relations, in a world where those relations are now in flux, is speculative. Yet there are signs that the strict definition of gender roles with respect to family and work has eroded dramatically. In developed countries, women have moved into the paid workforce in large numbers, often becoming primary breadwinners for their families (Galinsky, Aumann, and Bond, 2011). The definition of family has changed; both same-sex parenting and single-parent families require changes to traditional expectations about motherhood and fatherhood (Parke, 2013; Webb, Chonody, and Kavanagh, 2017). Women's increasing presence in the paid workforce has driven policy changes (parental leave, childcare arrangements, flexible work schedules) that support workers in balancing family and employment responsibilities. However, despite their increasing presence in the workforce, women everywhere still earn less than men for similar work (Organization for Economic Cooperation and Development, 2017a, 2017b), and workplace sexism has proven to be a daunting barrier to women's full participation, as evidenced by the accounts of women in technology industries (e.g., Pao, 2017).

There are still too many regions of the world where education for women is a low priority; however, in countries where women have equal access to education, women are quickly becoming more highly educated than men. Women hold more public leadership positions than ever before, although they still form a small minority in such roles. Thus, in terms of women's movement into roles traditionally reserved for men, there is evidence of a momentum that, although not unstoppable, is unlikely to be easily reversed.

Gender-based violence presents a deep-rooted barrier to such momentum. As noted in Chapter 7, violence remains a stubborn and serious problem, entwined in gender prejudice and in power disparities between women and men. At the time of writing, for example, thousands are marching in Mexico to protest the murder of 19-year-old Mara Fernanda Castilla—the eighty-fourth "feminicidio" (act of extreme violence against a woman) to occur in her city in 2017. In Canada, an ongoing inquiry to discover the truth about disappearances and murders of up to 4000 indigenous women over the past three decades moves ahead with agonizing inefficiency. And in India, some women have donned cow masks to dramatize their point that there is less outrage over violence against women than over harm to cows.

Even in the face of violent threats, and in regions of the world where restrictions on them are most draconian, women and girls are pushing up against barriers, often risking their lives to gain opportunities for education, self-expression, healthcare for themselves and their families, and protection from sexual violence. It does not seem unreasonable to predict that women's roles will continue to expand, and that these changes will result in greater gender equality. Since a significant body of research suggests that greater societal gender equality is associated with lower levels of sexual violence, intimate partner violence, and maternal and child mortality, and with higher levels of economic prosperity, health, and happiness, the goal of increasing equality has been adopted by many world organizations.

What of changes in men's roles? In some contexts and on some dimensions, women have been encouraged to be more flexible in the ways they enact femininity. However, social definitions of masculinity are often more rigid, and pressures on men to live up to masculine ideals are strong. Men have been slower to change, most likely because societies have traditionally assigned lower status to feminine-stereotyped behaviors. However, men have also moved into roles previously restricted to the other gender. There are more men in traditionally female "caring" professions such as nursing and social work, and even a small but significant minority of men who are full-time homemakers. Both men and women are now less likely than in earlier years to insist on a traditional division of family roles in which the man earns more money and the woman is the primary caretaker of the home and children—and men's attitudes have changed more than women's toward acceptance of the notion that employed women can be good mothers. However, for men, the biggest change may be more subtle than a change in jobs or primary roles. Once sharing or ceding the role of main breadwinner in the family, a man may have to shift his sources of identity and self-esteem away from a traditional (and higher status) masculine emphasis on successful competition and external accomplishments. Instead, his contributions to childrearing, keeping the home running smoothly, and maintaining a good relationship with his spouse become more important. If men have difficulty adapting to this change, they may struggle with lowered self-esteem, psychological distress, and even depression

(Dunlop and Mletzko, 2011). Yet some men have found these changes liberating, exhilarating, and meaningful (Chabon, 2009; Round, 2006).

What about changes in the understanding of gender itself? As explored in Chapters 1 and 2, the notion of gender as a simple binary is now challenged; advances in the science of gender have led many to think of gender as a spectrum rather than as two discrete categories (e.g., Henig, 2017). Whereas many people prefer the traditional categories of female and male, a significant minority do not identify comfortably with either one, and social institutions are beginning to adjust to this reality. Facebook allows users to select from more than 70 options in listing gender—along with a fill-in-the-blank option for those who want to describe their identity freely. Google+ provides an "infinite" gender category for people who feel constrained by listed options. Some countries (Australia, Bangladesh, Canada, Germany, India, Nepal, New Zealand, Pakistan) allow citizens to designate their sex as "X" or "O" rather than "F" or "M" on passports and other documents.

Social change is an uneven and sometimes frustrating process— and its results are rarely unequivocally positive. Some people fear that blurring the distinctions among genders causes confusion and threatens social stability. Some worry that values traditionally associated with femininity, such as care for others, may lose prominence as more women move into more competitive and individualistic lifestyles. Some worry that societies will lose their competitive edge if they restructure institutions to accommodate the demands of family responsibilities for all their workers and encourage men to share those responsibilities. It can hardly be denied that change is unsettling. It seems clear that both caring and achievement, both the capacity for empathy and the capacity for toughness, both openness to compromise and unwavering determination, are qualities much needed for the smooth functioning of societies, institutions, families, and interpersonal relationships. Yet if all such qualities are useful, why insist on dividing them up between women and men? Why, in particular, assign lower status to those "soft" qualities linked to femininity? And why insist that every individual must conform neatly to one of two well-defined gender categories?

Debates persist, but in a context of rapidly changing technology and global media reach, the tide of change in gender roles is unlikely to reverse. And because we are connected, because we live and work together, changes in gender roles and in the ways we think about gender categories are bound to ripple outward from the people most directly affected—until they touch everyone. As we journey into a future that appears dynamic and uncertain, there will be a continuing necessity to question long-held assumptions and experiment with new roles. Perhaps the greatest allure of the journey is in not knowing exactly where it will lead.

FOR FURTHER EXPLORATION

National Geographic Society (2017, January). Special Issue: The shifting landscape of gender. *National Geographic, 231*(1). This special issue tackles gender issues using a global lens and from multiple perspectives. In first-person accounts, photographs, statistics, and analysis, it explores how children form a gender identity, how societies define femininity and masculinity, inequality between genders, and changing gender roles.

World Economic Forum (2016). *The global gender gap report 2017*(Geneva, Switzerland: Author). www.weforum.org/reports/the-global-gender-gap-report-2017. This report details recent progress on gender equality around the world, using measures of health, education, economy, and politics, revealing where change has been fast and slow. It illustrates the connections between gender equality and a variety of positive outcomes, explores the factors that tend to promote and retard change in the direction of greater equality between women and men, and makes policy recommendations. The report concludes that, with current trends, the overall gender gap may close in 83 years, but the gaps in the spheres of economics and health will not close for 170 years.

REFERENCES

Chabon, M. (2009). *Manhood for amateurs: The pleasures and regrets of a husband, father, and son.* New York: Harper Collins.

Firestone, S. (1970). *The dialectic of sex*. New York: William Morrow and Company.

Dunlop, B.W. and Mletzko, T. (2011). Will current socioeconomic trends produce a depressing future for men? *The British Journal of Psychiatry, 198*, 167–168. doi: 10.1192/bjp.bp.110.084210.

Galinsky, E., Aumann, K., and Bond, J.T. (2011). *Times are changing. Gender and generation at work and at home*. Families and Work Institute. http://familiesandwork.org/site/research/reports/Times_Are_Changing.pdf.

Henig, R.M. (2017). Rethinking gender. *National Geographic, 231*(1), 48–73.

LeGuin, U.K. (1969). *The left hand of darkness*. New York: Ace Books.

Organization for Economic Cooperation and Development (2017a). *Interim Economic Outlook release of 20 September 2017*. www.oecd.org/economy/outlook/economic-outlook/.

Organization for Economic Cooperation and Development (2017b). Gender wage gap (indicator). doi: 10.1787/7cee77aa-en (Available at https://data.oecd.org/earnwage/gender-wage-gap.htm (accessed September 21, 2017).

Pao, E. (2017). *Reset: My fight for inclusion and lasting change*. New York: Spiegel & Grau.

Parke, R.D. (2013). *Future families: Diverse forms, rich possibilities*. New York: Wiley Blackwell.

Round, A. (2006). The happy house-husbands of Brussels. *The Telegraph*, May 17. www.telegraph.co.uk/expat/4200102/The-happyhouse-husbands-of-Brussels.html.

Webb, S.N., Chonody, J.M., and Kavanagh, P.S. (2017). Attitudes toward same-sex parenting: An effect of gender. *Journal of Homosexuality, 64*, 1583–1595. http://dx.doi.org/10.1080/00918369.2016.1247540.

GLOSSARY

Affirmative action: a constellation of proactive intervention strategies aimed at increasing the proportion of women and other underrepresented groups who have access to educational and employment opportunities.

Ageism: bias against and/or stereotyping of individuals because of their age.

Ambivalent sexism: a constellation of attitudes made up of both negative and positive feelings and beliefs about women or men.

Androgyny: the combination of both feminine and masculine qualities.

Bases of power: resources (such as reward, punishment, legitimacy, expertise) that may be used to back up attempts to exert power.

Benevolent sexism: warm but condescending stereotypic attitudes toward women or men. Includes attitudes that each gender is naturally better at certain things, and that women and men need each other to be complete.

Cisgender: an individual who identifies with the gender to which she or he has been assigned.

Cognitive approach to gender development: theories that emphasize the child's role as an active seeker of the correct ways to be and behave as a boy or a girl.

Descriptive gender stereotypes: beliefs about what typical men and women are like.

Double bind: for women in leadership roles this refers to the dilemma that, if they behave in too feminine a way, they will not be seen as effective leaders, but if they behave in too masculine a way, they will be disliked and disparaged.

Double standard: the use of different standards of acceptable sexual behavior for women and for men.

Evolutionary psychology: theoretical approach that locates the origin of male–female behavioral differences in the pressures for reproductive success. This approach says men and women are different because different qualities and strategies have led to reproductive success for the two groups across many generations.

Fatherhood premium: tendency for male workers who are fathers to be paid more than non-fathers.

Feminism: a set of diverse ideologies which center on the idea that inequalities between women and men should be challenged.

Feminist studies of men: theoretical approach which focuses on the dominance relations between men and the ways in which, within categories such as race and class, male perspectives and male dominance tend to prevail,

Gender: socially constructed category involving a constellation of stereotypes, norms, and roles for various forms of masculinity, femininity, and androgyny.

Gender identity: the private sense of oneself as male or female, or as a member of a third gender category.

Gender role: a set of behaviors culturally prescribed for women or for men.

Gender schema theory: posits that children develop a network of cognitive associations (schema) for gender based on the degree to which a gender dichotomy is emphasized during their socialization. They then use this schema to organize incoming information.

Gender/sex: an umbrella term used for both gender and sex to reflect identities or social locations where gender and sex are intertwined and cannot be separated

Gender token: the only woman or man (one of very few) in a particular occupational or educational setting numerically dominated by members of the other gender.

Glass ceiling: metaphor used to describe the situation where women appear to encounter an invisible barrier as they try to advance to higher levels of leadership.

Glass escalator: metaphor used to describe a constellation of subtle mechanisms and pressures that enhance men's advancement in female-dominated professions.

Hegemonic masculinity: a cultural ideal of manhood that underlies male dominance over women and some men's dominance over other men.

Heteronormative: embodying the attitude that heterosexuality is the normal sexual orientation and that sexual relationships between women and men are the only normal and natural expressions of sexuality

Honor killing: sanctioned killing of a wife or daughter who has behaved "inappropriately" in order to protect the honor of her family.

Hook-up: sexual activity with no expectation of commitment.

Hostile sexism: derogatory beliefs about women or men based on their gender.

Human capital model: an economic model which describes differences in employment earnings as explainable by differences in employment-related investments (e.g., education, time at work) workers make.

Implicit stereotypes: stereotypes that operate automatically, below the level of awareness.

Influence styles: approaches to making requests or demands of others (direct or indirect).

Interactionist theories: theories based on the idea that biology and environment interact to influence developmental outcomes.

Intersectionality: the ways in which different statuses based on gender, race/ethnicity, and class operate together to produce various levels and types of advantage/disadvantage.

Intersex: having both male and female biological markers.

Intimate justice: a theory that focuses on the way in which social and political inequalities can affect women's and men's experiences of intimate relationships.

Lack of fit: the notion that, because of a mismatch between her or his qualities and the requirements of the job, a certain type of individual is not a good match for a certain type of job. Used in the literature on gender and work to describe the assumed mismatch between women and managerial jobs.

Liberal feminism: posits that gender inequality stems from the different opportunities and choices available to women and men, the different socialization of boys and girls, and the devaluing of women and their work.

Marxist feminism: views gender inequality as a symptom of the larger problem of class inequality.

Misogyny: hatred of, or disdain for, women.

Modern sexism: a subtle form of sexism which entails a lack of support for policies designed to promote equality-oriented changes in gender relations, antagonism toward women's demands for access and inclusion, and denial that gender discrimination still exists (also called **neosexism**).

Motherhood penalty: tendency for women workers who are mothers to experience a loss of cumulative employment earnings.

Multiracial/multiethnic feminism: focuses on the intersecting effects of multiple categories of identity, status, and dominance: gender, race, ethnicity, social class, sexuality, and others.

Nature versus nurture: debate about the relative contributions of biology and environment to human (and other animal) development.

Neosexism: a subtle form of sexism that entails a lack of support for policies designed to promote equality-oriented changes in gender relations, antagonism toward women's demands for access and inclusion, and denial that gender discrimination still exists (also called **modern sexism**).

Old-fashioned sexism: the open endorsement of stereotypic judgments about, and differential treatment of, women and men.

Patriarchy: a system of male dominance that involves male authority figures, competitiveness among men, and restrictions on women.

Performativity: the idea that gender categories are not essential but are constructed by the behavior (performances) of people endeavoring to conform to cultural structures of power and knowledge that organize human beings into female–male binary categories.

Positivity effect: the tendency found among older people to devote more of their attention and memory to positive rather than negative stimuli (see also **socio-emotional selectivity theory**).

Possible selves: individuals' specific images and fantasies of what they could be or become in the future.

Postmodern feminism: posits that gender categories such as male and female are not real, but are modifiable performances.

Prescriptive gender stereotypes: beliefs about what men and women should be like in order to conform to society's expectations.

Psychoanalytic theory: theoretical approach which locates differences between women and men in early childhood relationships with parents.

Queer theories: challenge the binary gender system by arguing that the dualities of sex (female–male), gender (feminine–masculine), and sexuality (heterosexuality–homosexuality) are blurry, arbitrary, and fluid.

Relational aggression: aggression which hurts or threatens another person by damaging her or his relationships and/or social status.

Role incongruity: the situation where two roles an individual is trying to fulfill have conflicting requirements. This concept is sometimes invoked to describe the difficulty of fulfilling contradictory requirements of the female role and those of a leadership role.

Selective optimization with compensation: process by which older individuals are theorized to adapt to losses in functioning: by targeting their resources to a narrower set of goals and priorities, and compensating for any deficiencies by using alternative approaches.

Sex: biological category of male or female.

Sexism: evaluative judgments of individuals based on gender.

Sex chromosomes: the twenty-third pair of chromosomes in humans: XX for females, XY for males.

Sexual orientation: tendency to be attracted sexually to members of one's own or the other sex, or to both.

Sexual self-schema: the way in which a person conceptualizes her- or himself as a sexual being.

Social cognitive theory: suggests that children initially learn gender roles through external rewards and punishments, but, as they mature, begin to regulate their own actions via internal rewards and punishments.

Social construction feminism: posits that gender categories are created and kept in place by behaviors and social organizational structures that emphasize the differences between two non-overlapping categories: "male" and "female."

Social dominance theory: theoretical approach which posits that, in hierarchically oriented societies, women are socialized toward values that are hierarchy-attenuating and men toward values that are hierarchy-enhancing.

Social roles theory: argues that women and men occupy different roles because each gender is expected to have the qualities necessary for those roles, and that performing those roles reinforces and develops these qualities, thus supporting gender stereotypes.

Socialist feminism: theoretical approach which focuses on the complex inequalities that exist between people and groups with different dimensions, such as gender, race, ethnicity, and class.

Socialization: processes used to teach and encourage individuals to conform to societal norms and expectations.

Social-cultural theories: theories which emphasize the role of social structures and power relations in the production of behavioral differences between groups (in this case, women and men).

Socio-emotional selectivity theory: theory that, as they grow older, adults realize their remaining life is short, and so tend to reduce the amount of time they devote to negative emotions and experiences (see also **positivity effect**).

Stereotype embodiment theory: theory which suggests that people incorporate cultural stereotypes (for example, of frailty associated with aging) into self-definitions that, in turn, affect their own physical functioning and health.

Stereotype threat: awareness of being judged according to negative stereotypes about one's group.

Transactional leadership: a style that focuses on reaching set goals, completing tasks, assigning rewards and punishments based on performance, and detecting errors.

Transformational leadership: a style of leadership which focuses on motivating followers to perform at a high level and, in the process, to develop their own leadership potential. The style includes four aspects: stimulating followers to think innovatively, motivating followers to contribute to a shared vision, showing consideration and support for followers' concerns and development, and modeling one's own ideals, values, and beliefs.

Transgender (or trans): an individual who is not comfortable with the gender category to which she or he has been assigned.

Transnational feminism: examines the ways that the global movements of persons, goods, the production of goods, and ideas are gendered, and how this contributes to gender inequality

INDEX